大学入試 全レベル問題集

英語長文

2 共通テストレベル

三訂版

JN036249

Obunsha

大学入試　全レベル問題集　英語長文
レベル２　［三訂版］ 別冊（問題編）

目　次

┌ **編集部より** ┤
│ 問題を解くときには英文音声は必要ありませんが，復習の際にはぜひ音声を利用して英
文の通し聞きを繰り返しおこなってください。語彙やイントネーションの定着に，音声
を介したインプットは非常に効果的です。

次の英文を読んで，あとの問いに答えなさい。

　　If someone were to ask you what language people in the United States speak in their own homes, your answer would probably be, "English, of course!" You might be surprised to learn, however, that that answer would be only 　(ア)　 correct.

　　For many years, *the U.S. Census Bureau, a part of the American government, has been investigating this language question. Currently, this is being done by asking people whether they (and/or their children 5 years old or older) speak something other than English at home. If the answer is "yes," then *follow-up questions are asked about which language is used and how well the person can speak English. Two important purposes of asking these 3 questions are to learn how many people have difficulty using English and to better understand (イ)how efforts to assist such people should be made.

　　Recent Census Bureau results indicate that about 79% of the 291.5 million people (aged 5 and over) in the U.S. speak only English at home. (ウ)Stated another way, about 21% of the people speak a language other than

English. Many of those people (about 58%), however, apparently can also speak English "very well."

The Census Bureau results show that speakers of "Spanish or Spanish *Creole" are, [(エ)   ], the largest group of "other language" users. They account for more than 60% of the "other language" people. After them come the speakers of Chinese, and then the speakers of *Tagalog, *Vietnamese, and French, in that order.

Just [(オ)   ] how many different languages are spoken in American homes? The Census Bureau says that (カ)it doesn't have a definite answer to this, but that data collected several years ago indicated that more than 300 of them were being used at that time.

*the U.S. Census Bureau「アメリカ国勢調査局」　*follow-up「引き続いての」
*Creole「クレオール語」　*Tagalog「タガログ語」
*Vietnamese「ベトナム語」

問1 空所 (ア), (エ), (オ) に入る3つの語 (句) が, 順不同で, 次のA〜Cに示されている。意味の通る文章にするのに最も適切な配列を, ①〜④の中から1つ選びなさい。

A. exactly   B. by far   C. partly

① A-B-C   ② B-C-A   ③ C-A-B   ④ C-B-A

問2 下線部(イ)の内容を最もよく表している日本語を①〜④の中から1つ選びなさい。

① そのような人々を援助する取り組みがどのようになされるべきか

② 英語を使うのに苦労する人々を支援するために, いかなる試みが行われるべきだとしても

③ 英語を使えない人々が支援を受けるためにどれほどの努力をするべきか

④ そのような人々を援助することがいかに効果的であるべきか

問3 下線部(ウ)に最も近い意味を表す語を①〜④の中から1つ選びなさい。

① exchanged   ② exercised   ③ expressed   ④ expected

問4 下線部(カ)が指しているものはどれか, ①〜④の中から1つ選びなさい。

① the U.S.   ② the Census Bureau

③ English   ④ a language

問5 次の中で本文の内容と一致するものを次の①〜⑥の中から2つ選びなさい。ただし, 解答の順序は問いません。

① アメリカでは家庭でどんな言語を話しているかという調査が毎年行われている。

② 使用言語に関する調査では, 英語をどの程度話せるかという問いも含まれている。

③ アメリカの全人口の約79%が家庭で英語を使っていると回答した。

④ アメリカでは家庭で英語を使わない人の約21%が英語を流ちょうに話せることがわかった。

⑤ アメリカの家庭で英語以外に多く使われている言語の順は, スペイン語, 中国語, フランス語, ベトナム語, タガログ語である。

⑥ 数年前に集計されたデータによると, アメリカの家庭では当時, 300より多くの言語が話されていることが明らかになった。

次の英文を読んで, あとの問いに答えなさい。

Doctors say the most effective way to prevent the spread of disease is for people to wash their hands with soap and water. There are programs around the world to increase hand-washing with soap. One million lives could be saved each year if people washed their hands with soap often.

Hand-washing kills *germs from other people, animals or objects a person has touched. When people get *bacteria on their hands, they can *infect themselves by touching their eyes, nose or mouth. Then these people can infect other people. The easiest way to catch a cold is to touch your nose or eyes after someone nearby has *sneezed or coughed. Another way to become sick is to eat food prepared by someone whose hands are not clean.

Hand-washing is especially important before and after preparing food, before eating, and after using the toilet. People should wash their hands after handling animals and after cleaning a baby. Doctors say it is also a good idea to wash your hands after handling money and after sneezing or coughing. It is important to wash your hands often when someone in your home is sick.

The most effective way to wash your hands is to rub them together after putting soap and warm water on them. Doctors say you do not have to use special *anti-bacterial soap. Be sure to rub all areas of the hands for about ten to fifteen seconds. The soap and the rubbing action remove germs. Rinse the hands with water and dry them.

People using public restrooms should dry their hands with a paper towel and use the towel to turn off the water. Doctors also advise using the paper towel to open the restroom door before throwing the towel away in order to help you avoid getting the germs of people who did not wash well.

*germ「病原菌」　*bacteria「ばい菌」　*infect「感染させる」
*sneezed「くしゃみをした」　*anti-bacterial「抗菌用の」

問 次の英文 (ア) ～ (ソ) の中から，本文の内容と一致するものを 5 つ選びなさい。

(ア) Washing your hands is an effective way to spread disease.

(イ) There are programs around the world to prevent people from washing their hands with soap and water.

(ウ) If people washed their hands with soap often, one million lives could be saved each year.

(エ) Hand-washing can prevent disease by killing germs.

(オ) People never infect themselves by touching their eyes, nose or mouth.

(カ) Touching your nose or eyes after someone nearby has sneezed or coughed can cause you to catch a cold.

(キ) It is important to wash your hands before preparing food but not after.

(ク) Handling animals and cleaning babies is a good way to keep your hands clean.

(ケ) When someone in your home is sick, it is always because they have handled money after sneezing or coughing.

(コ) Rubbing your hands together after putting soap and warm water on them is the most effective way to wash your hands.

(サ) Doctors say that it is important to use special anti-bacterial soap.

(シ) You should rinse hands with very hot water before rubbing them for about ten to fifteen seconds.

(ス) There are many germs on paper towels in public restrooms, so you should not turn off the water with them.

(セ) Doctors also advise people not to use public restrooms.

(ソ) Opening a public restroom door with the towel you used to dry your hands can help you avoid getting germs on your hands.

次の英文を読んで，あとの問いに答えなさい。

Although people everywhere seem to enjoy drinking coffee, they do not all have the same coffee culture. (ア)In Europe, for example, coffee shops are common places for people to meet friends and to talk while they drink coffee. On the other hand, locations like this were not as common in North America in the past. Instead, people in North America tended to drink coffee in their homes with their friends. The coffee culture in the USA changed when Starbucks coffee shops spread across the country.

The first Starbucks coffee shop opened in 1971 in downtown Seattle, Washington, in the USA. It was a small coffee shop that 　　(イ)　　 its own coffee beans. The coffee shop's business did well, and by 1981 there were three more Starbucks stores in Seattle.

Things really began to change for the company in 1981. That year, (ウ)Howard Schultz met the three men who ran Starbucks. Schultz worked in New York for a company that made kitchen equipment. He noticed that Starbucks ordered a large number of special coffee makers, and he was curious. Schultz went to Seattle to see what Starbucks did. In 1982, the original Starbucks owners hired Schultz as the company's head of marketing.

In 1983, Schultz traveled to Italy. The unique atmosphere of the espresso bars there caught his ____(エ)____. (オ)Back in the USA, Schultz created an atmosphere for Starbucks coffee shops that was comfortable and casual, and customers everywhere seemed to like it. Starbucks began opening more locations across the USA. Then the company opened coffee shops in other countries as well. Today, there are more than 16,000 Starbucks coffee shops worldwide.

____(カ)____, that does not mean Starbucks has not had problems. As a matter of fact, many Starbucks locations have closed over the past few years. In some cases, this is because there were too many coffee shops competing for business in one small area. In other cases, locations in some countries closed because the coffee culture there did not match with the "feel the same everywhere" atmosphere offered by Starbucks.

問1 下線部(ア)を日本語に直しなさい。

_____

_____

問2 空所(イ)に入れるのに最も適した語を次から1つ選びなさい。
① cooked ② boiled ③ roasted ④ burned

問3 下線部(ウ)について本文中に述べられているものに〇, 述べられていないものに×をつけなさい。
(1) ニューヨークで生まれた。
(2) スターバックスの創業者である。
(3) 台所用品の製造会社に勤めていた。
(4) コーヒーメーカーを大量に注文した。

(1)　　　　(2)　　　　(3)　　　　(4)

問4 空所(エ)に入れるのに最も適した語を次から1つ選びなさい。
① ear ② eye ③ arm ④ heart

問5 下線部（オ）を日本語に直しなさい。

_____

_____

_____

問6 空所（カ）に入れるのに最も適した語を次から1つ選びなさい。
① So   ② Therefore   ③ Though   ④ However

問7 本文の内容に合っているものを次から2つ選びなさい。
① かつてのアメリカ合衆国では，コーヒーはあまり飲まれなかった。
② スターバックスの第1号店はシアトルでオープンした。
③ ハワード・シュルツは多くの優秀な人材をヘッドハンティングした。
④ ハワード・シュルツはイタリアを旅行して大のエスプレッソ好きになった。
⑤ アメリカ以外で16,000以上のスターバックスがある。
⑥ ヨーロッパでは，最近数年間で多くのスターバックスが閉店に追い込まれた。
⑦ スターバックスの店はどこでも同じ感じがする。

次の英文を読んで，あとの問いに答えなさい。

The Internet has become an important part of our modern lives. In fact, it is impossible for many people to imagine a day without some contact with the Internet. Most people use it to shop, send e-mail, and for social networking. However, some people (ア) [much / find / they / time / control / online / how / it / to / spend / hard].

So, how much Internet is too much Internet? (イ)Experts agree that people who use the Internet so much that it causes problems with their daily activities are spending too much time online. They say that some people may actually be *addicted to the Internet in ┌─── (ウ) ───┐ the same way as some people are addicted to gambling or alcohol. Signs of Internet addiction include spending more and more time online, reducing or giving up social, work-related, or hobby-related activities in favor of spending time online, and giving up sleep to spend time on the Internet.

Experts say that this becomes a real problem when a person starts experiencing problems sleeping, problems in their home and work life, or problems in social relationships. People who use the Internet excessively also seem to be more likely to show signs of *depression.

How do you know if you are spending too much time online? Some common warning signs include checking your e-mail every few minutes, always thinking about your next online session, and getting complaints from the people around you about how much time you spend online.

Showing any of these signs may mean that you are on your way to becoming addicted to the Internet. However, experts agree that there is hope. They say that simply understanding that spending too much time online is a problem may be the first step to solving the problem. They believe that, in most cases, doing something as simple as creating a better system for managing your time online can solve the problem.

The Internet is a wonderful tool for communicating and finding information. However, as with most things in life, you have to learn to use it carefully, and make sure you keep a healthy balance between being online and the other important things in your life.

✝addicted「中毒の」　＊depression「うつ病」

問1 （ア）の [　　　] 内の語を文意に合うように並べ替えなさい。

_____

問2 下線部（イ）を日本語にしなさい。

_____

_____

_____

問3 空所（ウ）に入れるのに最も適当なものを①〜④の中から１つ選びなさい。

① very　　　　② much　　　　③ more　　　　④ most

[　　　　]

問4 以下の問いに対する答えとして最も適当なものを，それぞれ①〜④の中から１つずつ選びなさい。

(1) In the passage, which of the following is <u>NOT</u> mentioned about most people's use of the Internet?
　① They use it for shopping.
　② They use it for hobby-related activities.
　③ They use it to send e-mail.
　④ They use it for social networking.

(2) What does the author say about Internet addiction?
　① Those who are addicted to gambling are also addicted to the Internet.
　② Spending more time in work-related activities is a sign of Internet addiction.
　③ Giving up social activities is a sign of Internet addiction.
　④ Those who are addicted to the Internet are also addicted to alcohol.

(3) According to the passage, which of the following is <u>NOT</u> true about people who use the Internet too much?

① They sleep very well.

② They are more likely to show signs of depression.

③ They check their e-mail every few minutes.

④ They have problems in their home and work life.

(4) What is suggested as the first step to overcoming the problem of Internet addiction?

① To get complaints from the people around you.

② To recognize that too much time spent online is a problem.

③ To create a better system for checking your e-mail.

④ To think about your next online session every few minutes.

(5) Which of the following should be the title of this passage?

① Signs and solutions of Internet addiction

② History of Internet addiction

③ Advantages and disadvantages of the Internet

④ Young people with Internet addiction

(1)	(2)	(3)	(4)	(5)

次の英文を読んで, あとの問いに答えなさい。

The United Nations has named March 22nd World Water Day to focus attention on the importance of fresh, clean water and to promote the (ア)<u>sustainable</u> management of fresh water resources.

Almost one billion people — one seventh of the world's population — suffer from constant hunger, a crisis that could become (イ)<u>more intense</u> as the global population grows. Our ability to increase food production will require (ウ)<u>sufficient</u> water and ways to predict how much water will be available for people to grow food. More than 70 percent of the water used in the world goes towards agriculture. In many developing countries, the amount used for agriculture is more than 90 percent.

Seven billion people live on this planet, with another 2 billion predicted by 2050. Each one of us drinks two to four liters of water daily, but we consume much more as part of the food we eat. It takes around 1,500 liters of water to (エ)<u>produce</u> a kilo of wheat and ten times that amount for a kilo of beef.

As urban populations and economies increase, so do water demands for cities and industry, leaving less for agriculture. Competition between cities and the countryside is increasing. That means there will be less water for small farmers and fishermen who cannot _(オ)make a living without it.

Food security is critically dependent on a supply of clean water. We must make it a priority to reduce water pollution. We must develop more efficient water supply systems, _(カ)eliminate leaks, and make sure that water is stored and _(キ)distributed properly.

We also need to protect the purity of water resources and wetlands that support fisheries. They provide a significant source of protein to 2.5 billion people in developing countries.

Water and sanitation should be priorities in national development plans and strategies. Money should also be provided to meet these goals. Communities and governments should work towards meeting the basic needs of their people to _(ク)achieve food security.

We need to increase water supplies through better resource management. We also need to reduce the demand for water by _(ケ)employing more efficient irrigation technology. Individuals, communities and governments must all work together. Water scarcity is a global challenge, but the solutions are often local.

下線部（ア）～（ケ）の語句の文中での意味に最も近いものを，（A）～（D）の中から1つ選びなさい。

（ア）（A）lasting　（B）risky　（C）temporal　（D）natural
（イ）（A）better　（B）lighter　（C）calmer　（D）worse
（ウ）（A）fluent　（B）enough　（C）wealthy　（D）efficient
（エ）（A）include　（B）dispose　（C）grow　（D）flood
（オ）（A）get shelter　（B）lack food　（C）save face　（D）earn money
（カ）（A）stop　（B）start　（C）increase　（D）rise
（キ）（A）put off　（B）left off　（C）taken out　（D）given out
（ク）（A）lose　（B）ruin　（C）gain　（D）collect
（ケ）（A）inventing　（B）working　（C）modifying　（D）using

（ア）☐　（イ）☐　（ウ）☐　（エ）☐　（オ）☐

（カ）☐　（キ）☐　（ク）☐　（ケ）☐

問2 次の(1)～(6)の英文の空所に入る最も適切なものを，（A）～（D）の中から1つ選びなさい。

(1) According to paragraphs 1 and 2, _____
 （A） the United Nations has focused on a market for fresh water.
 （B） about one out of seven people is under the threat of hunger.
 （C） world population growth isn't connected with the management of water resources.
 （D） only a small amount of water is used for agriculture in many developing countries.

(2) According to paragraphs 2 and 3, _____
 （A） we should improve our ability to predict when to grow more food.
 （B） world population is expected to reach 9 million in 2050.
 （C） one person drinks about 14 to 28 liters of water a week.

(D) 1,500 liters of water are needed to produce a kilo of beef.

(3) According to paragraph 4, _____
  (A) people living in urban areas do not need much water.
  (B) farmers always compete with fishermen to make a living.
  (C) economic growth has made more water available for agriculture.
  (D) some people won't be able to live by farming due to competition for water.

(4) According to paragraphs 5 and 6, _____
  (A) food security is subject to the availability of water.
  (B) if we reduce water pollution, efficient water supply systems won't be necessary.
  (C) fisheries have a positive effect on water purity.
  (D) people in developing countries need to get more protein.

(5) According to paragraphs 7 and 8, _____
  (A) communities and governments should work independently on water issues.
  (B) financial support isn't necessary for food security.
  (C) water supplies can be maintained by good resource management and efficient technology.
  (D) people don't need a global perspective when they try to solve local problems.

(6) The best title for the passage is "_____"
  (A) The Population Explosion.
  (B) Water and Food Security.
  (C) An Analysis of Public Sanitation.
  (D) Water Shortage in Africa.

(1) [ ]　(2) [ ]　(3) [ ]　(4) [ ]　(5) [ ]　(6) [ ]

次の英文を読んで，あとの問いに答えなさい。

A cat's home range has no specific boundaries; it is simply the area within which there are a number of favorite places which it regularly visits, plus a network of pathways which it ⎡ (ア) ⎤ to get to them. Country cats may range over as much as sixty acres. Suburban and city cats are much more restricted because of such ⎡ (イ) ⎤ as streets and buildings.

In either situation, though, several cats may use the same geographical area as a home range, each having its own special hunting grounds or resting places within it.

Researchers have watched how cats whose ranges overlap solve the problem of using the same pathways. ⎡ (ⅰ) ⎤ cat, upon spotting ⎡ (ⅱ) ⎤ moving along a path, holds back until ⎡ (ⅲ) ⎤ cat has disappeared. If two cats see each other approaching a junction of two paths, both may sit down at a distance from the crossroads and try to wait longer than the other. One cat may eventually make a fast run across the junction, or both may turn around and go back in the ⎡ (ウ) ⎤ from which they originally came. They try to 	 (エ) 	 confrontation, even if one of the cats has already established itself as dominant to the other. If, for example, an inferior cat is already walking down a pathway when a superior cat approaches, the 	 (iv) 	 cat sits down and waits until the road is 	 (v) 	 . Nor does it drive an inferior cat away from its own favorite sunning spot.

For many small animals, (A)the mere sight of another of its species is not enough to cause aggressive behavior. That cats know what cats look like has been shown by researchers who have watched *feline reactions to pictures of variously shaped abstract forms and animal silhouettes. The usual behavior of a cat in this test situation is to approach the cat silhouette cautiously and then, sometimes, to make an angry sound when the pictured cat 	 (オ) 	 to respond to its signals. A cat who sees itself in a mirror also approaches the "animal" it has just sighted in a friendly spirit. Unable to locate a flesh-and-blood cat in front of the mirror, the real cat often searches behind the mirror, and (B)when this does not work, it rapidly loses interest.

*feline「ネコ科の」

問1 空所(ア)から(オ)に入れるのに最も適切なものをそれぞれ1つ選びなさい。

(ア) ① catches　　② loses　　③ misses　　④ travels

(イ) ① attempts　② barriers　③ favorites　④ symbols

(ウ) ① country　　② direction　③ distance　④ time

(エ) ① avoid　　　② expect　　③ understand　④ watch

(オ) ① cares　　　② fails　　　③ forgets　　④ stops

(ア)[　　　　]　(イ)[　　　　]　(ウ)[　　　　]　(エ)[　　　　]　(オ)[　　　　]

問2 空所(ⅰ)(ⅱ)(ⅲ)に入る言葉の並びとして最も適切なものを, ①～④の中から1つ選びなさい。

　① Another - one - the other　　② Another - the other - one

　③ One - another - the other　　④ One - the other - another

[　　　　]

問3 空所(ⅳ), (ⅴ)に入る言葉の並びとして最も適切なものを, ①～④の中から1つ選びなさい。

　① inferior - clean　　　　② inferior - clear

　③ superior - clean　　　　④ superior - clear

[　　　　]

24

問4 下線部 (A) (B) の意味として最も適切なものをそれぞれ 1 つ選びなさい。

(A) ① 同じ種類の動物を目にするだけでは

② 別の種類の動物を目にするだけでは

③ 同じ種類の動物によって見られるだけでは

④ 別の種類の動物によって見られるだけでは

(B) ① 鏡に映る猫がいなくなると

② 鏡の前にいる猫を探すことができないと

③ 鏡の後ろを探しても猫が見つからないと

④ 鏡に映る猫を見つけることができないと

(A) ☐ (B) ☐

問5 次の各文について，本文の内容と一致するものには①を，一致しないものには②を，それぞれ書きなさい。

(a) Country cats use a very big area as a home range, which they rarely share with other cats.

(b) When two cats see each other approaching a junction of two paths, they try not to cross it at the same time.

(c) A cat can distinguish another cat from other animals.

(d) When a cat sees its own shape in the mirror, it walks up to the "animal" it has seen.

(a) ☐ (b) ☐ (c) ☐ (d) ☐

次の英文を読んで，あとの問いに答えなさい。

When people travel, they sometimes prefer not to stay in hotels. Then, they stay in other people's homes. These accommodations are called "Bed and Breakfast", or "B & B". These places are a nice way to meet people, but it is not always easy to find the right one. Recently, a service has started (ア)that helps people find places to stay when they travel. The service is called Airbnb. Airbnb has a free website (イ)that lets people find accommodation which is similar to a "B & B" before they go on their holidays. It works like any holiday booking site: travelers go online, select the dates they wish to travel and pick a place to stay. The places on offer tend to be the apartments and houses of ordinary people who are looking to make some extra money.

Hosts can register on the site for free, set a price per night for their accommodation and upload pictures of their homes. They can even set house rules. A stay in an Airbnb property is thought to be cheaper than one in a hotel.

Airbnb began in 2008 after two of its founders decided to offer their San Francisco apartment to travelers coming to the city for a conference. Since then it has become very popular. People can now stay in Airbnbs in 34,000 cities in 190 countries. More than 40 million people have booked a trip using the site. Airbnb charges both its guests and its hosts a fee for arranging stays. Hosts are charged 3% of the cost of the room to pay for expenses. Guests are charged 6-12% depending on the price of the room.

In some areas in which Airbnb is operating, there are rules about renting out a home. New York, [　　(A)　　] , does not allow short-term rentals (fewer than 30 days) unless the owner is also living there.

Other concerns include standards of local housing, laws and regulations, and security risks. There have been some cases of guests stealing or destroying property. Some owners have complained about people renting houses to hold parties (ウ)that have caused damage to homes.

[　　(B)　　] , there are no signs (エ)that Airbnb's growth is slowing. It has recently started to use TV advertisements in order to attract even more people to the site. In the future, Airbnb hopes to expand into the Chinese and the business travel markets.

問1 下線部（ア）～（エ）の中から，ほかと異なる用法のものを１つ選びなさい。

問2 本文中の空所（A）・（B）に入るべき適切なものを，①～④の中から１つずつ選びなさい。なお，文頭に来るべきものも小文字で示してある。

① for example　② therefore　③ on the other hand　④ however

(A) ☐　(B) ☐

問3 本文の内容に合うように，次の(1)～(6)の各質問に対する適切な答えを，それぞれ①～④の中から１つずつ選びなさい。

(1) What is Airbnb?

① It is a holiday booking site for people who run hotels and apartments.

② It is a website for people to provide information about free rooms.

③ It is a website which allows people to rent their homes and apartments to travelers.

④ It is a website for people to sell their houses or apartments to make money.

(2) What has happened to Airbnb recently?

① The number of Airbnb users has increased quite rapidly.

② The founders of Airbnb have become very popular at conferences.

③ It has become popular among people who love to stay at expensive homes.

④ About 34,000 cities in 190 countries have developed their own websites.

(3) How does Airbnb make money?

    ① The service is free for both its hosts and guests.

    ② It charges some amount of money for accessing the site.

    ③ The owner of the website charges people when they log in.

    ④ Both hosts and guests pay a fee when an arrangement to stay is made.

(4) Which of the following risks for owners of Airbnb is NOT mentioned in the passage?

    ① Some guests may steal from the owners.

    ② The owners' property might get damaged.

    ③ Some guests may try to avoid paying for their stay.

    ④ The owners' property might be used for parties.

(5) Who can be an Airbnb host?

    ① Anyone without houses or apartments.

    ② Home owners who can offer their property to travelers.

    ③ People who have trouble with their own houses.

    ④ People who pay taxes to the city.

(6) What is the future for Airbnb?

    ① The business will probably continue to expand.

    ② The business is certain to slow down in a few years.

    ③ Airbnb will need more Chinese and business travelers to survive.

    ④ People are having problems with Airbnb, and it may end the service soon.

(1) ☐   (2) ☐   (3) ☐   (4) ☐   (5) ☐   (6) ☐

問4 本文のタイトルとして最も適切なものを①〜④の中から1つ選びなさい。

① A New Type of Accommodation System

② A Travel Style Becoming Popular Around the World

③ How to Find a Cheaper Place to Stay

④ Where to Stay for an Overseas Trip

問5 次のグラフのうち，Airbnb の利用者数の推移を表すグラフとして，本文の内容に合致するものを①〜④の中から選びなさい。

①

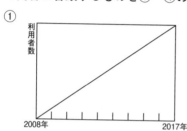

②

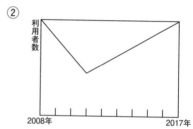

③

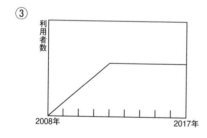

④

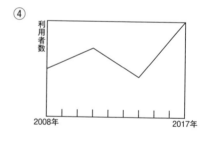

次の英文を読んで，あとの問いに答えなさい。

　　If human beings train their bodies, they can become fine athletes. The best of us can achieve great feats of speed and endurance. For example, in 1996, an Ethiopian farm boy, Haile Gebreselassie, set an Olympic record in the 10-kilometer race. Haile developed his speed and endurance by running barefoot every day from his farm to his school six miles away. Yet even this elite runner would be left behind in a race with certain animals. While human beings race for fun or to win prizes, these animals primarily run (ア)for their lives.

　　The cheetah, the world's swiftest land animal, can reach speeds of 70 miles per hour. But it can sprint at this top speed for only a few seconds. The *American pronghorn antelope, however, may be the world's greatest all-round athlete. Although its greatest speed is only 60 miles per hour, the pronghorn has superb (イ)endurance. It can run at this speed for an hour. A physiologist has explained the pronghorn's athletic superiority. "Pronghorns have evolved over millennia. In ancient times, they probably developed speed to evade cheetahs. They developed endurance to escape wolf packs, which hunted over long distances."

Much smaller animals are also superb athletes. The tiny California *hummingbird, for instance, migrates enormous distances. To do this, it beats its wings thousands of times per minute for 24 hours at a time. (A) To match the hummingbird's energy, a human being would have to work hard for a week without a minute's rest. Another example is the *Etruscan shrew. This mouse-like creature is only two inches long and thin as a *dime. Yet it can run more swiftly than the fastest human. If the tiny shrew were the size of a human being, it could sprint a mile in about forty seconds. Even the great Olympic runner Jesse Owens couldn't do that!

Every creature's speed and endurance depends on how well oxygen is transported by the aerobic system. Each breath of air we take contains oxygen that passes into the lungs. The oxygen travels from the lungs into the blood; then the bloodstream moves the oxygen into the heart. The heart pumps this oxygen-filled blood into the muscles. There, the life-giving oxygen is transformed into energy. The aerobic system of the pronghorn is five to ten times more (C) efficient than the human aerobic system. (B) This is the secret of the pronghorn's athletic superiority.

Unfortunately, the peerless pronghorn pays a high price for its aerobic efficiency. The pronghorn has almost no body fat. Therefore, while it can outrun its enemies, it may starve to death in a harsh winter.

＊American pronghorn antelope「プロングホーン (カモシカに似た動物)」
＊hummingbird「ハチドリ」
＊Etruscan shrew「コビトジャコウネズミ」
＊dime「10セントコイン」

問1 下線部 (ア)〜(ウ) が本文中で表している内容に最も近いものを①〜④の中から1つ選びなさい。

(**ア**) for their lives
　　① 成長するために　　　② 元気いっぱいで
　　③ 生きるために　　　　④ 楽しんで

(**イ**) endurance
　　① 生命力　　　　　　② 回復力
　　③ 速力　　　　　　　④ 持久力

(**ウ**) efficient
　　① 珍しい　　　　　　② 複雑な
　　③ 浪費する　　　　　④ 効率のよい

(ア)　　　　　(イ)　　　　　(ウ)

問2 下線部(A)の内容として最も適当なものを①〜④の中から1つ選びなさい。

① ハチドリの活動量を人間に置きかえると，人間は1週間の間1分も休まずに働き続けなくてはいけない。

② ハチドリの力を解明するために，人類は1分も休まず努力しなくてはいけない。

③ ハチドリの行動力を見習って，人類も休みなく働くべきである。

④ ハチドリの活動量と比較すると，人間はわずかな休息しか取らず働きすぎている。

問3 下線部(B)が示す内容として最も適当なものを①〜④の中から1つ選びなさい。

① プロングホーンは地上で最も優れた万能な陸上選手であること

② プロングホーンは人間のオリンピック選手よりも速く走れること

③ プロングホーンの酸素消費システムは人間よりも優れていること

④ プロングホーンより小さくても優れた運動能力を持つ動物がいること

問4 本文の内容と合致しないものを①〜⑥の中から2つ選びなさい。ただし、解答の順序は問わない。

① エチオピア出身のオリンピック選手 Haile Gebreselassie は毎日はだしで学校まで走ることでその能力を鍛えた。

② チーターとプロングホーンでは最高速度もその速度を持続できる時間もプロングホーンの方が勝っている。

③ 長距離を追ってくるオオカミの群れから逃れようとして、プロングホーンはその運動能力を伸ばしてきたと考えられる。

④ コビトジャコウネズミがもし人間と同じサイズなら、オリンピック選手よりもはるかに速く走ることができるだろう。

⑤ 動物の運動能力は、酸素がいかに有効に酸素消費システムに取り込まれるかに関係している。

⑥ プロングホーンは万能な運動選手なので、体脂肪が少ないことは不利にならない。

問5 以下は本文中で説明されている酸素消費の仕組みを簡単に図式化したものです。空所（ア）〜（ウ）に(a)〜(c)を入れる場合、最も適当な組み合わせを①〜④の中から1つ選びなさい。

The animal takes a breath of air.
↓

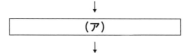

|（ア）|

↓

The lungs carry oxgen into the bloodstream.
↓

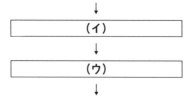

|（イ）|

↓

|（ウ）|

↓

The oxygen turns into energy.

(a) The heart pumps oxygen-filled blood into the muscles.

(b) Blood-carrying oxygen enters the heart.

(c) Oxygen goes into the lungs.

① (ア) ―(a)　　(イ) ―(b)　　(ウ) ―(c)

② (ア) ―(b)　　(イ) ―(a)　　(ウ) ―(c)

③ (ア) ―(c)　　(イ) ―(a)　　(ウ) ―(b)

④ (ア) ―(c)　　(イ) ―(b)　　(ウ) ―(a)

問6 この文章のタイトルとして最も適当なものを①~④の中から１つ選びな
さい。

① Species with High Speed and Endurance

② The Fastest Land Animal in History

③ How Oxygen Travels in Your Body

④ How Pronghorns Have Evolved over Millennia

次の英文を読んで，あとの問いに答えなさい。

Many people worry about memory loss. It is normal to lose memory as you get older. In fact, memory loss can begin when someone is in their twenties. But how much of your memory do you have to lose, and how quickly does it have to happen? Research on the brain and memory is a huge area these days. Doctors are looking for ways to help people improve their memory and possibly prevent loss.

Let us look at one program to help memory, called The Boot Camp for the Brain. What is The Boot Camp for the Brain? It is a two-week program developed by a *psychiatrist named Gary Small. His program (ア)combines four elements: a special diet, daily physical activity, stress relieving exercises and, of course, memory exercises. The memory exercises take about 15 minutes a day. Dr. Small claims that this combination can improve your brain's function.

Michele Rubin is one of Dr. Small's success stories. Rubin is a 46-year-old mother of three teenagers. At the start of the program, her memory tested as average for her age. When she took memory tests after the program, her memory was equal to a 20-year-old person. Rubin says that a few years ago she started to feel that she was forgetting things and that her memory was not as good as it used to be. She says that the program was life-changing. Since completing the program, in addition to exercising more and improving her diet, she has started using memory (1)strategies, reading non-fiction and doing crossword puzzles. She also helps her children with their math homework as a way to work her brain.

Dr. Small says that he has evidence that the two-week boot camp program (2)does in fact change the brain. He did a study with 17 volunteers. All of the volunteers had mild memory complaints. Dr. Small randomly chose eight people to participate in The Boot Camp for the Brain, and the remaining nine people did nothing different.

They did brain scans on all 17 people before and after the program. Dr. Small says that the eight people who participated developed significantly more efficient brain cell activity in a front part of the brain that controls everyday memory tasks. The people who participated also said that they felt less forgetful after the program.

Dr. Small emphasizes that this study was very

small and that a larger study is needed. But he still feels that the results are important. Other scientists say they are cautiously optimistic about Small's approach. They feel more research is needed, but say it is possible that The Boot Camp for the Brain could (エ)<u>delay</u> serious memory problems.

＊psychiatrist「精神科医」

問1 記憶力低下はどの年代から始まる可能性があるか, 最も適当なものを①〜④の中から 1 つ選びなさい。

① 10 代　　　② 20 代　　　③ 30 代　　　④ 40 代

問2 下線部(ア)の意味として最も適当なものを①〜④の中から 1 つ選びなさい。

① features　② includes　③ improves　④ selects

問3 Gary Small の考案したプログラムに<u>含まれていない</u>と推測されるものを①〜④の中から 1 つ選びなさい。

① jogging, swimming, or walking every day
② eating something good for the brain and memory
③ 15 minutes of memory exercises a day
④ watching a show on the television and reading fiction

問4 Michele Rubin について述べられているものを①〜④の中から１つ選びなさい。

① Her memory is much worse than that of the average people of her age.

② Dr. Small failed to improve her memory with his memory exercises.

③ She has three children who each raise teenagers of their own.

④ She exercises her brain by helping her children with their studies.

問5 下線部（イ）の意味に最も近いものを①〜④の中から１つ選びなさい。

① methods   ② records   ③ guidances   ④ contests

問6 下線部（ウ）の does に最も近い用法のものを①〜④の中から１つ選びなさい。

① He usually does his homework after dinner.

② It is widely known that smoking does us more harm than good.

③ He does love his wife, but she doesn't.

④ I can write better than my brother does.

問7 第4段落の内容に<u>合致しない</u>ものはどれか，①〜④の中から1つ選びなさい。

① Seventeen people were studied in the research.

② Dr. Small chose eight people to do the two-week program.

③ Before the test, some of the volunteers had a problem in their memory.

④ Nine people were chosen for comparison and did nothing special.

問8 第5段落では，2週間のプログラムを受けた人にはどのような変化があると書かれているか，最も適当なものを①〜④の中から1つ選びなさい。

① プログラムの成果を調べて欲しいと言う人が多くなる。

② 記憶力が良くなるので，頭の回転が速くなる。

③ 脳の記憶に関係する部分が活発に活動するようになる。

④ 少しだが忘れやすくなったという人があることも報告されている。

問9 下線部（エ）の delay の意味に最も近いものを①〜④の中から1つ選びなさい。

① slow　　② lighten　　③ protect　　④ solve

問10 この文章のタイトルとして最も適当なものを①～④の中から１つ選びな
さい。
① Memory and Exercise
② Age and Memory Loss
③ What Are Brain Cells?
④ The Boot Camp for the Brain

次の英文を読んで，あとの問いに答えなさい。

In Istanbul, Yesim Yilmaz is getting ready for class. Her mother brings her some breakfast, which Yesim eats while looking at her e-mail on her phone. She has forgotten to read a chapter for her biology class. No problem. She opens up her laptop and downloads a chapter from her online textbook to read on the train.

On Sunday afternoon next to his apartment complex in Seoul, Min-ho Park is waiting for the bus. At lightning speed, he types a text message to let his friend know he's on his way. Min-ho is never without his phone. In fact, he's already bought a ticket on his phone for a movie he and his friends will see this afternoon. Min-ho laughs （　ア　） he checks some funny photos his friend Jae-sung has just posted online. His bus soon arrives. Min-ho gets on, sits down, opens a game app on his phone, and puts his earphones in his ears. Most of the other people on the bus who are Min-ho's age are doing exactly the same thing.

Yesim and Min-ho are members of Generation Z. They are sometimes called "digital natives" because they have grown up with the Internet, mobile phones, and social media since they were children. In fact, many have never seen a *VCR or a telephone with a dial. Members of Gen-Z are people born (イ) the mid-1990s and the early 2000s.

Their parents spent most of their teenage years listening to cassette players, playing early video games, and calling friends on their families' telephones. Generation Z, however, is connected to its music, videos, games, and friends online all day, every day. Recent surveys show that young people in Asia spend an average of 9.5 hours per day online. And marketing companies know this.

Every time they open their page on a social networking site, Gen-Z members don't see only friends' *updates and photos. They also see ads for products they might want to buy. Marketing companies work with social media sites to find out where their customers live, what movies, books, and music they like, and who their friends are. The companies use this information to show their customers the advertisements they want them to see.

What does this generation think about marketing companies knowing so much about them? Are they worried about losing their privacy? Not many seem to be very worried about companies knowing how to sell things to them. Many Gen-Z members are more concerned about keeping their private information from their parents. For example, Valerie Chen in *Kaohsiung is upset because her parents want to watch everything she does online. But her parents' eyes are not (ウ) to make her stop using social media. Valerie knows how to limit what her parents can see about her on the social networking sites she uses.

However, keeping information private from parents may not be the only challenge. Many people are now finding out that posting funny pictures on the Web can be a problem when they finish school and start looking for a job. In fact, some studies show that more than 70% of companies reject people who are looking for jobs because of what they can see about young people online. (エ) they grew up using social media, maybe Generation Z will be better at protecting their personal information online than the generation before them. Only time will tell.

*VCR「ビデオテープレコーダー」　　*updates「最新情報」
*Kaohsiung「(台湾の) 高雄市」

文中の空所(ア)～(エ)に入れるのに最も適当なものを, それぞれ①～④
の中から1つずつ選びなさい。

(ア) ① at　　　② as　　　③ loudly　　④ what

(イ) ① between　② among　③ for　　④ at

(ウ) ① work　　② bad　　③ enough　④ effect

(エ) ① Before　② Although　③ When　④ Because

(ア)	(イ)	(ウ)	(エ)

問2 次の問いの答えとして最も適当なものを, それぞれ①～④の中から1つず
つ選びなさい。

(a) Which of the following is true of Yesim Yilmaz?

① She often skips breakfast.

② She doesn't belong to Generation Z.

③ She sometimes leaves her textbook on the train.

④ She doesn't get upset if she forgets to do her homework.

(b) Which of the following is NOT stated of Min-ho Park?

① He is good at typing text messages.

② He always carries his phone with him.

③ He often takes funny photos and shows them to his friends.

④ He plays games on his phone on the bus.

(c) Which of the following is true of Valerie Chen?

① Her parents don't worry about what she does online.

② Her parents don't know that she is using social media.

③ She keeps in touch with her parents using social media.

④ She is successful in hiding her sensitive information from her
parents.

(a)	(b)	(c)

問3 最後の段落の内容に最も近いものを, ①〜④の中から１つ選びなさい。

① It will become harder for Generation Z to keep their private information secret from their parents.

② People should be careful not to lose their chance to get a job because of what they post online.

③ Social media will teach Generation Z how to protect their privacy from marketing companies.

④ It will be impossible even for Generation Z to protect their personal information.

問4 次の各文が本文の内容と一致するように, 空所に入れるのに最も適当なものを, それぞれ①〜④の中から１つずつ選びなさい。

(a) This article is primarily about ( ).

① Generation Z and its use of technology

② how to use technology to find a job

③ how social media affects parents of Gen-Z

④ the difference between Gen-Z members and their parents

(b) Many Gen-Z members ( ).

① are encouraged to spend more time using social media by marketing companies

② decide what items to buy based on their friends' advice on social networking sites

③ don't seem to care how much of their personal information is collected by marketing companies

④ seem to be more afraid of having their privacy invaded by marketing companies than by their parents

(a) [　　] (b) [　　]

問5 本文の内容に一致するものを，次の①〜④の中から 1 つ選びなさい。

① Most Gen-Z members have never used VCRs or desktop computers.

② The parents of Generation Z had no access to a computer.

③ Some members of Gen-Z were born in the 21st century.

④ Gen-Z's parents didn't have telephones in the house when they were children.

次の英文と図表を読んで, 解答番号 [1] ～ [6] にあてはまるものとして最も適当な選択肢を選びなさい。

Your teacher has asked you to read two articles about effective ways to study. You will discuss what you learned in your next class.

How to Study Effectively: Contextual Learning!
Tim Oxford
Science Teacher, Stone City Junior High School

As a science teacher, I am always concerned about how to help students who struggle to learn. Recently, I found that their main way of learning was to study new information repeatedly until they could recall it all. For example, when they studied for a test, they would use a workbook like the example below and repeatedly say the terms that go in the blanks: "Obsidian is igneous, dark, and glassy. Obsidian is igneous, dark, and glassy...." These students would feel as if they had learned the information, but would quickly forget it and get low scores on the test. Also, this sort of repetitive learning is dull and demotivating.

To help them learn, I tried applying "contextual learning." In this kind of learning, new knowledge is constructed through students' own experiences. For my science class, students learned the properties of different kinds of rocks. Rather than having them memorize the terms from a workbook, I brought a big box of various rocks to the class. Students examined the rocks and identified their names based on the characteristics they observed.

Thanks to this experience, I think these students will always be able to describe the properties of the rocks they studied. One issue, however, is that we don't always have the time to do contextual learning, so students will still study by doing drills. I don't think this is the best way. I'm still searching for ways to improve their learning.

Rock name	Obsidian
Rock type	igneous
Coloring	dark
Texture	glassy
Picture	

How to Make Repetitive Learning Effective

Cheng Lee

Professor, Stone City University

Mr. Oxford's thoughts on contextual learning were insightful. I agree that it can be beneficial. Repetition, though, can also work well. However, the repetitive learning strategy he discussed, which is called "massed learning," is not effective. There is another kind of repetitive learning called "spaced learning," in which students memorize new information and then review it over longer intervals.

The interval between studying is the key difference. In Mr. Oxford's example, his students probably used their workbooks to study over a short period of time. In this case, they might have paid less attention to the content as they continued to review it. The reason for this is that the content was no longer new and could easily be ignored. In contrast, when the intervals are longer, the students' memory of the content is weaker. Therefore, they pay more attention because they have to make a greater effort to recall what they had learned before. For example, if students study with their workbooks, wait three days, and then study again, they are likely to learn the material better.

Previous research has provided evidence for the advantages of spaced learning. In one experiment, students in Groups A and B tried to memorize the names of 50 animals. Both groups studied four times, but Group A studied at one-day intervals while Group B studied at one-week intervals. As the figure to the right shows, 28 days after the last learning session, the average ratio of recalled names on a test was higher for the spaced learning group.

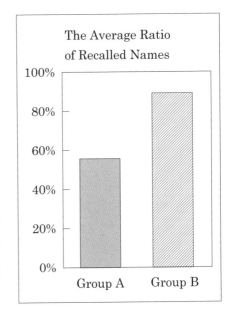

The Average Ratio of Recalled Names

I understand that students often need to learn a lot of information in a short period of time, and long intervals between studying might not be practical. You should understand, though, that massed learning might not be good for long-term recall.

問1 Oxford believes that [1] .

　① continuous drilling is boring

　② reading an explanation of terms is helpful

　③ students are not interested in science

　④ studying with a workbook leads to success

問2 In the study discussed by Lee, students took a test [2] after their final session.

　① four weeks　　　　　　② immediately

　③ one day　　　　　　　④ one week

問3 Lee introduces spaced learning, which involves studying at [3] intervals, in order to overcome the disadvantage of [4] learning that Oxford discussed. (Choose the best one for each box from options ①～⑥.)

　① contextual　　② extended　　③ fixed　　　　④ irregular

　⑤ massed　　　　⑥ practical

3 [　　　　]　　4 [　　　　]

問4 Both writers agree that [5] is helpful for remembering new information.

　① experiential learning　　　② having proper rest

　③ long-term attention　　　　④ studying with workbooks

問5 Which additional information would be the best to further support Lee's argument for spaced learning? **6**

① The main factor that makes a science class attractive

② The most effective length of intervals for spaced learning

③ Whether students' workbooks include visuals or not

④ Why Oxford's students could not memorize information well

次の英文を読んで, あとの問いに答えなさい。

Your English teacher has told everyone in your class to choose a short story in English to read. You will introduce the following story to your classmates, using a worksheet.

Becoming an Artist

Lucy smiled in anticipation. In a moment she would walk onto the stage and receive her prize from the mayor and the judges of the drawing contest. The microphone screeched and then came the mayor's announcement. "And the winner of the drawing contest is... Robert McGinnis! Congratulations!"

Lucy stood up, still smiling. Then, her face blazing red with embarrassment, abruptly sat down again. What? There must be a mistake! But the boy named Robert McGinnis was already on the stage, shaking hands with the mayor and accepting the prize. She glanced at her parents, her eyes filled with tears of disappointment. They had expected her to do well, especially her father. "Oh Daddy, I'm sorry I didn't win," she whispered.

Lucy had enjoyed drawing since she was a little

girl. She did her first drawing of her father when she was in kindergarten. Although it was only a child's drawing, it really looked like him. He was delighted, and, from that day, Lucy spent many happy hours drawing pictures to give to Mommy and Daddy.

As she got older, her parents continued to encourage her. Her mother, a busy translator, was happy that her daughter was doing something creative. Her father bought her art books. He was no artist himself, but sometimes gave her advice, suggesting that she look very carefully at what she was drawing and copy as accurately as possible. Lucy tried hard, wanting to improve her technique and please her father.

It had been Lucy's idea to enter the town drawing contest. She thought that if she won, her artistic ability would be recognized. She practiced every evening after school. She also spent all her weekends working quietly on her drawings, copying her subjects as carefully as she could.

Her failure to do well came as a great shock. She had worked so hard and her parents had been so supportive. Her father, however, was puzzled. Why did Lucy apologize at the end of the contest? There was no need to do so. Later, Lucy asked him why she had failed to win the competition. He answered sympathetically, "To me, your drawing was perfect." Then he smiled, and added, "But perhaps you should talk to your mother. She understands art better than I do."

Her mother was thoughtful. She wanted to give Lucy advice without damaging her daughter's self-esteem. "Your drawing was good," she told her, "but I think it lacked something. I think you only drew what you could see. When I translate a novel, I need to capture not only the meaning, but also the spirit of the original. To do that, I need to consider the meaning behind the words. Perhaps drawing is the same; you need to look under the surface."

Lucy continued to draw, but her art left her feeling unsatisfied. She couldn't understand what her mother meant. What was wrong with drawing what she could see? What else could she do?

Around this time, Lucy became friends with a girl called Cathy. They became close friends and Lucy grew to appreciate her for her kindness and humorous personality. Cathy often made Lucy laugh, telling jokes, saying ridiculous things, and making funny faces. One afternoon, Cathy had such a funny expression on her face that Lucy felt she had to draw it. "Hold that pose!" she told Cathy, laughing. She drew quickly, enjoying her friend's expression so much that she didn't really think about what she was doing.

When Lucy entered art college three years later, she still had that sketch. It had caught Cathy exactly, not only her odd expression but also her friend's kindness and her sense of humor — the things that are found under the surface.

Your worksheet:

---

1. Story title

"Becoming an Artist"

2. People in the story

Lucy: She loves to draw.

Lucy's father: He ⬚ 1 ⬚ .

Lucy's mother: She is a translator and supports Lucy.

Cathy: She becomes Lucy's close friend.

---

3. What the story is about

Lucy's growth as an artist:

> 2
>
> 3
>
> 4
>
> 5

Her drawing improves thanks to 6 and 7 .

4. My favorite part of the story

When the result of the contest is announced, Lucy says, "Oh Daddy, I'm sorry I didn't win."
This shows that Lucy 8 .

5. Why I chose this story

Because I want to be a voice actor and this story taught me the importance of trying to 9 to make the characters I play seem more real.

問1 Choose the best option for ☐ 1 ☐.

① gives Lucy some drawing tips

② has Lucy make drawings of him often

③ spends weekends drawing with Lucy

④ wants Lucy to work as an artist

問2 Choose **four** out of the five descriptions (①〜⑤) and rearrange them in the order they happened. ☐ 2 ☐ → ☐ 3 ☐ → ☐ 4 ☐ → ☐ 5 ☐

① She becomes frustrated with her drawing.

② She decides not to show anyone her drawings.

③ She draws with her feelings as well as her eyes.

④ She has fun making drawings as gifts.

⑤ She works hard to prove her talent at drawing.

	→	→	→	

問3 Choose the best two options for ☐ 6 ☐ and ☐ 7 ☐. (The order does not matter.)

① a friend she couldn't help sketching

② a message she got from a novel

③ advice she received from her mother

④ her attempt to make a friend laugh

⑤ spending weekends drawing indoors

問4 Choose the best option for ⌊ 8 ⌋.

① didn't practice as much as her father expected

② knew her father didn't like her entering the contest

③ thought she should have followed her father's advice

④ was worried she had disappointed her father

問5 Choose the best option for ⌊ 9 ⌋.

① achieve a better understanding of people

② analyze my own feelings more deeply

③ describe accurately what is happening around me

④ use different techniques depending on the situation

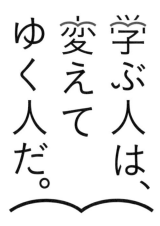

学ぶ人は、
変えて
ゆく人だ。

目の前にある問題はもちろん、

人生の問いや、

社会の課題を自ら見つけ、

挑み続けるために、人は学ぶ。

「学び」で、

少しずつ世界は変えてゆける。

いつでも、どこでも、誰でも、

学ぶことができる世の中へ。

旺文社

大学入試 全レベル問題集

英語長文

駿台予備学校講師 三浦淳一 著

2 共通テストレベル

三訂版

はじめに

　大学受験に向けた英語学習は，書店の学習参考書コーナーに行けばすぐにわかるとおり，とても細分化されています。単語・熟語，文法・語法，構文，英作文，長文読解，リスニング，会話表現，発音・アクセント…

　これを1つずつやっていたら，何年かかっても終わりそうにありません。

　「一石二鳥」という言葉がありますが，短期間で英語の学習を仕上げるには，いわば「一石五鳥」「一石六鳥」の学習をすることです。つまり，1つの学習で複数の効果を得られるような学習をすべきなのです。

　『大学入試 全レベル問題集 英語長文』シリーズは，長文読解の問題集という形をとっていますが，これにとどまらず，語彙力をつけたり，重要な文法事項の確認をしたり，音声を用いた学習により，発音・アクセント，リスニングの力をつけることも目指しています。

　本シリーズはレベル別に6段階で構成されており，必ず自分にピッタリ合った1冊があるはずです。また，現時点の実力と志望校のレベルにギャップがあるなら，1～2段階レベルを下げて，英語力を基礎から鍛え直すのもおすすめです。受験生はもちろん，高校1・2年生からスタートすることもできます。

　本シリーズは最新の大学入試問題の傾向に対応し，さらに，英語4技能（Reading ／ Listening ／ Writing ／ Speaking）を今後ますます重視する入試制度にも対応しうる，本質的・普遍的な英語力をつけることを目的にしています。

　本シリーズを利用して，皆さんが第一志望の大学に合格することはもちろん，その先，一生の武器となる確固たる英語力を身につけてほしいと願っています。

三浦　淳一

目　次

音声について

本書の英文を読み上げた音声を，専用ウェブサイト・スマートフォンアプリで聞くことができます。英文ごとに，2種類の音声を収録しています。全文通し読みの音声と，段落ごとに区切ったややゆっくりめの音声があります。段落ごとに区切った音声は，ディクテーションでご利用ください。🔊 01 のように示しています。

●ウェブサイトで聞く方法
・以下のサイトにアクセスし，パスワードを入力してください。
　https://service.obunsha.co.jp/tokuten/zlr3/
　※すべて半角英数字。検索エンジンの「検索欄」は不可。
　パスワード：zlr3w

●スマートフォンアプリで聞く方法
・音声をスマートフォンアプリ「英語の友」で聞くことができます。「英語の友」で検索するか，右の二次元コードからアクセスしてください。
・パスワードを求められたら，上と同じパスワードを入力してください。

　ご注意ください　◆音声を再生する際の通信料にご注意ください。◆音声は MP3 形式となっています。音声の再生には MP3 を再生できる機器などが別途必要です。デジタルオーディオプレーヤーなどの機器への音声ファイルの転送方法は，各製品の取り扱い説明書などをご覧ください。ご使用機器，音声再生ソフトなどに関する技術的なご質問は，ハードメーカーもしくはソフトメーカーにお問い合わせください。◆スマートフォンやタブレットでは音声をダウンロードできないことがあります。◆本サービスは予告なく終了することがあります。

自動採点について

採点・見直しができる無料の学習アプリ「学びの友」で，簡単に自動採点ができます。

① 以下の URL か右の二次元コードから，公式サイトにアクセスしてください。
　https://manatomo.obunsha.co.jp/
② アプリを起動後，「旺文社まなび ID」に会員登録してください（無料）。
③ アプリ内のライブラリより本書を選び，「追加」ボタンをタップしてください。

※ iOS ／ Android 端末，Web ブラウザよりご利用いただけます。
※ 本サービスは予告なく終了することがあります。

本シリーズの特長

「大学入試全レベル問題集 英語長文」シリーズには，以下の特長があります。

1．細かく分かれたレベル設定
本シリーズはレベル別からなる6冊で構成されており，学習者の皆さんそれぞれがベストな1冊を選んで大学入試対策をスタートできるようにしています。各書がレベルに応じた収録英文数と設問構成になっています。

2．語彙力を重視
語彙力は語学学習における基本です。単語がわからなければ英文を読むにも書くにも不自由します。本書ではオールラウンドな語彙力をつけられるよう，幅広いテーマの英文を選びました。各ユニットの最後に，本文の単熟語や英文が復習できる確認問題や，音声を利用した単語のディクテーション問題を設け，語彙力が増強できるよう工夫しています。

3．英文構造の明示
すべての英文の構造を示し（SVOC分析），英文を完全に理解できるようにしました。さらに，本文の和訳例も，あまり意訳をせず，文構造を反映させた直訳に近い日本語にしました。

4．文法事項のわかりやすい解説
近年の入試問題では，難関大学を中心に文法問題の出題が減少しており，「**文法問題を解くための文法学習**」は，もはや時代遅れです。本書では「**英文を正しく読むための文法**」を心がけて解説しています。

5．設問の的確な解説
すべての設問に，なるべく短く的確な解説をつけました。特に本文の内容に関する設問は，根拠となる箇所を明示して解説しています。類書と比較しても，わかりやすく論理的な解説にしています。これは，解説を読んで納得してほしいということもありますが，それ以上に，読者の皆さんが自分で問題を解くときにも，このように論理的に考えて，正解を導き出せるようになってほしいからです。

6．音声による学習
付属の音声には本書に掲載した**英文の音声が2パターンで収録**されています。主にリスニング力UPを目的としたナチュラルに近いスピードのものは，シャドーイング*1やオーバーラッピング*2用です。また1つ1つの単語の発音がわかるようなややゆっくりしたスピードのものは，ディクテーション問題用です。

> *1　シャドーイング・・・すぐ後から音声を追いかけて、同じ内容を口に出す練習方法
> *2　オーバーラッピング・・・流れてくる音声とぴったり重なるように口に出す練習方法

著者紹介： **三浦淳一**（みうら じゅんいち）

早稲田大学文学部卒。現在，駿台予備学校・医学部受験専門予備校 YMS 講師。『全国大学入試問題正解 英語』（旺文社）解答・解説執筆者。『入門英語長文問題精講［3 訂版］』『医学部の英語』『大学入学共通テスト英語〔リーディング〕集中講義』（以上，旺文社），『世界一覚えやすい中学英語の基本文例 100』（以上，KADOKAWA）ほか著書多数。「N予備校」「学びエイド」などで映像授業も担当する。

〔協力各氏・各社〕

装丁デザイン：ライトパブリシティ	録 音・編 集：ユニバ合同会社
本文デザイン：イイタカデザイン	ナレーション：Ann Slater, Guy Perryman, Katie Adler
校　　　正：大河恭子，関花々，株式会社友人社， 　　　　　　渡邉聖子，Jason A. Chau	編 集 協 力：株式会社オルタナプロ 編 集 担 当：高杉健太郎

志望校レベルと「全レベル問題集 英語長文」シリーズのレベル対応表

* 掲載の大学名は本シリーズを購入していただく際の目安です。また, 大学名は刊行時のものです。

本書のレベル	各レベルの該当大学
① 基礎レベル	高校基礎〜大学受験準備
② 共通テストレベル	共通テストレベル
③ 私大標準レベル	日本大学・東洋大学・駒澤大学・専修大学・京都産業大学・近畿大学・甲南大学・龍谷大学・札幌大学・亜細亜大学・國學院大學・東京電機大学・武蔵大学・神奈川大学・愛知大学・東海大学・名城大学・追手門学院大学・神戸学院大学・広島国際大学・松山大学・福岡大学 他
④ 私大上位レベル	学習院大学・明治大学・青山学院大学・立教大学・中央大学・法政大学・芝浦工業大学・成城大学・成蹊大学・津田塾大学・東京理科大学・日本女子大学・明治学院大学・獨協大学・北里大学・南山大学・関西外国語大学・西南学院大学 他
⑤ 私大最難関レベル	早稲田大学・慶應義塾大学・上智大学・関西大学・関西学院大学・同志社大学・立命館大学 他
⑥ 国公立大レベル	北海道大学・東北大学・東京大学・一橋大学・東京工業大学・名古屋大学・京都大学・大阪大学・神戸大学・広島大学・九州大学 他

本書で使用している記号一覧

 …………… 文法事項の説明
🔊 …………… 音声番号

SVOC分析

S, V, O, C ……… 主節における文の要素
S, V, O, C ……… 従属節における文の要素
S′, V′, O′, C′ …… 意味上の関係
① ② ③ ………… 並列関係にある要素
〈　　〉………… 名詞句, 名詞節
〔　　〕………… 形容詞句, 形容詞節
（　　）………… 副詞句, 副詞節
関代 …………… 関係代名詞
関副 …………… 関係副詞
等接 …………… 等位接続詞
従接 …………… 従属接続詞
疑 ……………… 疑問詞
… so ～ that … 相関語句

語句リスト

動 ……………… 動詞
名 ……………… 名詞
形 ……………… 形容詞
副 ……………… 副詞
接 ……………… 接続詞
前 ……………… 前置詞
熟 ……………… 熟語

英文を読むための基礎知識

英文を読む上で，単語や熟語の知識が必要なのは当然である。しかし，語句の意味がわかれば英文を正しく理解できるというわけではない。英文は日本語とは異なる「構造」を持っているので，「構造」を把握することが英文を読むときには不可欠だ。

そこで，英文の「構造」を把握する前提となる知識を解説する。正直言って面白みがある内容ではないが，英文読解力をつける上で避けては通れない道である。何とかがんばって熟読し，完全理解に努めてほしい。

解説の構成
❶ 品詞
❷ 文型
 1. 文型と文の要素　 2. 文型の見分け方　 3. 自動詞と他動詞
❸ 句と節
 1. 句と節とは
 2. 句 ——（1）名詞句　（2）形容詞句　（3）副詞句
 3. 節 ——（1）名詞節　（2）形容詞節　（3）副詞節
 4. 句と節の文中での位置
❹ 並列
 1. 等位接続詞　 2. 並列　 3. 様々な等位接続詞　 4. 等位接続詞による相関語句
❺ 語順変化を意識する読み方
 1. 英文の語順変化　 2. 語順変化が起こる場合

❶ 品詞

　品詞は細かく分類すると相当な数になってしまうが，とりあえず「名詞」「動詞」「形容詞」「副詞」の4品詞を押さえよう。

　「名詞」とは人や事物の名称などを表す語。例を挙げたほうが早いだろう。student や car などだ。Japan のような固有名詞，he や this のような代名詞も，このグループに含まれる。名詞の働きは，**S（主語），O（目的語），C（補語）になったり，前置詞の後ろに置かれる**（これを「前置詞の目的語」という）。

　「動詞」は動作や状態などを表す語。walk や know などだ。be 動詞（is や are）もこのグループに属する。動詞の働きは **V（述語）になる**ことだ。

　「形容詞」は，**①名詞を修飾する，②C（補語）になる**，という2つの働きを持っている。
　①の例としては

例 She is a **pretty** girl.　「彼女は**可愛い**女の子だ」
　 S　V　　　 C

pretty という形容詞が girl という名詞を修飾（詳しく説明）している。
　②の例としては

例 The girl is **pretty**.　「その女の子は**可愛い**」
　 S　　 V　　 C

　The girl が S, is が V, pretty が C という〈S＋V＋C〉の第2文型だ。文型の説明はあとで行う。

6

「副詞」の働きは，名詞以外を修飾することだ。**ほとんどの場合に動詞を修飾する**のだが，**形容詞やほかの副詞を修飾することもあるし，文全体を修飾したりもする**から，「名詞以外を修飾する」というのが正確なんだ。

例えば，

例 He walks **slowly**.　「彼は**ゆっくりと**歩く」
　　S　　V

という文では，副詞の slowly が動詞の walks を修飾している。

例 He walks **very** slowly.　「彼は**とても**ゆっくりと歩く」
　　S　　V

という文はどうだろう。

slowly が walks を修飾するのは前の文と同じだが，今度は very という副詞が slowly という副詞を修飾している。つまり，very → slowly → walks というふうに，二重の修飾になっている。

整理すると以下のようになる。

品詞	例	働き
名詞	student, car, advice, Japan, he (代名詞)	S, O, C, 前置詞の目的語になる
動詞	walk, run, know, do, believe, be	V になる
形容詞	small, pretty, old, tall, wonderful	①名詞を修飾　②Cになる
副詞	slowly, very, soon, too, easily	名詞以外を修飾

② 文型

1. 文型と文の要素

文型とは，英語の文のパターンを分類したものだ。英語の文には5つの文型がある。

第1文型：**S ＋ V**
第2文型：**S ＋ V ＋ C**
第3文型：**S ＋ V ＋ O**
第4文型：**S ＋ V ＋ O ＋ O**
第5文型：**S ＋ V ＋ O ＋ C**

そして，文型を構成する1つ1つのパーツのことを，文の要素と呼んでいる。これも5つある。

S（主語）：「～は」「～が」と訳す。**名詞**。
V（述語）：「～する」「～である」と訳す。**動詞**。
O（目的語）：「～を」「～に」と訳す。**名詞**。
C（補語）：決まった訳し方はない。**名詞**または**形容詞**。
M（修飾語）：決まった訳し方はない。**形容詞**または**副詞**。

Mという要素は5文型の中には出てこない。これは，M（修飾語）とは文字通り「飾り物」であって，文の中で不可欠な要素ではないからである。文型とは，**このような「飾り物」を取り除いたあとに残るパターンを分類したものだ**，と理解しよう。

例えば，第1文型は〈S+V〉という2つの要素しかないが，だからといって文が短いということにはならない。〈S+V〉のあとにたくさんのM（修飾語）がくっついて，とても長い英文になることもある。

2. 文型の見分け方

この5つの文型の見分け方について説明しよう。

まず，**M（修飾語）をすべて取り除く。**このとき，**〈S+V〉しか残らなかったら，もちろん第1文型だ。**何がMになるのか，が問題だが，これには後述の「句」や「節」の理解が欠かせない。とりあえず，副詞や〈前置詞＋名詞〉はMになると考えてよい。

例 He usually goes to school by bus. 「彼はふだん，バスで学校に行く」

この英文では，usually が副詞だから取り除く。to school と by bus は〈前置詞＋名詞〉だから，これも取り除く。

$$\underset{S}{\text{He}} \; \cancel{\text{usually}} \; \underset{V}{\text{goes}} \; \cancel{\text{to school by bus}}.$$

というわけで，SとVしか残らないから，第1文型だ。

次に，Mを取り除いたときに，〈S+V〉の後ろに1つの要素（Xとする）が残っている場合は次のように考える。

> **S+V+X の場合**　「SはXだ」と言える　→　**S + V + C**
> 　　　　　　　　　「SはXだ」と言えない →　**S + V + O**

要するに，SとXが「主語－述語」の関係かどうか，ということだ。例文を見てみよう。

例 $\underset{S}{\text{The girl}}$ finally $\underset{V}{\text{became}}$ $\underset{C}{\text{a nurse}}$. 「その女の子は結局看護師になった」

finally が副詞なのでMと考え，取り除く。そうすると，The girl became という〈S+V〉のあとに，a nurse という要素が残った。そこでこれをXと考えると「その女の子は看護師だ」となり，これは特に不自然ではない。よって，〈S+V+C〉の第2文型。

例 $\underset{S}{\text{Her new dress}}$ $\underset{V}{\text{becomes}}$ $\underset{O}{\text{her}}$ very well.
「彼女の新しいドレスは彼女にとてもよく似合っている」

very も well も副詞なのでM。よって，これを取り除く。Her new dress がSでbecomes がVだ（細かいことを言えば，Her と new は dress を修飾しているからいずれもMだが，Her new dress をワンセットでSと考えたほうがわかりやすいだろう）。そこで，her をXと考えると「新しいドレスは彼女だ」となり，これは明らかにおかしい。よって，〈S+V+O〉

の第3文型。なお，become には第3文型で用いた場合に「似合う」という意味がある。

　最後に，M を取り除いたときに，〈S+V〉の後ろに2つの要素（X, Y とする）が残っている場合は次のように考える。

> **S+V+X+Y の場合**　「X は Y だ」と言える　→　**S ＋ V ＋ O ＋ C**
> 　　　　　　　　　　　「X は Y だ」と言えない　→　**S ＋ V ＋ O ＋ O**

例 <u>He</u> <u>made</u> <u>his daughter</u> <u>a doll</u>.　「彼は娘に人形を作ってあげた」
　　S　V　　O₁　　　O₂

　He が S, made が V。そのあとに his daughter と a doll という2つの要素がある。そこで，それぞれ X, Y と考える。「娘は人形だ」。これは無理。したがって，〈S+V+O₁+O₂〉の第4文型とわかった。make は第4文型で「O₁ に O₂ を作ってあげる」という意味だ。

例 <u>He</u> <u>made</u> <u>his daughter</u> <u>a nurse</u>.　「彼は娘を看護師にした」
　　S　V　　O　　　　C

　同じく，his daughter を X, a nurse を Y と考えると，今度は「娘は看護師だ」と言えるので〈S+V+O+C〉の第5文型となる。make は第5文型で「O を C にする」という意味だ。

例 <u>He</u> <u>made</u> <u>his daughter</u> <u>go to school</u>.　「彼は娘を学校に行かせた」
　　S　V　　O　　　　C

　his daughter を X, go (to school) を Y と考えると，「娘は（学校に）行くのだ」と言えるので，やはり〈S+V+O+C〉の第5文型となる。〈make+O+ 原形〉は「O に〜させる」という意味。このように，C には動詞の変形；原形，〈to+ 原形〉，現在分詞 (-ing 形)，過去分詞 (-ed 形，ただし不規則変化あり) が入ることもある。

　補足的に，O (目的語) と C (補語) の理解のしかたについて説明しよう。
　O (目的語) は V (述語) で表される行為などの対象 (相手) で，**必ず名詞**だ。
　C (補語) は，**第2文型〈S+V+C〉においては S と，第5文型〈S+V+O+C〉においては O と，それぞれ「主語－述語」の関係にある要素**，ということになる。そして，C は**名詞でも形容詞でもいいし**，前述のように動詞の変形の場合もある。

3. 自動詞と他動詞

　「自動詞」「他動詞」については，以下のように理解しよう。**O (目的語) がない動詞を「自動詞」，O がある動詞を「他動詞」**という。つまり，第1文型，第2文型の動詞は「自動詞」，第3文型，第4文型，第5文型の動詞は「他動詞」ということになる。

自動詞	第1文型：**S ＋ V**
	第2文型：**S ＋ V ＋ C**
他動詞	第3文型：**S ＋ V ＋ O**
	第4文型：**S ＋ V ＋ O ＋ O**
	第5文型：**S ＋ V ＋ O ＋ C**

自動詞, 他動詞の簡単な区別の仕方は, **「〜を」をつけられるかどうか**で考えるとわかりやすい。O は一般に「〜を」と訳すからだ。たとえば, go は, 「学校を行く」とは言わないから自動詞。visit は, 「学校を訪問する」と言えるから他動詞だ。

　もっとも, このやり方も万能ではない。marry や enter は他動詞だが, 「彼を結婚する」「部屋を入る」とは言わない。このようなものは, 文法・語法問題で問われるので, 整理しておく必要がある。

❸ 句と節

1. 句と節とは

　「句」も「節」も, 2語以上のカタマリを意味するが, 以下のような違いがある。

> 「句」→〈S+V〉を含まないカタマリ　　「節」→〈S+V〉を含むカタマリ

　たとえば, on the desk や playing the piano というカタマリは「句」で, if it rains や what I want というカタマリは「節」ということになる。そして「句」には, その働きにより, 「名詞句」「形容詞句」「副詞句」がある。節にも, 「名詞節」「形容詞節」「副詞節」がある(名詞, 形容詞, 副詞の働きについては, 6 ページを参照)。それぞれの「句」や「節」にはどんなものがあるのか, 表にまとめてみよう。

	種　類	働　き	句 や 節 を 作 る も の
句	名詞句	S, O, C になる	不定詞, 動名詞
	形容詞句	名詞を修飾	不定詞, 分詞, 前置詞
	副詞句	名詞以外を修飾	不定詞, 分詞, 前置詞
節	名詞節	S, O, C になる	従属接続詞 (that / if / whether), 疑問詞, 関係詞
	形容詞節	名詞を修飾	関係詞
	副詞節	名詞以外を修飾	従属接続詞, 関係詞

　以下, 表の上のほうから順に説明する。

2. 句

(1) 名詞句

　S, O, C になる句。**不定詞や動名詞のカタマリ**である。どちらも, 「**〜すること**」と訳す場合が多い。

> 例 <u>My desire</u> <u>is</u> 〈to study abroad〉.　　「私の希望は留学することだ」
> 　　S　　　　V　C

> 例 <u>He</u> <u>enjoyed</u> 〈swimming in the sea〉.　　「彼は海水浴(海で泳ぐこと)を楽しんだ」
> 　S　　V　　　　O

　それ以外には, 〈疑問詞+to *do*〉も名詞句を作る。

例 I didn't know 〈which way to go〉. 「私はどちらの道に行くべきかわからなかった」
　　S　　V　　　　O

名詞を修飾する句。**不定詞，分詞，前置詞のカタマリ**がこれにあたる。

例 I have a lot of *homework* [to do]. 「私にはやるべき宿題がたくさんある」
　　S　V　　　　　　　O

to do が homework という名詞を修飾している。

例 Look at *the dog* [running in the park]. 「公園で走っている犬を見なさい」
　　　V　　　　O

running in the park というカタマリが the dog という名詞を修飾している。

例 I bought *a ticket* [for the concert]. 「私はコンサートのチケットを買った」
　　S　　V　　　O

for the concert という前置詞のカタマリが，a ticket という名詞を修飾している。

名詞以外（主に動詞）を修飾する句。**不定詞，分詞，前置詞のカタマリ**がこれにあたる。なお，分詞が副詞句を作ると，「分詞構文」と呼ばれ，**【時】【理由】【付帯状況】**などの意味を表す。

例 He *went* to America (to study jazz). 「彼はジャズの研究をするためにアメリカへ行った」
　　S　V

to study jazz という不定詞のカタマリが went という動詞を修飾している。ここでは「〜するために」という**【目的】**の意味。

例 He *entered* the room, (taking off his hat). 「彼は帽子を脱ぎながら部屋に入った」
　　S　　V　　　O

taking off his hat という分詞のカタマリ（分詞構文）が entered という動詞を修飾している。ここでは「〜しながら」という**【付帯状況】**の意味。

例 I *got* (to the station) (at ten). 「私は 10 時に 駅に到着した」
　　S　V

to the station と at ten という2つの前置詞のカタマリが，いずれも got という動詞を修飾している。

3. 節

S，O，C になる節。**従属接続詞（that / if / whether），疑問詞，関係詞**が名詞節を作る。ここで，「従属接続詞」について説明しよう。

接続詞には，「等位接続詞」「従属接続詞」の2種類がある。「等位接続詞」は and や or のように，前後を対等に結ぶ（並列する）接続詞だ（14 ページ参照）。これに対して，「従属

接続詞」とは，**節を作るタイプの接続詞**のこと。従属接続詞は数多くあるが，その中で**名詞節を作るのは that「…こと」／ if「…かどうか」／ whether「…かどうか」の3つだけ**で，それ以外のすべての従属接続詞は副詞節しか作れない。

　例文を見てみよう。

例 〈**That** <u>you</u> <u>study</u> <u>Spanish</u> now〉 <u>is</u> <u>a good idea</u>.
　　　　S　　　S　　V　　　O　　　　　V　　C

「あなたが今スペイン語を勉強する**こと**はいい考えだ」

例 <u>I</u> <u>don't know</u> 〈**if**[**whether**]〉 <u>he</u> <u>will come</u> here tomorrow〉.
　　S　　V　　　　　　　　　　　　S　　　V

「明日彼がここに来る**のかどうか**わからない」

　このほか，**疑問詞も名詞節を作る**。前提として，まず，疑問詞について確認しよう。what「何」，who「誰」，which「どちら」，when「いつ」，where「どこ」，why「なぜ」，how「どのように」といった語を疑問詞という。これらの最も基本的な働きは，疑問文で文頭に置かれる用法だ。

例 What <u>does</u> <u>he</u> <u>want</u>?　「彼は何が欲しいのですか」
　　　　(V)　S　　V

この疑問詞が，名詞節を作って，文中で S, O, C になることがある。

例 <u>I</u> <u>don't know</u> 〈**what** <u>he</u> <u>wants</u>〉.　「私は，彼が**何を**欲しがっているのか知らない」
　　S　　V　　　　　　O　　　S　　V

このような文のことを「**間接疑問文**」という。上の2つの例文で，what のあとの語順を比較してほしい。文中に what がある場合は，そのあとが does he want という疑問文の語順ではなく，he wants という**平叙文の語順**になる。

　最後に，**一部の関係詞も名詞節を作る**ことがある。これは，関係詞の中では少数派であり，関係詞の大半は，次に述べる形容詞節を作る。名詞節を作る関係詞は，**what「…すること／…するもの」**と **how「…する方法」**を押さえておこう。

例 〈**What** <u>I</u> <u>want</u>〉 <u>is</u> <u>a new car</u>.　「私が欲しい**もの**は新しい車だ」
　　　　S　　S　V　　V　　C

例 This <u>is</u> 〈**how** <u>I</u> <u>solved</u> <u>the problem</u>〉.
　　S　V　C　　　S　　V　　　O

「これが，私が問題を解決した**方法**だ（→このようにして私は問題を解決した）」

（2）形容詞節

　名詞を修飾する働きをする節。これを作るのは**関係詞だけ**だ。関係詞には，関係代名詞と関係副詞の2つがある。関係代名詞は**後ろに「不完全な文」**（S や O などが欠けている文），関係副詞は**後ろに「完全な文」**（S や O などが欠けていない文）が続く。例文で確認してみよう。

例 I have *a friend* 〔**who** lives in Osaka〕. 「私には大阪に住んでいる友人がいる」
　S　V　　O　　　　　　V

関係代名詞 who から始まるカタマリが a friend という名詞を修飾している。who の後ろには lives に対する S が欠けた文（＝不完全な文）が続いている。

例 This is *the place* 〔**where** I met her first〕.「ここは私が初めて彼女に会った場所だ」
　S　V　　C　　　　　　　　S　V　O

関係副詞 where から始まるカタマリが the place という名詞を修飾している。where の後ろには，I (S) met (V) her (O) という，何も欠けていない文（＝完全な文）が続いている。

（3）副詞節

名詞以外（主に動詞）を修飾する節。従属接続詞はすべて，副詞節を作ることができる。

例 I like him （**because** he is generous）.　「彼は気前がいいので，私は彼が好きだ」
　S　V　O　　　　　　　　S　V　　C

従属接続詞 because から始まるカタマリが like という動詞を修飾している。

先ほど名詞節のところで出てきた that / if / whether は，名詞節だけではなく副詞節も作ることができる（ただし，that は so ～ that … 構文など，特殊な構文に限られる）。**if は「もし…すれば」，whether は「…であろうとなかろうと」の意味では副詞節**である。

例 I will stay home （**if** it rains tomorrow）. 「もし明日雨が降ったら，私は家にいるつも
　S　　V　　　　　　　　S　V　　　　　　　　りだ」

従属接続詞 if から始まるカタマリが stay という動詞を修飾している。

このほか，「複合関係詞」と呼ばれる特殊な関係詞が副詞節を作ることができる。これは，**関係詞の後ろに -ever をくっつけたもの**で，whoever, whatever のように〈関係代名詞 + -ever〉のタイプと，whenever, wherever のように〈関係副詞 + -ever〉のタイプがある。

例 I will reject your offer （**whatever** you say）.
　S　　V　　　O　　　　　　　　S　V

「たとえ君が何を言っても，私は君の申し出を断ります」

複合関係詞 whatever から始まるカタマリが reject という動詞を修飾している。

4. 句と節の文中での位置

ここまで述べた，合計6種類の句・節のうち，**副詞句・副詞節の2つは基本的に文中での位置が自由である。**

前述の副詞句の例文は，以下のように書き換えてもよい。

例 He went to America （to study jazz）.

= （To study jazz）, he went to America.

副詞節の例文も同様。

例 I will stay home (if it rains tomorrow).
　＝(If it rains tomorrow), I will stay home.

より長い文だと, 副詞句・副詞節が文の中ほどに挿入されることもある。

これに対して, 名詞句・名詞節は, S, O, C などのあるべき位置に, 形容詞句・形容詞節は, 修飾する名詞の後ろに置かれる。したがって, 文中での位置は自由ではない。

④ 並 列

1. 等位接続詞

and や or などのように, **前後を対等の関係に結ぶ接続詞**を「等位接続詞」という。これに対し, 前述の that や because など, 節を導く接続詞を「従属接続詞」という。

2. 並列

等位接続詞によって対等の関係に結ばれることを「**並列**」という。

例 He studied English and mathematics. 「彼は**英語**と**数学**を勉強した」
　　　　　　　　①　　　　　　　②

English と mathematics が並列されている。つまり, O が2つ並列されている。
＊なお, 本書では並列されているもの同士を①, ②, ③……のように示す。

例 He studied English, mathematics and science. 「彼は**英語**と**数学**と**理科**を勉強した」
　　　　　　　　①　　　　　　②　　　　　　③

English, mathematics, science が並列されている。つまり, O が3つ並列されている。3つ以上の並列の場合, 〈① and ② and ③〉としてもよいが, 〈①, ② and ③〉のように, 等位接続詞は最後に1回だけ用いるのがふつう。

例 He studied English and read a comic book. 「彼は**英語を勉強**し, **漫画を読んだ**」
　　　①　　　　　　　　　　②

studied English と read a comic book が並列されている。つまり, 〈V+O〉が2つ並列されている。

例 He studied English and his brother read a comic book.
　　①　　　　　　　　　　　②

「彼は**英語を勉強**し, **彼の弟は漫画を読んだ**」

He studied English と his brother read a comic book が並列されている。つまり, 〈S+V+O〉が2つ並列されている。

14

3. 様々な等位接続詞

　and 以外の等位接続詞としては，or「または」／ but「しかし」／ yet「しかし」／ so「だから」／ nor「～も～ない」／ for「というのは～だからだ」がある。**and と or は語，句，節を並列するのに対し，その他は主に節を並列する。**

例 Which do you like better, tea or coffee?
　　　　　　　　　　　　　　 ①　②

　　「**紅茶**と**コーヒー**ではどちらのほうが好きですか」

例 She is wealthy, but [yet] she is unhappy.　「彼女は裕福なのに**不幸**だ」
　　　　　①　　　　　　　　　②

例 This is a simple but [yet] important question.　「これは**単純**だが**重要**な問題だ」
　　　　　　①　　　　　　　②

＊but や yet が語を並列することもある。

例 He worked hard, so he passed the entrance examination.
　　　　①　　　　　　②

　　「**彼は一生懸命勉強した**，だから**入学試験に合格した**」

例 He isn't rich, nor has he ever been.「彼は**金持ち**ではないし**金持ちだったこともない**」
　　　①　　　　　　②

＊nor のあとは倒置が起こり，疑問文のような語順になる。

例 He felt no fear, for he was a brave man.
　　　①　　　　　②

　　「**彼は恐怖を感じなかった**，というのは**勇敢な男だったからだ**」

4. 等位接続詞による相関語句

以下も A と B が文法上対等になる。
□ not A but B　　　　　　「A ではなくて B」（= B, not A）
□ both A and B　　　　　　「A と B の両方」（= at once A and B ）
□ either A or B　　　　　　「A か B のどちらか」
□ neither A nor B　　　　　「A も B もどちらも～ない」（= not ～ either A or B）
□ not only A but also B　　「A だけでなく B も」（= B as well as A）

例 He studied both English and French.　「彼は**英語**と**フランス語**の両方を勉強した」
　　　　　　　①　　　　②

　そのほか，A rather than B [rather A than B]「B というよりむしろ A」，A, if not B「B ではないとしても A」なども並列構造を作り，A と B が文法上対等となる。

❺ 語順変化を意識する読み方

1. 英文の語順変化

英語の語順は，〈S + V + O〉，〈S + V + O + C〉などの「文型」に従ったものになるのが原則である。しかし，様々な要因により，この原則的な語順が変化することがある。

例えば，He ate spaghetti. 「彼はスパゲティを食べた」という英文は，He が S，ate が V，spaghetti が O であり，〈S + V + O〉の原則通りの語順である。

これに対し，What did he eat? 「彼は何を食べましたか？」という英文は，he が S，〈did + eat〉が V，What が O であり，**本来なら eat の後にあるはずの O が文頭に移動している**ことがわかる。これは，疑問詞を含む疑問文で，**「疑問詞は文頭に置かれる」という**ルールが，**文型の語順のルールよりも優先される**からである。

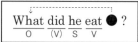

さて，このレベルの英文であれば，語順変化を意識しなくてもスムーズに読むことができるだろう。だが，より複雑な英文になると，語順変化をしっかり意識しなければ，正しく理解できないケースが出てくる。

その場合，上の図の●のように，元の位置を自分でマークし，その位置に戻して考えてみることが有効である。

2. 語順変化が起こる場合

では，実際にどのような場合に語順変化が起こるのだろうか。

整理すると，以下の 8 つのケースが重要である。

| ① 疑問文　② 関係代名詞　③〈C + as + S + V〉　④〈the + 比較級〉 |
| ⑤ 強調構文　⑥ 形容詞用法の不定詞　⑦ no matter ... / -ever　⑧ 倒置 |

例を挙げながら解説していこう。

① 疑問文

疑問詞を含む疑問文で，語順変化が起こる。

例 How much attention did you pay to his proposal?

　「彼の提案にどれほどの注意を払いましたか？」

pay attention to 〜「〜に注意を払う」という熟語だが，attention が How much と結びついて文頭に移動している。せっかく熟語を知っていても，語順変化を意識しないと，「pay to って何だろう？」となってしまう。

$$\underset{\text{O}}{\text{How much attention}} \; \underset{\text{(V)}}{\text{did}} \; \underset{\text{S}}{\text{you}} \; \underset{\text{V}}{\text{pay}} \; \bullet \; \text{to his proposal?}$$

このように，元の位置を意識すれば，熟語を発見し，正しく解釈できるのである。

② 関係代名詞

関係代名詞の先行詞にあたる名詞は，後ろから前へと移動する。

例 This is the bike I had repaired yesterday.

「これは私が昨日修理してもらった自転車だ」

この英文を和訳させると，ほとんどの受験生が「これは私が昨日修理した自転車だ」と答える。しかし，yesterday という単なる過去の出来事を〈had + P.P.〉(過去完了形) で書くことはないので，この解釈は無理。

※間違った考え方

This is the bike 〔(which) $\underset{\text{S}}{\text{I}}$ $\underset{\text{V}}{\text{had repaired}}$ $\underset{\text{(O)}}{\bullet}$ yesterday.〕

以下のように考える。

※正しい考え方

This is the bike 〔(which) $\underset{\text{S}}{\text{I}}$ $\underset{\text{V}}{\text{had}}$ $\underset{\text{(O)}}{\bullet}$ $\underset{\text{C}}{\text{repaired}}$ yesterday.〕

つまり，〈have + O + P.P.〉「O を〜してもらう」の have が過去形になっているのだ。

③ 〈C + as + S + V〉

〈S + V + C〉の C が前に移動し，〈C + as + S + V〉の形で，「…であるが」という【譲歩】の意味を表す。

例 Reluctant as he was to attend the party, he accepted her invitation.

「彼はパーティーに出席したくなかったが，彼女の招待を受け入れた」

be reluctant to *do* で「〜したがらない」の意味。この形容詞 reluctant が前に移動した結果，was と to がくっついている。

(Reluctant $\underset{\text{C}}{}$ *as* $\underset{\text{S}}{\text{he}}$ $\underset{\text{V}}{\text{was}}$ $\bullet$ to attend the party,) he accepted her invitation.

---

④ 〈the + 比較級〉

〈the + 比較級 〜, the + 比較級 ...〉で「〜すればするほど…」の意味を表す。この構文

では，比較級の部分が移動してきていることが多い。

例 The harder you study English, the more interesting you will find it.

「英語を一生懸命に学べば学ぶほど，それが面白いものであることがわかるだろう」

harder は副詞で，元の位置は English の後。You study English hard.「あなたは一生懸命に英語を勉強する」という文をイメージする。more interesting は〈find ＋ O ＋ C〉「O が C だとわかる」という第 5 文型の C が前に移動したもの。元の位置を意識しないと，find の意味（文型ごとに異なる）を正しく理解できない。

⑤ 強調構文

〈It is ～ that ...〉の形で「～」の部分を強調するのが強調構文。「…するのは～だ」などと訳す。この構文でも，強調される「～」は本来は that 以下の文の要素なのだが，前に移動している。

例 It is with political systems in the past that historians have to deal.

「歴史家が扱わなくてはならないのは，過去の政治体制だ」

deal with ～「～を扱う」という熟語の with ～ が前に移動し，強調されている。

It is (with political systems in the past) *that* <u>historians</u> <u>have to deal</u> ●.
　　　　　　　　　　　　　　　　　　　　　　　　　　　S　　　　　V

⑥ 形容詞用法の不定詞

不定詞の形容詞用法とは，不定詞が直前の名詞を修飾する用法である。

例 He has many friends to support him.　「彼には支えてくれる友達がたくさんいる」
　 He has many friends to support.　「彼には支えるべき友達がたくさんいる」

上の例文は，many friends (S') ⇒ support (V') という関係が成立する。
下の例文は，support (V') ⇒ many friends (O') という関係が成立する。
語順変化が起こるのは，下のパターンである。

He has <u>many friends</u> [to <u>support</u> ●].
　　　　　　O'　　　　　　　　V'

もう 1 つ例を見てみよう。

例 I need a knife to cut meat with.　「私は肉を切るためのナイフが必要だ」

【道具・手段】を表す前置詞 with が文末にあり，本来なら with の後にあったはずの a knife が前に移動している。cut meat *with* a knife「ナイフを使って肉を切る」というつながりを意識して解釈する。

I need a knife [to cut meat with ●].

⑦ no matter … / -ever

no matter … / -ever は「たとえ…しても」の意味。「…」の部分には who / which / what / when / where / how などが入る。

例 He looks young whatever clothes he wears.
  ＝He looks young no matter what clothes he wears.

「彼はどんな服を着ても若く見える」

wears の目的語である clothes が whatever [no matter what] と結びついて前に移動している。

He looks young (*whatever* clothes he wears ●).
　　　　　　　　　　　 O　　 S　 V

特に注意が必要なのは，however [no matter how] で，形容詞や副詞と結びつく。

例 However absorbed he seemed to be in his work, he lacked concentration.
  ＝No matter how absorbed he seemed to be in his work, he lacked concentration.
「彼はどんなに仕事に熱中しているように見えても，集中力を欠いていた」

be absorbed in ～「～に没頭して，～に熱中して」の absorbed が however [no matter how] と結びついて前に移動している。

(*However* absorbed he seemed to be ● in his work), he lacked concentration.
　　　　　　 C　　 S　　　 V

⑧ 倒置

倒置には様々なパターンがあるが，特に O や C が前に移動するタイプの倒置（〈S ＋ V ＋ C〉⇒〈C ＋ S ＋ V〉，〈S ＋ V ＋ O〉⇒〈O ＋ S ＋ V〉など）は語順変化に注意が必要である。

例 All my spare time I spent in reading comic books.

「余暇の時間はすべて，漫画を読んで過ごした」

〈spend ＋ 時間 ＋ (in) *doing*〉「～して 時間 を過ごす」の 時間 (O) が前に移動している。

All my spare time I spent ● (in reading comic books).
　　　　　 O　　　　 S　 V

1 解答・解説

解答

問1	④	問2	①	問3	③
問4	②	問5	②, ⑥		

解説

問1

(ア) 直後の correct を修飾する副詞を選ぶ。直前の文の「(家庭で話す言語は) 英語だ」という答えは，第3段落によれば79%の人々にあてはまる。つまり100%ではないので **partly**「部分的に」が正解。

(エ) 直後に最上級が続く。 **by far** は最上級を強調し，「ずば抜けて〜，断トツで〜」の意味。

(オ) 直後に how many が続く副詞としては，**exactly**「正確に」が適切。

問2

疑問詞 how は，形容詞や副詞とセットで用いると「どれほど〜か」という【程度】を表すが，単独で用いると「どのように[どう]〜か」という【方法】または【様子】を表す。ここでは how の後に形容詞・副詞ではなく名詞 efforts が続いているので後者。選択肢①がこれにあたる。選択肢③は【程度】の意味で解釈している点に注意。

問3

各選択肢の動詞 (現在形) の意味は以下の通り。
①「交換する」　②「運動する」　**③「表現する」**　④「予期[期待]する」
state は動詞で用いると「言う，述べる」の意味なので，③が最も近い。なお，下線部は Stated と【受動】を表す過去分詞になっており，直訳すれば「ほかの方法で述べられると」となる。

問4

直後に doesn't have a definite answer とあるので，異なる言語の数はいく

つあるかという問いに対する「答え」を持ちうる立場にあるものは何か，と考える。第3〜4段落で国勢調査局（the Census Bureau）が言語の使用状況を調査し把握していることがわかる。

問5

① 「毎年」行われているという記述はない。

② 第2段落第3文に how well the person can speak English 「その人がどれほどうまく英語を話せるのか」という質問が含まれるとあるので，これと一致する。

③ 第3段落第1文参照。79%は家庭で英語「だけ」を話す人々の割合である。複数言語を話す人々もいると考えられるので，実際にはこれより多くなるはず。また，調査対象は5歳以上のため，「全人口の」も誤り。

④ 第3段落第2文によれば，21%とは英語以外の言語を家庭で話す人々の割合。また，同段落最終文によれば，そのうち58%が流ちょうに英語を話せる。

⑤ 第4段落第1文および最終文参照。スペイン語，中国語，タガログ語，ベトナム語，フランス語の順である。なお，第4段落最終文の in that order は「その順番に」の意味。

⑥ 第5段落最終文の後半部分と一致。

▼

それでは次に，段落ごとに詳しくみていこう。

第1段落　文の構造と語句のチェック

¹(If someone were to ask you 〈 what language people 〔 in the United States 〕
　　従接　 S　　　 V　　　 O₁ O₂　疑　　 O　　　　　　　 S

speak (in their own homes)〉〉), your answer would probably be,
　 V　　　　　　　　　　　　　　　　　 S　　　　　 V

"English, of course!" ²You might be surprised (to learn, however, 〈 that
　　　　　 C　　　　　 S　　 V　　　 C　　　　　　　　　　　　　　 従接

that answer would be only partly correct 〉).
　　 S　　　　 V　　　　 C

語句

probably	副	おそらく, たぶん	**however**	副	しかしながら, けれども	
of course	熟	もちろん	**partly**	副	部分的に, 一部分は	
			correct	形	正しい, 正確な	

第2段落 文の構造と語句のチェック

¹(For many years), the U.S. Census Bureau, a part of the American government,
　　　　　　　　　　　　　　 S　　　└──同格──┘

has been investigating this language question. ²Currently, this is being done (by
　　　　　 V　　　　　　　　　 O　　　　　　　　　　　　　 S　　 V

asking people ⟨ whether they (and/or their children 5 years old or older) speak
　　　　　　　　 従接　 S　　　　　　　　　　　　　　　　　　　　　　　　　 V

something other than English (at home))). ³(If the answer is "yes,") then
　　　　 O　　　　　　　　　　　　　　　　　　 従接　 S　 V　　 C

follow-up questions are asked 〔 about ⟨ which language is used ⟩ and ⟨ how well
　　 S　　　　　　 V　　　　　　　　　 疑　　 S　　 V　 等接　 疑

the person can speak English 〕. ⁴Two important purposes 〔 of asking these 3
　 S　　 V　　 O　　　　　　　　　 S
　　　　　　　　　　　　　　　　　　①

questions 〕 are ⟨ to learn ⟨ how many people have difficulty (using English)⟩⟩ and
　　　　 V　 C　　　　　　 疑　　　 S　　 V　　 O　　　　　　　　 等接
②
⟨ to better understand ⟨ how efforts 〔 to assist such people 〕 should be made ⟩⟩.
C　　　　　　　　　　 疑　 S　　　　　　　　　　　　　　　 V

語句

government	名	政府
investigate	動	調査する
currently	副	現在(は), 今のところ
whether	接	…かどうか
other than ~	熟	~以外に
purpose	名	目的

difficulty	名	困難, 苦労
▶ have difficulty (in) *doing*		
	熟	~するのに苦労する
effort	名	取り組み, 試み
▶ make efforts [an effort]		
		取り組み [試み] を行う, 努力する
assist	動	助ける, 支援する

第3段落　文の構造と語句のチェック

¹Recent Census Bureau results indicate 〈 that about 79% of the 291.5
　S　　　　　　　　　　　　　　 V　　　 O 従接

million people (aged 5 and over) 〔 in the U.S. 〕 speak only English (at home)〉.
　　S　　　　　　　　　　　　　　　　　　　 V　　　　 O

²(Stated another way), about 21% of the people speak a language 〔 other than
　　　　　　　　　　　　　　　　　 S　　　　　　 V　　　 O

English 〕. ³Many of those people (about 58%), however, apparently can also speak
　　　　　　 S　　　　　　　　　　　　　　　　　　　　　　　　 V

English ("very well.")
　O

> **訳** ¹最近の国勢調査の結果が示すように, アメリカの2億9150万人の人々(5歳以上)のうち約79%は家庭で英語しか話さない。²別の言い方をすると, 約21%の人々は英語以外の言語を話している。³しかし, そのような人々の多く(約58%)は, どうやら英語を「とても上手に」話すこともできるようだ。

語句

recent	形	最近の
result	名	結果
indicate	動	示す

aged	形	~歳の
state	動	言う, 述べる
apparently	副	どうやら…らしい

第4段落　文の構造と語句のチェック

¹The Census Bureau results show 〈 that speakers 〔 of "Spanish or Spanish Creole" 〕
　S　　　　　　　　　　　　 V　O 従接　 S　　　　　　 ①　　等接　　　②

23

are, (by far), the largest group 〔 of "other language" users 〕〉. ²They account for
‾ V‾   ‾‾‾‾‾‾‾‾C‾‾‾‾‾‾‾‾   ‾S‾ ‾‾‾V‾‾‾

more than 60% 〔 of the "other language" people 〕. ³(After them) come
‾‾‾‾‾‾O‾‾‾‾‾‾   ‾V‾

the speakers 〔 of Chinese 〕, and then the speakers 〔 of Tagalog, Vietnamese, and
‾‾‾S‾‾‾‾   等接   ‾‾‾S‾‾‾‾   ①   ②   等接

French, (in that order)〕.
‾‾‾‾‾
③

訳 ¹国勢調査の結果は, スペイン語またはスペイン系クレオール語の話者が「他の言語」を
使う人々の中でずば抜けて最大の集団であることを示している。²彼らは「他の言語」の人々
のうち60%以上を占めている。³それに次ぐのが中国語話者であり, そしてタガログ語, ベ
トナム語, フランス語話者がその順番で続く。

語句
by far   熟 断トツで, ずば抜けて

account for 〜   熟 〜の割合を占める
order   名 順番, 順序

第5段落 文の構造と語句のチェック

¹Just exactly how many different languages are spoken (in American homes)?
‾‾‾‾‾‾‾‾疑 ‾‾‾‾‾‾‾‾‾‾‾S‾‾‾‾‾‾‾‾‾‾ ‾‾‾V‾‾‾
①

²The Census Bureau says 〈 that it doesn't have a definite answer 〔 to this 〕〉,
‾‾‾‾‾‾S‾‾‾‾‾‾ ‾V‾ O 従接 S ‾‾‾V‾‾‾ ‾‾‾‾‾‾‾O‾‾‾‾‾‾
②

but 〈 that data 〔 collected several years ago 〕 indicated 〈 that more than 300 of
等接 O 従接 ‾S‾   ‾‾‾V‾‾‾ O 従接 ‾‾‾‾‾S‾‾‾‾‾

them were being used (at that time)〉〉.
      ‾‾‾‾‾V‾‾‾‾‾

訳 ¹正確にはいくつの異なる言語がアメリカの家庭で話されているのだろうか。²国勢調査
局は, これに対する明確な答えはないが, 数年前に集められたデータの示すところでは, 当
時300を超える言語が使われていたと述べる。

語句
exactly   副 正確に, 厳密に
definite   形 明確な

data   名 資料, データ
　　　　　　　　　＊datumの複数形
collect   動 集める
at that time   熟 当時

24

文法事項の整理 ① 進行形・完了形の受動態

第2段落第2文の進行形の受動態を見てみよう。

Currently, this **is being done** by asking people whether they (and/or their children 5 years old or older) speak something other than English at home.

受動態の基本パターンは〈be P.P.〉。進行形や完了形の文を受動態にすると以下のようなパターンになる。

①　進行形の受動態：〈be being P.P.〉「～されている，～されつつある」

例 Two workers are repairing the elevator.

　「2人の作業員がエレベーターを修理している」

　⇒ The elevator **is being repaired** by two workers.

　　「エレベーターが2人の作業員によって修理されている」

　＊以下のようなイメージで考えるとわかりやすい。

進行形	be	*doing*	
＋受動態		be	P.P.
	be	**being**	**P.P.**

②　完了形の受動態：〈have been P.P.〉「もう～された【完了】，～されたことがある【経験】，ずっと～されている【継続】」

例 Mr. Ito has already finished the work.

　「伊藤さんはもうその仕事を仕上げた」

　⇒ The work **has** already **been finished** by Mr. Ito.

　　「その仕事は伊藤さんによってもう仕上げられた」

　＊以下のようなイメージで考えるとわかりやすい。

完了形	have	P.P.	
＋受動態		be	P.P.
	have	**been**	**P.P.**

▶第５段落最終文

The Census Bureau says that it doesn't have a definite answer to this, but that data collected several years ago indicated that more than 300 of them <u>were being used</u> at that time.

▶過去進行形の受動態。

確認問題

/40点

1. 次の和訳と対応する英語の語句を, 頭文字を参考にして書き, 空欄を完成させよう。

(各1点×20)

①	of c____	熟	もちろん
②	h____	副	しかしながら, けれども
③	p____	副	部分的に, 一部分は
④	c____	形	正しい, 正確な
⑤	g____	名	政府
⑥	i____	動	調査する
⑦	p____	名	目的
⑧	d____	名	困難, 苦労
⑨	e____	名	取り組み, 試み
⑩	a____	動	助ける, 支援する
⑪	r____	形	最近の
⑫	i____	動	示す
⑬	s____	動	言う, 述べる
⑭	a____	副	どうやら…らしい
⑮	by f____	熟	断トツで, ずば抜けて
⑯	a____ for ~	熟	～の割合を占める
⑰	o____	名	順番, 順序
⑱	d____	形	明確な
⑲	c____	動	集める
⑳	a____ that time	熟	当時

2. 次の [　] 内の語句を並べ替えて, 意味の通る英文を完成させよう。(各5点×2)

① Currently, this [asking / being / is / people / by / done] whether they speak something other than English at home.

② Just exactly [how / languages / spoken / many / are / different] in American homes?

3. 次の英文を和訳してみよう。(10点)

For many years, the U.S. Census Bureau, a part of the American government, has been investigating this language question.

*Census Bureau「国勢調査局」

ディクテーションしてみよう！

今回学習した英文に出てきた単語を，音声を聞いて □□□□ に書き取ろう。

 02・06

02　If someone were to ask you what language people in the United States speak in their own homes, your answer would probably be, "English, of course!" You might be surprised to learn, however, that that answer would be only partly ❶ c□□□□□□□ .

03　For many years, the U.S. Census Bureau, a part of the American ❷ g□□□□□□□□□□□ , has been investigating this language question. Currently, this is being done by asking people whether they (and/or their children 5 years old or older) speak something other than English at home. If the answer is "yes," then follow-up questions are asked about which language is used and how well the person can speak English. Two important ❸ p□□□□□□□ of asking these 3 questions are to learn how many people have difficulty using English and to better understand how ❹ e□□□□□ to assist such people should be made.

04　Recent Census Bureau results ❺ i□□□□□□□ that about 79% of the 291.5 million people (aged 5 and over) in the U.S. speak only English at home. Stated another way, about 21% of the people speak a language other than English. Many of those people (about 58%), however, ❻ a□□□□□□□□ can also speak English "very well."

05　The Census Bureau results show that speakers of "Spanish or

28

Spanish Creole" are, by far, the largest group of "other language" users. They **❼** a   for more than 60% of the "other language" people. After them come the speakers of Chinese, and then the speakers of Tagalog, Vietnamese, and French, in that **❽** o   .

06   Just exactly how many different languages are spoken in American homes? The Census Bureau says that it doesn't have a **❾** d   answer to this, but that data collected several years ago indicated that more than 300 of them were being used **❿** a   that time.

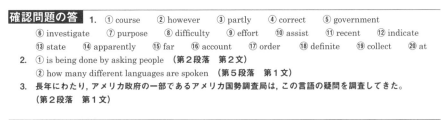

確認問題の答   **1.** ① course   ② however   ③ partly   ④ correct   ⑤ government
    ⑥ investigate   ⑦ purpose   ⑧ difficulty   ⑨ effort   ⑩ assist   ⑪ recent   ⑫ indicate
    ⑬ state   ⑭ apparently   ⑮ far   ⑯ account   ⑰ order   ⑱ definite   ⑲ collect   ⑳ at

2. ① is being done by asking people （第2段落　第2文）
   ② how many different languages are spoken （第5段落　第1文）

3. 長年にわたり，アメリカ政府の一部であるアメリカ国勢調査局は，この言語の疑問を調査してきた。
   （第2段落　第1文）

ディクテーションしてみよう！の答 ❶ correct   ❷ government   ❸ purposes
  ❹ efforts   ❺ indicate   ❻ apparently   ❼ account   ❽ order   ❾ definite
  ❿ at

解答

問	(ウ)	(エ)	(カ)	(コ)	(ソ)

解説

問

(ア)「手洗いは病気を蔓延させるための効果的な方法である」

▶第1段落第1文と不一致。病気の蔓延を防ぐための効果的な方法として手洗いが挙げられている。

(イ)「人々に石けんと水で手洗いをさせないようにするプログラムが世界中にある」▶第1段落第2文と不一致。手洗いを推進するプログラムがあると書かれている。

(ウ)「**もし人々が頻繁に石けんで手を洗えば，毎年100万人の命が救われるだろう**」▶第1段落第3文と一致。

(エ)「**手洗いは病原菌を死滅させることにより病気を予防し得る**」

▶第2段落第1文と一致。

(オ)「人々は自分の目，鼻，口を触ることで自らを感染させることはない」

▶第2段落第2文と不一致。

(カ)「**近くの人がくしゃみやせきをしたあとに自分の鼻や目を触ることは，風邪をひく原因となり得る**」▶第2段落第4文と一致。

(キ)「食べ物を調理する前に手を洗うことは重要だが，調理のあとはそうではない」▶第3段落第1文と不一致。調理の前後ともに重要だとある。

(ク)「動物を扱ったり赤ん坊をきれいに拭いたりすることは手を清潔に保つよい方法である」▶第3段落第2文と不一致。

(ケ)「家の中の誰かが病気になるのは，常にくしゃみやせきのあとにお金を扱ったことが原因である」▶このような記述はない。第3段落第3・4文参照。

(コ)「**石けんとお湯をかけたあとに手をこすり合わせることは，最も効果的な手洗いの方法である**」▶第4段落第1文と一致。

(サ)「特別な抗菌用の石けんを使うことが重要であると医者は言う」

▶第4段落第2文と不一致。

(シ)「手をこする前に 10〜15 秒間, 高温の湯で手をゆすぐべきだ」
　▶このような記述はない。第 4 段落第 3 文には,「手のすべての部分を 10
　　〜15 秒間こするように」とある。

(ス)「公衆トイレのペーパータオルには多くの病原菌がついているので, それ
　　を使って水を止めるべきではない」▶第 5 段落第 1 文と不一致。

(セ)「医者は人々に公衆トイレを使わないようにとの忠告もする」
　▶このような記述はない。

**(ソ)「手を乾かすのに使ったタオルで公衆トイレの扉を開けることは, 手に病
　　原菌がつくのを避けるのに役立ち得る」**▶第 5 段落第 2 文と一致。

▼

それでは次に, 段落ごとに詳しくみていこう。

第1段落　文の構造と語句のチェック

> ──従接 that 省略
>
> ¹Doctors say ⟨ the most effective way 〔 to prevent the spread of disease 〕 is ⟨ for
> 　　S　　V　O　　　　　　　S　　　　　　　　　　　　　　　　　　　　　　V　C
>
> people to wash their hands (with soap and water)⟩⟩. ²There are programs
> 　S′　　V′　　　O′　　　　　　　　　　　　　　　　　　　　　V　　　S
>
> (around the world) 〔 to increase hand-washing with soap 〕. ³One million lives
> 　　　　　　　　　　　　　　　　　　　　　　　　　　　　　　　　　S
>
> could be saved (each year)(if people washed their hands (with soap) often).
> 　　V　　　　　　　　　　　　従接　S　　V　　　O

> **訳** ¹病気の蔓延を防ぐ最も効果的な方法は, 人々が石けんと水で手を洗うことだと医者は言う。²石けんで手を洗うことを増やすためのプログラムが世界中にある。³もし人々が石けんで頻繁に手を洗っていれば, 100万人の命が毎年救われるであろう。

Check! 第 1 文 ... is for people to wash their hands with soap and water の部分は　不定詞の意味上の主語が　for A で表されている。このように, **for A to do** の形で**不定詞の意味上の主語**を示し,「A が〜すること [〜すべき／〜するために／〜するには]」などの意味を表す。

第2段落　文の構造と語句のチェック

関代 that 省略

¹Hand-washing kills germs〔from other people, animals or objects〔a person
S　　　　　　V　　O　　　　①　　　②　等接　③　　　　S

has touched〕〕. ²(When people get bacteria (on their hands)), they can infect
V　　　　　従接　S　　V　　O　　　　　　　　S　　V

themselves (by touching their eyes, nose or mouth). ³Then these people
O　　　　　　　　　　　①　　②　等接　③　　　　　　　S

can infect other people. ⁴The easiest way〔to catch a cold〕is〈to touch your
V　　O　　　　　S　　　　　　　　V C

nose or eyes (after someone nearby has sneezed or coughed)). ⁵Another way
①　等接　②　　従接　　S　　　　　V　　等接　　　　　S

〔to become sick〕is〈to eat food〔prepared by someone〔whose hands are not
V C　　　　　　　　　　　　　　　　　　　関代　S　　V

clean〕〕〉.
C

> **訳** ¹手洗いにより, 接触したほかの人, 動物, 物から来た病原菌は死滅する。²手にばい菌が
> ついていると, 人々は目や鼻や口を触ることにより自ら感染してしまう可能性がある。³そ
> の後, このような人々が他人に感染させてしまう可能性がある。⁴風邪をひく最も簡単な方
> 法は, 近くにいる人がくしゃみやせきをしたあとに自分の鼻や目を触ることである。⁵病気
> になるもう1つの方法は, 手が清潔でない人が調理した食べ物を食べることである。

person	名	人, 個人
eye	名	目
nose	名	鼻
mouth	名	口
easy	形	簡単な
＊比較変化：easy-easier-easiest		
catch a cold	熟	風邪をひく

nearby	形	近くの
cough	動	せきをする
another	形	ほかの, もう1つの
sick	形	病気の
prepare	動	調理する
clean	形	清潔な, きれいな

第3段落 文の構造と語句のチェック

¹Hand-washing is especially important (before and after preparing food),
　　　S　　　　V　　　　　　　C　　　　①　等接　②

(before eating), and (after using the toilet). ²People should wash their hands
　②　　　　　等接　③　　　　　　　　　　　　　　S　　　V　　　　　O
　　　　　　　　　　　　　　　　　　　　　　　　　　従接 that 省略

(after handling animals) and (after cleaning a baby). ³Doctors say 〈 it is
　①　　　　　　　　　　等接　②　　　　　　　　　　　　S　　V　O仮S V

also a good idea 〈 to wash your hands (after handling money) and (after
　　　C　　真S　　　　　　　　　　①　　　　　　　　　等接　②

sneezing or coughing)〉〉. ⁴It is important 〈 to wash your hands often 〉
　　　　　　　　　　　仮S V　　C　　　　真S

(when someone 〔 in your home 〕 is sick).
　従接　S　　　　　　　　　　V　C

訳 ¹手洗いは食べ物の調理の前後, 食事の前, そしてトイレを使ったあとには特に重要である。²動物に触れたあとや赤ちゃんをきれいに拭いたあとには手を洗うべきである。³お金を扱ったり, くしゃみやせきをしたあとに手を洗うのもいい考えだと医者は言う。⁴自分の家の誰かが病気のときには頻繁に手を洗うことが重要である。

語句

especially	副	特に
important	形	重要な
toilet	名	トイレ, 便器

handle	動	扱う, 手を触れる
clean	動	きれいにする, 掃除する
also	副	～も, ～もまた
idea	名	考え

¹The most effective way〔to wash your hands〕is〈to rub them together（after
  S   V C

putting soap and warm water on them）〉. ²Doctors say〈you do not have to use
        ① 等接 ②   S   V O S   V
                                                      ┌─従接 that 省略

special anti-bacterial soap〉. ³Be sure to rub all areas of the hands（for about ten
        O   V   O

to fifteen seconds）. ⁴The soap and the rubbing action remove germs. ⁵Rinse
                              等接 S   V   O   V

the hands（with water）and dry them.
  O   等接 V O

訳 ¹手洗いの最も効果的な方法は，石けんをつけ，お湯をかけたあとに手をこすり合わせる
ことである。²特別な抗菌用の石けんを使う必要はないと医者は言う。³約10〜15秒，手の全
体を必ずこすりなさい。⁴石けんとこする行為が，病原菌を取り除くのだ。⁵水で手をゆすぎ，
乾かしなさい。

語句

rub	動 こする		**be sure to *do***	熟 必ず〜する，きっと〜する
▶ rub 〜 together	〜をこすり合わせる		**area**	名 場所，範囲，部位
warm	形 温かい		**second**	名 秒
have to *do*	熟 〜しなければならない		**action**	名 行為，行動
▶ don't have to *do*	〜する必要はない		**remove**	動 取り除く
special	形 特別な		**rinse**	動 ゆすぐ，すすぐ
			dry	動 乾かす

¹People〔using public restrooms〕should dry their hands（with a paper towel）
  S   V   O
        ┌─（should）

and use the towel（to turn off the water）. ²Doctors also advise〈using the paper
等接 V   O   S   V   O

towel（to open the restroom door）（before throwing the towel away）（in order to

34

help you avoid getting the germs of people 〔 who did not wash well 〕)〉.
関代　　　V′

> **訳** ¹公衆トイレを使う人は，ペーパータオルで手を乾かし，水を止めるのにそのペーパータオルを使うべきだ。²しっかり洗わない人々の病原菌をもらうのを避けられるようにするため，ペーパータオルを捨てる前に，トイレの扉を開けるのにペーパータオルを使うことも医者は勧める。

Check! 第2文 in order to help you avoid getting the germs of people who did not wash well の help の用法に注目しよう。〈**help＋O＋to** *do*〉で「**O が〜するのを助ける**」の意味だが，to が省略され〈help＋O＋*do*〉も可。

語句

public	形	公の，公共の
restroom	名	トイレ
towel	名	タオル
turn off ~	熟	~を止める，消す，切る

advise	動	勧める
throw away ~	熟	~を捨てる
in order to *do*	熟	~するために
well	副	よく，十分に

文法事項の整理 ②　仮定法の基本パターン

第1段落第3文の仮定法過去について見てみよう。

One million lives **could be saved** each year if people **washed** their hands with soap often.

「仮定法」とは，事実に反することを仮定する表現方法である。これに対し，事実をそのまま述べる方法は「直説法」という。

仮定法の特徴は，現在の内容が過去形で，過去の内容が過去完了形で書かれる，つまり，時制が1つ前にずれるという点である。

例 ① If I were rich, I could buy the house.

「(今)私が金持ちなら,(今)その家を買えるのだが」

  ▶現実は,金持ちでないから買えない。

  (≒As I am not rich, I can't buy the house.)

例 ② If I had been rich, I could have bought the house.

「(あのとき)私が金持ちだったら,(あのとき)その家を買えたのだが」

  ▶現実は,金持ちでなかったから買えなかった。

  (≒As I was not rich, I couldn't buy the house.)

例 ③ If I had worked hard, I could buy the house.

「(あのとき)熱心に働いていたら,(今)その家を買えるのだが」

  ▶現実は,熱心に働かなかったから買えない。

  (≒As I did not work hard, I can't buy the house.)

パターンを整理すると以下のようになる。

If+S+動詞の過去形〜 ──①➤ **S+助動詞の過去形+*do* ...**

「(今)S が〜すれば」 ③ 「(今)S は…するだろう」

If+S+had+過去分詞〜 ──②➤ **S+助動詞の過去形+have+過去分詞 ...**

「(あのとき)S が〜したら」 「(あのとき)S は…しただろう」

  (①②③は,上の例文に対応)

①のパターンを「仮定法過去」,②のパターンを「仮定法過去完了」という。③は①+②の混合である。

▶第１段落第３文は仮定法過去(上記①のパターン)である。

文法事項の整理 ③ 分詞の形容詞用法

第2段落第5文の分詞の形容詞用法について見てみよう。

Another way to become sick is to eat <u>food</u> **prepared** by someone whose hands are not clean.

　現在分詞（動詞の -ing 形），過去分詞（動詞の -ed 形，ただし不規則活用に注意）は，名詞を修飾する用法を持つ。これを，「分詞の形容詞用法」という。

　現在分詞は「〜している」，過去分詞は「〜される［た］」の意味を表す。分詞が単独の場合は，名詞の前に置かれるのがふつう。

例　Look at the <u>walking</u> <u>dog</u>. 「歩いている犬を見なさい」

　　Look at the <u>broken</u> <u>vase</u>. 「割られた花瓶を見なさい」

分詞が2語以上のかたまりになるときは，名詞のあとに置く。

例　Look at the <u>dog</u> walking in the park.

　　「公園で歩いている犬を見なさい」

例　Look at the <u>vase</u> broken by your son.

　　「あなたの息子によって割られた花瓶を見なさい」

▶ 第2段落第5文は，prepared（過去分詞）以降がかたまりを作り，前のfoodを修飾している。

▶ 第5段落第1文は，using（現在分詞）以降がかたまりを作り，前のPeopleを修飾している。

<u>People</u> using public restrooms should dry their hands with ...

確認問題

1. 次の和訳と対応する英語の語句を, 頭文字を参考にして書き, 空欄を完成させよう。

(各1点×20)

①	e	形	効果的な
②	p	動	防ぐ, 予防する
③	s	名	広がり, 蔓延, 普及
④	d	名	病気
⑤	i	動	増やす, 高める
⑥	s	動	救う
⑦	o	名	物, 物体
⑧	p	名	人, 個人
⑨	n	形	近くの
⑩	c	動	せきをする
⑪	p	動	調理する
⑫	e	副	特に
⑬	h	動	扱う, 手を触れる
⑭	i	名	考え
⑮	r	動	こする
⑯	w	形	温かい
⑰	a	名	行為, 行動
⑱	r	動	取り除く
⑲	p	形	公の, 公共の
⑳	t away 〜	熟	〜を捨てる

2. 次の [ ] 内の語句を並べ替えて, 意味の通る英文を完成させよう。(各5点×2)

① Doctors say the most effective way to prevent the spread [for / to / is / wash / of / people / disease] their hands with soap and water.

② Another way to become sick is to eat food [by / are / whose / prepared / hands / someone] not clean.

3. 次の英文を和訳してみよう。(10点)

One million lives could be saved each year if people washed their hands with soap often.

ディクテーションしてみよう！

今回学習した英文に出てきた単語を、音声を聞いて □□□ に書き取ろう。

08/12

08　Doctors say the most effective way to prevent the spread of ❶d□□□□□□ is for people to wash their hands with soap and water. There are programs around the world to increase hand-washing with soap. One million lives could be ❷s□□□□ each year if people washed their hands with soap often.

09　Hand-washing kills germs from other people, animals or ❸o□□□□□□ a person has touched. When people get bacteria on their hands, they can infect themselves by touching their eyes, nose or mouth. Then these people can infect other people. The easiest way to catch a cold is to touch your nose or eyes after someone nearby has sneezed or ❹c□□□□□. Another way to become sick is to eat food ❺p□□□□□□ by someone whose hands are not clean.

10　Hand-washing is ❻e□□□□□□□ important before and after preparing food, before eating, and after using the toilet. People should wash their hands after ❼h□□□□□ animals and after cleaning a baby. Doctors say it is also a good idea to wash your hands after handling money and after sneezing or coughing. It is important to wash your hands often when someone in your home is sick.

11　The most effective way to wash your hands is to ❽r□□ them together after putting soap and warm water on them. Doctors say you do not have to use special anti-bacterial soap. Be sure to rub all areas of the hands for about ten to fifteen seconds. The soap and the rubbing action

❾ `r` ⬚⬚⬚⬚⬚⬚ germs. Rinse the hands with water and dry them.

12 People using **❿** `p` ⬚⬚⬚⬚⬚⬚ restrooms should dry their hands with a paper towel and use the towel to turn off the water. Doctors also advise using the paper towel to open the restroom door before **⓫** `t` ⬚⬚⬚⬚⬚⬚⬚ the towel away in order to help you avoid getting the germs of people who did not wash well.

3 解答・解説

解 答

問1	たとえばヨーロッパでは，コーヒーショップは人々がコーヒーを飲みながら友人と会ったり，おしゃべりをしたりする，一般的な場所である。

| 問2 | ③ | 問3 | (1)× | (2)× | (3)○ | (4)× | 問4 | ② |

問5	アメリカに戻ってから，シュルツはスターバックスコーヒーに快適で気楽な雰囲気を作り出した。そして，あらゆる場所の客がそれを気に入ったようであった。

| 問6 | ④ | 問7 | ②，⑦ |

解 説

問1

以下のポイントをおさえよう！

☑ for example「たとえば」は，最初に訳す。このように，直前の文との論理関係を示す副詞語句は，文中での位置にかかわらず最初に訳す。however「しかし」や therefore「したがって」も同様。

☑ coffee shop(s) は「コーヒーショップ」「喫茶店」などと訳す。

☑ common は①「ふつうの，ありふれた」②「共通の」③「公共の」などの意味を持つ。ここでは①。

☑ to 不定詞の前に for A があると，**不定詞の意味上の主語**を表す（▶ 48 ページ「文法事項の整理④」参照）。

☑ to meet friends と to talk が and により並列。places を修飾する形容詞用法の不定詞。

☑ while は①「～している間に」【時】②「～だけど」【譲歩】③「～の一方で」【対比】の意味がある。ここでは①。同時進行を表すので，「～しながら」などと訳してもよい。

☑ while が導く副詞節は meet friends と talk を修飾。

空所の後ろには its own coffee beans とあり，これが空所に入るべき動詞の目的語であると考える。各選択肢の意味は，①「料理した」②「沸かした」③「**炒った**」④「燃やした」。

(1) ▶第3段落第3文に「ニューヨークで働いていた」とあるが，ニューヨークで生まれたとは書いていない。

(2) ▶第3段落第6文に「スターバックスの創業者がシュルツを雇った」とあるので，シュルツ自身は経創業者ではないことがわかる。

(3) ▶第3段落第3文と一致。

(4) ▶第3段落第4文によれば，コーヒーメーカーを大量に注文したのはスターバックスであり，シュルツではない。

catch *one's* eye で「～の目にとまる，～の注意を引く」の意味。

以下のポイントをおさえよう！

☑ Back in the USA は，アメリカ人のシュルツがイタリアに旅行したという文脈を踏まえ，「アメリカに戻って」などと訳す。

☑ atmosphere は①「空気，大気」②「雰囲気，ムード」の意味がある。ここでは②。

☑ that は主格の関係代名詞。先行詞は直前の Starbucks coffee shops ではなく（仮にこれが先行詞なら，複数扱いなので that *were* … となるはず），an atmosphere。that の導く節は casual まで。

☑ seem to *do* は「～するようだ」の意味。

☑ 文末の it は an atmosphere を指す。

空所の後ろには，that does not mean Starbucks has not had problems「それ

はスターバックスに問題がなかったということを意味するわけではない」とある。not が2回使われて**二重否定**になっているので,「スターバックスにも問題はあった」という内容。これに対し, 前の段落ではスターバックスが全世界で店舗を増やして成功している様子が記述されている。そこで,【逆接】を表す However が正しいとわかる。各選択肢の意味は, ①「そこで, だから」(等位接続詞) ②「したがって」(副詞) ③「～だけど」(従属接続詞) ④「**しかし**」(副詞)。なお, ③の though は however と同様の副詞の働きもあるが, その場合は文頭には置かない。

問7

① ▶第1段落第4文によれば, 家庭でコーヒーを飲む文化は従来からあったとわかる。

② ▶第2段落第1文と一致。

③ ▶そのような記述はない。

④ ▶そのような記述はない。第4段落第2文でエスプレッソ・バーに注目したとの記述があるのみ。

⑤ ▶第4段落第6文に there are more than 16,000 Starbucks coffee shops worldwide との記述がある。worldwide は「世界中に, 全世界に」の意味。つまり, アメリカを含めての数字である。

⑥ ▶第5段落第2文に many Starbucks locations have closed over the past few years との記述があるが,「ヨーロッパで」とは書かれていない。

⑦ ▶第5段落第4文の the "feel the same everywhere" atmosphere offered by Starbucks の部分と一致する。

▼

それでは次に, 段落ごとに詳しくみていこう。

第1段落 文の構造と語句のチェック

¹(Although people everywhere seem to enjoy 〈 drinking coffee 〉), they do not
（従接）   S   V   O   S

all have the same coffee culture. ²(In Europe), (for example), coffee shops are
V   O   S   V

<u>common places</u> 〔for people to meet friends and to talk (while they drink coffee)〕.
　C　　　　　　　S'　　V'　　O'　等接　V'　従接　S　　V　　O

³(On the other hand), <u>locations</u> 〔 like this 〕 <u>were not</u> <u>as common</u> (in North
　　　　　　　　　　　S　　　　　　　　V　　C

America)(in the past). ⁴(Instead), <u>people</u> 〔 in North America 〕 <u>tended to drink</u>
　　　　　　　　　　　　　　　　　S　　　　　　　　　　　V

<u>coffee</u>(in their homes)(with their friends). ⁵<u>The coffee culture</u> 〔 in the USA 〕
　O　　　　　　　　　　　　　　　　　　　　　　　　　S

<u>changed</u>(when Starbucks coffee shops <u>spread</u>(across the country)).
　V　　　従接　　　　　S　　　　　V

訳 ¹あらゆる地域の人々がコーヒーを飲むことを楽しむようであるが, 皆が同じコーヒー文化を持っているというわけではない。²たとえばヨーロッパでは, コーヒーショップは人々がコーヒーを飲みながら友人と会ったり, おしゃべりをしたりする, 一般的な場所である。³他方, 北米ではかつて, このような店舗はそれほど一般的ではなかった。⁴その代わりに, 北米の人々は自宅で友人と一緒にコーヒーを飲む傾向があった。⁵アメリカのコーヒー文化は, スターバックスコーヒーが国中に広がったときに変化した。

 Check! 第1文 not all … は「すべてが…わけではない」という部分否定。

語句

although	接	…だが
everywhere	副	あらゆる所で
seem to *do*	熟	～するようだ
culture	名	文化
Europe	名	ヨーロッパ
for example	熟	たとえば
common	形	ふつうの, ありふれた
while	接	…する間に
on the other hand	熟	他方で, その一方で

location	名	位置, 場所
North America	名	北米, 北アメリカ
past	名	過去, 昔／形 過去の
▶ in the past		過去に, 昔は
instead	副	その代わりに
tend to *do*	熟	～する傾向がある
spread	動	広がる, 拡大する
		*活用：spread-spread-spread
across	前	～の至る所に
country	名	国, 国家

第2段落　文の構造と語句のチェック

¹<u>The first Starbucks coffee shop</u> <u>opened</u> (in 1971) (in downtown Seattle,
　　　　　　S　　　　　　　　　　V

Washington, in the USA). ²It was a small coffee shop 〔 that roasted its own coffee
　　　　　　　　　　　　　　S　V　　C　　　　　　関代　V　　　　　　O

beans 〕. ³The coffee shop's business did well, and (by 1981) there were
　　　　　　　S　　　　　　　V　　　　等接　　　　　　　　　　V

three more Starbucks stores (in Seattle).
　　　　S

訳 ¹スターバックスコーヒーの第1号店は1971年に, アメリカのワシントン州シアトルの繁華街
にオープンした。²それは, 自家製のコーヒー豆を炒る小さなコーヒーショップであった。³そのコー
ヒーショップの営業は順調で, 1981年までにシアトルにはさらに3軒のスターバックスができた。

語 句

downtown	形	中心部の, 繁華街の	**bean**	名	豆
roast	動	あぶる, 炒る	**business**	名	事業, 商売, 売り上げ
			do well	熟	うまくいく

第3段落　文の構造と語句のチェック

¹Things really began to change (for the company) (in 1981). ²(That year),
　S　　　　　　V

Howard Schultz met the three men 〔 who ran Starbucks 〕. ³Schultz worked (in
　　S　　　　V　　O　　　　　関代　V　　O　　　　　S　　　V

New York) (for a company 〔 that made kitchen equipment 〕). ⁴He noticed
　　　　　　　　　　　　関代　V　　　　O　　　　　　S　　V

⟨ that Starbucks ordered a large number of special coffee makers⟩, and he was
O　従接　S　　　V　　　　　　　　O　　　　　　　　　　等接　S　V

curious. ⁵Schultz went (to Seattle) (to see ⟨ what Starbucks did ⟩). ⁶(In 1982),
　C　　S　　V　　　　　　　　　　　　疑　　S　　V

the original Starbucks owners hired Schultz (as the company's head of
　　　　S　　　　　　　V　　O

marketing).

訳 ¹その会社にとって状況が本当に変化し始めたのは1981年であった。²その年, ハワード・
シュルツはスターバックスを経営する3人の男たちに会った。³シュルツはニューヨークで
台所用品を製造する会社に勤めていた。⁴彼は, スターバックスが多数の特殊なコーヒー

メーカーを注文するのに気づき，好奇心を持った。⁵シュルツはスターバックスが何をしているのか調べようとシアトルに行った。⁶1982年に，スターバックスの創業者たちはシュルツを会社の市場調査の責任者として雇った。

第4段落　文の構造と語句のチェック

¹(In 1983), Schultz traveled (to Italy). ²The unique atmosphere 〔 of the espresso
　　　　　　　　S　　V　　　　　　　　　　　　　　　　　　　　　　　S

bars there 〕 caught his eye. ³(Back in the USA), Schultz created an atmosphere
　　　　　　　V　　O　　　　　　　　　　　　　　　S　　V　　　　O

(for Starbucks coffee shops) 〔 that was comfortable and casual 〕, and
　　　　　　　　　　　　　　　　　　　　関代　V　　　　C　　等接　　　　　等接

customers everywhere seemed to like it. ⁴Starbucks began 〈 opening more locations
　　　　S　　　　　　　　V　　　　O　　　　S　　　　V　　　O

(across the USA)〉. ⁵Then the company opened coffee shops (in other countries)
　　　　　　　　　　　　　　　　S　　　V　　　O

(as well). ⁶Today, there are more than 16,000 Starbucks coffee shops worldwide.
　　　　　　　　　　　　　　V　　　　　　　S

訳 ¹1983年に，シュルツはイタリアに出かけた。²そこにあったエスプレッソ・バーの独特な雰囲気が彼の関心を引いた。³アメリカに戻ってから，シュルツはスターバックスコーヒーに快適で気楽な雰囲気を作り出した。そして，あらゆる場所の客がそれを気に入ったようであった。⁴スターバックスはアメリカ中にさらに多くの店舗をオープンし始めた。⁵その上，その会社はほかの国にもコーヒーショップをオープンした。⁶今日，全世界にスターバックスコーヒーの店舗は1万6千以上ある。

語句

travel	動	旅行する
unique	形	独特な
atmosphere	名	雰囲気
espresso	名	エスプレッソ(イタリア式のコーヒー)
catch *one's* eye	熟	~の目にとまる, ~の注意を引く
create	動	作り出す, 創造する
comfortable	形	心地よい
casual	形	形式張らない, カジュアルな
customer	名	客, 顧客
as well	熟	~も
worldwide	副	世界中で

第5段落　文の構造と語句のチェック

┌─従接 that 省略

¹However, that does not mean 〈 Starbucks has not had problems 〉. ²(As a
　　　　　　S　　　V　　　 O　　　 S　　　　　V　　　　O

matter of fact), many Starbucks locations have closed (over the past few years).
　　　　　　　　　　　　　S　　　　　　　　　V

³(In some cases), this is (because there were too many coffee shops 〔 competing
　　　　　　　　　　　 S　 V　 従接　　　　　 V　　　　　　　　S

for business 〕 (in one small area)). ⁴(In other cases), locations 〔 in some
　　　　　　　　　　　　　　　　　　　　　　　　　　　　　　　　S

countries 〕 closed (because the coffee culture there did not match (with the "feel
　　　　　　 V　 従接　　　　　　 S　　　　　　　　V

the same everywhere" atmosphere 〔 offered by Starbucks 〕)).

訳 ¹しかしながら, それはスターバックスに問題がなかったということを意味するわけでは
ない。²実は, ここ数年で多くのスターバックスの店舗が閉店している。³いくつかのケース
では, 1つの小さな地域であまりに多数のコーヒー店が売り上げを競っていたことが原因で
ある。⁴また, いくつかの国々の店舗が, スターバックスの提供する「どこでも同じ気分」とい
う雰囲気にその国のコーヒー文化が合わなかったせいで, 閉店したというケースもある。

Check! 第3文 this is because … は「これは…だからだ」の意味で, 前の文が【結果】,
because 以下が【原因】。なお, this is why … は「このようなわけで…」の意味で,
前の文が【原因】, why 以下が【結果】となるので, 区別すること。

however	副	しかしながら
mean	動	意味する
problem	名	問題, 課題
as a matter of fact	熟	実は, 実を言うと
close	動	閉じる, 閉店する
case	名	場合
compete	動	競争する
area	名	地域, 地方
match	動	合う, 調和する
offer	動	提供する

文法事項の整理④　不定詞の意味上の主語

第1段落第2文の不定詞の意味上の主語について見てみよう。

In Europe, for example, coffee shops are common places **for** people **to** meet friends and **to** talk while they drink coffee.

「不定詞の意味上の主語」とは, 不定詞が表す**〈行為・状態などの主体〉**のことである。

たとえば, I want to study abroad.「私は留学したい」という英文で, to study abroad の主体は I（私）なので, これが意味上の主語である。この場合,〈文の S＝意味上の主語〉という関係が成立する。

また, I want you to study abroad.「私はあなたに留学してほしい」という英文では, to study abroad の主体は you（あなた）なので, これが意味上の主語ということになる。この場合,〈文の O＝意味上の主語〉という関係が成立することになる。

意味上の主語が文の S や O と等しくない場合は, 次のパターンが基本となる。

for＋意味上の主語＋to *do*

例　It is important for you to study mathematics.
　　　　　　　　　　　　S′　　　V′
　　「あなたが数学を勉強することは重要だ」

例 This question is too difficult $\underset{S'}{\boxed{\text{for}}\ \text{me}}\ \underset{V'}{\boxed{\text{to}}\ \text{answer}}$.

「この問題は私<u>が</u>答えられないほど難しい」

例 He stepped aside $\underset{S'}{\boxed{\text{for}}\ \text{me}}\ \underset{V'}{\boxed{\text{to}}\ \text{enter}}$.

「彼は私<u>が</u>入るためにどいてくれた」

〈**It is＋人間の性質を表す形容詞＋of＋人＋to do**〉「〈人〉は～するとは…だ」のパターンもおさえておこう。

例 It was careless $\underset{S'}{\boxed{\text{of}}\ \text{you}}\ \underset{V'}{\boxed{\text{to}}\ \text{leave}}$ your keys on the train.

「<u>あなたは</u>電車にカギを忘れてくるとは不注意だった」

確認問題

1. 次の和訳と対応する英語の語句を, 頭文字を参考にして書き, 空欄を完成させよう。

(各1点×20)

①	s _____	to *do*	熟	～するようだ
②	c _____		名	文化
③	c _____		形	ふつうの, ありふれた
④	p _____		名	過去, 昔／形　過去の
⑤	i _____		副	その代わりに
⑥	t _____	to *do*	熟	～する傾向がある
⑦	d _____		形	中心部の, 繁華街の
⑧	r _____		動	経営する
⑨	e _____		名	備品, 装備, 機材
⑩	c _____		形	好奇心を持って
⑪	o _____		形	最初の
⑫	h _____		動	雇う
⑬	u _____		形	独特な
⑭	a _____		名	雰囲気
⑮	c _____		動	作り出す, 創造する
⑯	c _____		形	心地よい
⑰	c _____		名	客, 顧客
⑱	as a m _____ of fact		熟	実は, 実を言うと
⑲	c _____		動	競争する
⑳	o _____		動	提供する

2. 次の [　] 内の語句を並べ替えて, 意味の通る英文を完成させよう。(各5点×2)

① He noticed that Starbucks [coffee / number / a / special / ordered / of / large] makers.

② However, that [has / mean / Starbucks / not / not / had / does] problems.

3. 次の英文を和訳してみよう。(10 点)

In Europe coffee shops are common places for people to meet friends and to talk while they drink coffee.

ディクテーションしてみよう！

今回学習した英文に出てきた単語を，音声を聞いて ☐☐☐ に書き取ろう。

14
18

14 Although people everywhere seem to enjoy drinking coffee, they do not all have the same coffee culture. In Europe, for example, coffee shops are ❶ c☐☐☐☐☐ places for people to meet friends and to talk while they drink coffee. On the other hand, locations like this were not as common in North America in the ❷ p☐☐☐. ❸ I☐☐☐☐☐☐☐, people in North America tended to drink coffee in their homes with their friends. The coffee culture in the USA changed when Starbucks coffee shops spread across the country.

15 The first Starbucks coffee shop opened in 1971 in ❹ d☐☐☐☐☐☐ Seattle, Washington, in the USA. It was a small coffee shop that roasted its own coffee beans. The coffee shop's business did well, and by 1981 there were three more Starbucks stores in Seattle.

16 Things really began to change for the company in 1981. That year, Howard Schultz met the three men who ran Starbucks. Schultz worked in New York for a company that made kitchen equipment. He noticed that Starbucks ordered a large number of special coffee makers, and he was curious. Schultz went to Seattle to see what Starbucks did. In 1982, the original Starbucks owners hired Schultz as the company's head of marketing.

17 In 1983, Schultz traveled to Italy. The unique atmosphere of the espresso bars there caught his eye. Back in the USA, Schultz

❺ c ⬚⬚⬚⬚⬚⬚⬚ an atmosphere for Starbucks coffee shops that was
❻ c ⬚⬚⬚⬚⬚⬚⬚⬚⬚⬚ and casual, and customers everywhere seemed to like it. Starbucks began opening more locations across the USA. Then the company opened coffee shops in other countries as well. Today, there are more than 16,000 Starbucks coffee shops worldwide.

18 However, that does not mean Starbucks has not had problems. As a
❼ m ⬚⬚⬚⬚⬚ of fact, many Starbucks locations have closed over the past few years. In some cases, this is because there were too many coffee shops **❽** c ⬚⬚⬚⬚⬚⬚⬚⬚ for business in one small area. In other cases, locations in some countries closed because the coffee culture there did not match with the "feel the same everywhere" atmosphere
❾ o ⬚⬚⬚⬚⬚ by Starbucks.

解 答

問1	find it hard to control how much time they spend online				
問2	全訳参照	問3	②		
問4	(1) ②	(2) ③	(3) ①	(4) ②	(5) ①

解 説

問1

ポイントは仮目的語（▶60ページ「文法事項の整理⑤」参照）。

〈find＋O＋C〉で「OがCだとわかる，思う」の意味。このOの部分に仮目的語の it が入り，真目的語の to 不定詞が後ろに置かれると，find it ... to *do*「〜するのが…だとわかる，思う」という形になる。以上により，find it hard to control「制御するのが難しいとわかる」というつながりができる。

次に，control の目的語にあたる部分だが，疑問詞 how から始まる節を置くと考える。疑問詞から始まる節の中は平叙文の語順（間接疑問文）なので，how much time they spend online「どのくらいの時間をオンラインで過ごすか」となる。

問2

> Experts agree that people who use the Internet so much that it causes problems with their daily activities are spending too much time online.

Experts が S，agree が V，that 以下が O。that 節の中では，people が S，are spending が V，too much time が O となっている。people の後に関係代名詞 who の節が続いていることもポイント。〈so 〜 that ...〉の訳し方にも注意。

問3

much the same 〜で「ほぼ同じ〜」の意味（＝almost the same 〜）。in much the same way で「ほぼ同じように」という意味になる。

(1) 「本文において，ほとんどの人々のインターネット利用について言及されていないものは以下のうちどれか」

   ① 「彼らは買い物のためにそれを利用している」

   ② 「彼らは趣味に関する活動のためにそれを利用している」

   ③ 「彼らはメールを送るためにそれを利用している」

   ④ 「彼らはソーシャルネットワーキングのためにそれを利用している」

   ▶①③④は第1段落第3文で言及されている。

(2) 「筆者はインターネット中毒について何と述べているか」

   ① 「ギャンブル中毒の人々はインターネット中毒でもある」

   ② 「仕事関係の活動により多くの時間を費やすのはインターネット中毒の兆候である」

   ③ 「社交的活動をやめてしまうのはインターネット中毒の兆候である」

   ④ 「インターネット中毒の人々はアルコール中毒でもある」

   ▶第2段落最終文にインターネット中毒の兆候として giving up social, work-related, or hobby-related activities とあり，この部分と③が一致する。

(3) 「本文によれば，インターネットを使いすぎる人々について当てはまらないものは以下のうちどれか」

   ① 「とてもよく眠る」

   ② 「うつ病の兆候を示す可能性がより高い」

   ③ 「数分おきにメールをチェックする」

   ④ 「家庭生活や仕事生活に問題をかかえている」

   ▶②は第3段落最終文，③は第4段落第2文，④は第3段落第1文で言及されている。①は第3段落第1文の experiencing problems sleeping と矛盾する。

(4) 「インターネット中毒の問題を克服する第一歩としてどんなことが述べられているか」

   ① 「周囲の人々から文句を言われること」

② 「オンラインで費やされる時間があまりに長いのは問題であると認識すること」

③ 「メールをチェックするより良い方法を生み出すこと」

④ 「数分おきに次回のオンラインの時間について考えること」

▶②が第5段落第3文と一致。本文の understanding が recognize に言い換えられている。

(5) 「以下のうち本文のタイトルとすべきものはどれか」

① 「**インターネット中毒の兆候と解決策**」

② 「インターネット中毒の歴史」

③ 「インターネットの長所と短所」

④ 「インターネット中毒の若者」

▶第1～4段落はインターネット中毒の概要とその兆候について,5～6段落はインターネット中毒への対処法について書かれている。両者をカバーするものとして①が適切。

▼

それでは次に, 段落ごとに詳しくみていこう。

第1段落　文の構造と語句のチェック

¹The Internet has become an important part 〔 of our modern lives 〕. ²(In fact),
S ・・V・・ C

it is impossible (for many people)〈 to imagine a day 〔 without some contact with
仮SV C 真S V′ O′

the Internet 〕〉. ³Most people use it①(to shop), ②(send e-mail), and③(for social
S V O ┌to 省略 等接

networking). ⁴ However, some people find it hard 〈 to control 〈 how much time
S V 仮O C 真O 疑 O

they spend online 〉〉.
S V

訳 ¹インターネットは私たちの現代生活の重要な部分になった。²実際, インターネットに何らかの接触をしない1日を想像することは多くの人々にとって不可能である。³大半の人は買い物をしたり, Eメールを送ったり, ソーシャルネットワーキング(インターネットを通じた交流)のためにインターネットを利用する。⁴しかし, オンラインで過ごす時間の長さを制御するのが難しいと感じる人もいる。

語句

modern	形	現代の
imagine	動	想像する
contact	名	接触, ふれること
shop	動	買い物をする
e-mail	名	Eメール, 電子メール

social	形	社交のための, 社交上の
networking	名	人との交流, 人脈作り
control	動	管理する, 制御する
online	副	オンラインで, インターネットに接続して

第2段落 文の構造と語句のチェック

¹So, how much Internet is too much Internet? ²Experts agree 〈 that people [who use the Internet so much that it causes problems [with their daily activities]] are spending too much time online 〉. ³They say 〈 that some people may actually be addicted (to the Internet) (in much the same way as some people are addicted (to gambling or alcohol)))〉. ⁴Signs [of Internet addiction] include 〈 spending more and more time online 〉, 〈 reducing or giving up social, work-related, or hobby-related activities (in favor of spending time online)〉, and 〈 giving up sleep (to spend time on the Internet)〉.

訳 ¹では, どれほどインターネットをすると度がすぎるのだろうか。²専門家は, 日常の活動に問題を起こすほどインターネットを多く利用する人々はオンラインで過ごしている時間が長すぎるのだ, という点で意見が一致する。³彼らが言うには, ギャンブル中毒やアルコール中毒になる人が

いるのとほぼ同じように, 実際にインターネット中毒になる可能性がある人もいる。⁴インターネット中毒の兆候には, オンラインで過ごす時間がどんどん増えること, オンラインで時間を過ごすことを優先して社交上, 仕事関係あるいは趣味関係の活動を減らしたりやめてしまったりすること, そしてインターネットで時間を過ごすために眠らなくなってしまうことが含まれる。

語句

expert	名	専門家	alcohol	名	アルコール
agree	動	意見が一致する, 賛成する	sign	名	兆候
			addiction	名	中毒, 依存症
cause	動	引き起こす	include	動	含む
daily	形	毎日の, 日常の	reduce	動	減らす
activity	名	活動	give up	熟	やめる
actually	副	実際に	-related	形	～関連の
much the same ～	熟	ほぼ同じ～	hobby	名	趣味
gambling	名	ギャンブル, 賭け事	in favor of ～	熟	～の方を好んで, ～を選択して

第3段落　文の構造と語句のチェック

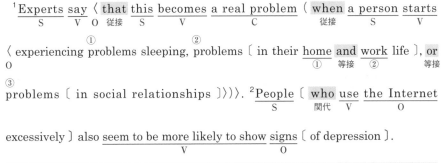

¹Experts say 〈 that this becomes a real problem 〈 when a person starts
S　　V　O　従接　S　　V　　　　　C　　　　　従接　　S　　　V

〈 experiencing problems sleeping, problems [in their home and work life], or
O ①　　　　　　　　　　　　　　　　②　　　　　　　　　　　①　等接　②　　　　　等接

③
problems [in social relationships]〉〉〉. ²People [who use the Internet
S　　関代　V　　O

excessively] also seem to be more likely to show signs [of depression].
　　　　　　　　　　V　　　　　　　　　　　　　　O

訳 ¹専門家が言うには, 人が睡眠の問題, 家庭生活と仕事生活の問題, あるいは社会的関係の問題を経験し始めると, このことが現実的な問題になる。²過剰にインターネットを利用する人はまた, うつ病の兆候を示す可能性も高いようである。

語句

experience	動	経験する	excessively	副	過度に
relationship	名	関係	be likely to *do*	熟	～しそうだ, ～する可能性が高い

第4段落　文の構造と語句のチェック

¹How do you know 〈 if you are spending too much time online 〉? ²Some common
　疑　(V)　S　　V　　O従接 S　　　V　　　　O　　　　　　　　　　　　　　S

warning signs include 〈 checking your e-mail (every few minutes)〉,〈 always
　　　　　　V　　O①　　　　　　　　　　　　　　　　　　　　　　　　　O②

thinking about your next online session 〉, and 〈 getting complaints (from the
　　　　　　　　　　　　　　　　　　　　　等接　　O③

people 〔 around you 〕)〔 about 〈 how much time you spend online 〉〕〉.
　　　　　　　　　　　　　　　　　疑　　　O　　S　　V

> **訳** ¹自分がオンラインで過ごす時間が長すぎるかどうかはどうしたらわかるのか。²一般的
> な前兆には、数分おきにメールをチェックすること，次回のオンラインの時間について常に
> 考えていること，そしてオンラインで過ごす時間が長いことについて周囲の人から文句を
> 言われることが含まれる。

語句

common 形 一般的な	**session** 名 (ある活動を行う) 時間
warning 名 警告, 前兆	**complaint** 名 文句, 苦情
▶ warning sign　警告標識, (病気などの) 前兆	

第5段落　文の構造と語句のチェック

¹〈 Showing any of these signs 〉 may mean 〈 that you are (on your way 〔 to
S　　　　　　　　　　　　　　V　　　O　従接　S　V

becoming addicted to the Internet 〕)〉. ²However, experts agree 〈 that there is
　　　　　　　　　　　　　　　　　　　　　　　　　S　　V　　O　従接　　　　V

hope 〉. ³They say 〈 that 〈 simply understanding 〈 that 〈 spending too much time
S　　　　S　V　O 従接 S　　　　　　　　　従接　S

online 〉 is a problem 〉〉 may be the first step 〔 to solving the problem 〕). ⁴They
　　　　V　　C　　　　　V　　　C　　　　　　　　　　　　　　　　　　　S

believe 〈 that , (in most cases) , 〈 doing something 〔 as simple as creating a
V　　O 従接　　　　　　　　　　　　　S

better system 〔 for managing your time online 〕〕〉 can solve the problem 〉.
　　　　　　　　　　　　　　　　　　　　　　　V　　　　O

58

訳 ¹こういった兆候のいずれかを示すことは, インターネット中毒になりつつあることを意味するかもしれない。²しかし, 希望はあるという点で専門家は意見が一致している。³彼らは, オンラインで過ごす時間が長すぎることは問題だと理解するだけでも問題解決の第一歩になるかもしれない, と言う。⁴ほとんどの場合, オンラインの時間を管理するより良い方法を生み出す程度の簡単なことをすることが問題を解決し得る, と彼らは考える。

語句

on *one's* way	熟	途中で
simply	副	単に, ただ
create	動	生み出す, 創り出す
system	名	方法, 方式
manage	動	管理する

第6段落 文の構造と語句のチェック

¹The Internet is a wonderful tool 〔for communicating and finding information 〕.
（S / V / C / ①・② 等接）

²However, (as with most things in life), you have to learn to use it carefully,
（S / V / O）

and make sure 〈 you keep a healthy balance 〔between being online and the
（等接 / V / O / S / V / O）
──従接 that 省略

other important things in your life〕〉.

訳 ¹インターネットはコミュニケーションを取ったり情報を見つけたりするためのすばらしい手段である。²しかし, 生活の大半の物事と同様に, それを慎重に使えるようになる必要があるし, 確実にオンラインにつながっていることと生活のほかの重要な物事との健全なバランスを保つようにしなければならない。

語句

wonderful	形	すばらしい
tool	名	道具, 手段
communicate	動	コミュニケーションを取る
as with 〜	熟	〜(の場合)と同様に
carefully	副	注意深く, 慎重に
make sure (that) ...	熟	確実に…する

文法事項の整理⑤　仮主語・仮目的語

第1段落第2文の it 〜 to ...について見てみよう。

In fact, **it** is impossible for many people **to** imagine a day without some contact with the Internet.

①　仮主語と真主語

It is important to study English.「英語を勉強することは重要だ」のような文で，It は主語の場所にあるが，実際の主語としての内容は to 以下にある。このような It のことを仮主語［形式主語］といい，to 以下を真主語という。

It は「それ」と訳すのではなく，to 以下の内容を It に代入して訳す。

仮主語のパターンは，不定詞のほか，動名詞，that 節，whether 節，疑問詞節でも使うことができる。

例　It is no use asking him.　　　　　　「彼に聞いてもむだだ」
　　仮S　　　　　真S

例　It is certain that he will win.　　　　「彼が勝つことは確実だ」
　　仮S　　　　　真S

例　It is doubtful whether he will win or not.
　　仮S　　　　　　真S
　　　　　　　　　　　　　　　　　　「彼が勝つのかどうか疑わしい」

例　It is a mystery why he won.　　　　「なぜ彼が勝ったのかは謎だ」
　　仮S　　　　　真S

▶ 第1段落第2文

In fact, it is impossible for many people to imagine a day without some contact with the Internet.

▶ it が仮主語，to 以下が真主語。to 不定詞の前に " for 〜" を置くと不定詞の意味上の主語を表す。

② 仮目的語と真目的語

I think it important to study English. 「英語を勉強することは重要だと思う」のような文で, it は第5文型 (S＋V＋O＋C) の O (目的語) の部分にあるが, 実際の O としての内容は to 以下にある。このような it のことを仮目的語 [形式目的語] といい, to 以下を真目的語という。

仮主語 [形式主語] の場合と同様, it は「それ」と訳すのではなく, to 以下の内容を it に代入して訳す。

形式目的語のパターンは, 上記のような不定詞のほか, 動名詞, that 節, whether 節, 疑問詞節でも使うことができる。

例 I believe [it] necessary to obey the law.
　　　　　　　 仮O　　　　　　　 真O
　　　　　　　　　　　　　　　「法律を守ることは必要だと思う」

例 He made [it] clear that he was opposed to the idea.
　　　　　　 仮O　　　　 真O
　　　　　　　　　「彼はその考えに反対であることを明らかにした」

例 He thinks [it] important how long it will take to finish the work.
　　　　　　　 仮O　　　　　　　　　　 真O
　「彼はその仕事を終えるのにどのくらい時間がかかるかが重要と考えている」

▶ 第1段落第4文

However, some people find [it] hard to control how much time they spend online.

▶ some people が S, find が V, it が仮目的語, hard が C, to 以下が真目的語。

確認問題

1. 次の和訳と対応する英語の語句を，頭文字を参考にして書き，空欄を完成させよう。

(各1点×20)

①	m	形	現代の	
②	i	動	想像する	
③	c	名	接触, ふれること	
④	d	形	毎日の, 日常の	
⑤	a	名	アルコール	
⑥	r	動	減らす	
⑦	e	動	経験する	
⑧	r	名	関係	
⑨	e	副	過度に	
⑩	be l ___ to *do*	熟	～しそうだ, ～する可能性が高い	
⑪	w	名	警告, 前兆	
⑫	s	名	(ある活動を行う)時間	
⑬	c	名	文句, 苦情	
⑭	o ___ *one's* way	熟	途中で	
⑮	s	副	単に, ただ	
⑯	s	名	方法, 方式	
⑰	m	動	管理する	
⑱	c	動	コミュニケーションを取る	
⑲	a ___ with ～	熟	～(の場合)と同様に	
⑳	make s ___ (that) ...	熟	確実に…する	

2. 次の[　]内の語句を並べ替えて，意味の通る英文を完成させよう。(各5点×2)

① It is impossible [a / people / imagine / many / to / day / for] without some

contact with the Internet.

② Some people [to / how / it / find / control / hard] much time they spend online.

3. 次の英文を和訳してみよう。(10点)

People who use the Internet so much that it causes problems with their daily activities are spending too much time online.

ディクテーションしてみよう！

今回学習した英文に出てきた単語を, 音声を聞いて [　｜　] に書き取ろう。

20
25

20　The Internet has become an important part of our
❶ [m　　　　　] lives.　In fact, it is impossible for many people to imagine a day without some contact with the Internet.　Most people use it to shop, send e-mail, and for social networking.　However, some people find it hard to control how much time they spend online.

21　So, how much Internet is too much Internet?　Experts agree that people who use the Internet so much that it causes problems with their
❷ [d　　　　] activities are spending too much time online.　They say that some people may actually be addicted to the Internet in much the same way as some people are addicted to gambling or ❸ [a　　　　　　].　Signs of Internet addiction include spending more and more time online,
❹ [r　　　　　　　] or giving up social, work-related, or hobby-related activities in favor of spending time online, and giving up sleep to spend time on the Internet.

22　Experts say that this becomes a real problem when a person starts
❺ [e　　　　　　　　　] problems sleeping, problems in their home and work life, or problems in social relationships.　People who use the Internet ❻ [e　　　　　　　　] also seem to be more likely to show signs of depression.

23　How do you know if you are spending too much time online?　Some common warning signs include checking your e-mail every few minutes, always thinking about your next online session, and getting **❼** c ⬚⬚⬚⬚⬚⬚⬚⬚⬚ from the people around you about how much time you spend online.

24 Showing any of these signs may mean that you are **❽** o ⬚⬚ your way to becoming addicted to the Internet. However, experts agree that there is hope. They say that simply understanding that spending too much time online is a problem may be the first step to solving the problem. They believe that, in most cases, doing something as simple as creating a better system for **❾** m ⬚⬚⬚⬚⬚⬚⬚ your time online can solve the problem.

25 The Internet is a wonderful tool for communicating and finding information. However, as with most things in life, you have to learn to use it carefully, and make **❿** s ⬚⬚⬚⬚ you keep a healthy balance between being online and the other important things in your life.

---

5 解答・解説

解 答

問1	(ア)(A)	(イ)(D)	(ウ)(B)	(エ)(C)	(オ)(D)	(カ)(A)
	(キ)(D)	(ク)(C)	(ケ)(D)			
問2	(1)(B)	(2)(C)	(3)(D)	(4)(A)	(5)(C)	(6)(B)

解 説

問1

下線部**(ア)～(ケ)**の意味は以下の通り。

(ア)「持続可能な」　　**(イ)**「より激しい，さらに強烈な」

(ウ)「十分な」　　**(エ)**「生産する」

(オ)「生計を立てる」　　**(カ)**「取り除く，排除する」

(キ)「分配される」　　**(ク)**「達成する，成し遂げる」

(ケ)「利用する」

各問の選択肢の意味は以下の通り。

(ア)(A)「**永続的な**」　(B)「危険な」　(C)「一時的な」　(D)「自然の」

(イ)(A)「よりよい」　(B)「より軽い」　(C)「より静かな」**(D)「より悪い」**

(ウ)(A)「流ちょうな」　**(B)「十分な」**　(C)「裕福な」　(D)「効率がよい」

(エ)(A)「含む」　(B)「配置する」　**(C)「栽培する」**　(D)「水浸しにする」

(オ)(A)「住まいを手に入れる」　(B)「食べ物が不足する」　(C)「面目を保つ」
　　(D)「金を稼ぐ」

(カ)(A)「やめる」　(B)「始める」　(C)「増やす」　(D)「上がる」

(キ)(A)「延期された」(B)「やめた」　(C)「持ち出された」**(D)「配られた」**

(ク)(A)「失う」　(B)「破滅させる」**(C)「得る」**　(D)「集める」

(ケ)(A)「発明する」　(B)「働く」　(C)「修正する」　**(D)「使う」**

問2

(1)「**第1・2パラグラフによれば，_____**」
　(A)「国連は真水（まみず）の市場に重点を置いてきた」▶第1段落第1文と不一致。
　(B)「およそ7人に1人が飢えの脅威にさらされている」▶第2段落第1

文と一致。

- (C)「世界の人口増加は水資源の管理とは関係がない」▶第2段落第1・2文と不一致。

- (D)「多くの発展途上国では，ごく少量の水だけが農業のために使われている」▶第2段落第4文と不一致。

(2)「**第2・3パラグラフによれば，_____**」

- (A)「私たちはいつ食物の栽培を増やすべきか，予測する能力を高めるべきだ」▶このような記述はない。

- (B)「世界の人口は2050年に900万人に達することが予想されている」▶第3段落第1文と不一致（本文は billion，選択肢は million）。

- (C)「**1人の人が1週間に飲む水はおよそ14〜28リットルだ**」▶第3段落第2文と一致（本文は1日あたりの量なので，これに7をかけて計算する）。

- (D)「1キロの牛肉を生産するために1,500リットルの水が必要とされる」▶第3段落第3文と不一致。小麦に1,500リットル，牛肉はその10倍と書かれている。

(3)「**第4パラグラフによれば，_____**」

- (A)「都心の地域に住んでいる人々は多くの水を必要としない」▶第4段落第1文と不一致。

- (B)「農家は常に生計を立てるために漁師と競争する」▶このような記述はない。また，第4段落第2〜3文から，農家の競争相手が漁師なのではなく，都市対田舎（農家や漁師）という対立構造が読み取れる。

- (C)「経済成長により農業のために利用可能な水が増えた」▶第4段落第1文と不一致。

- (D)「**水をめぐる競争のせいで，農業で生活できなくなるであろう人々もいる**」▶第4段落第2〜3文と一致。

(4)「**第5・6パラグラフによれば，_____**」

- (A)「**食の安全は水の入手しやすさに影響されやすい**」▶第5段落第1文と一致。

- (B)「水質汚染を減らせば，効率的な水の供給システムは必要なくなるだ

ろう」▶第5段落第2・3文によれば，いずれも必要である。

(C)「養殖場は水の清浄にプラスの影響を与える」▶そのような記述はない。第6段落第1文は，水の清潔さが養殖場にとって必要という内容である。

(D)「発展途上国の人々はより多くのたんぱく質を摂取する必要がある」▶そのような記述はない。第6段落第2文参照。

(5)「**第7・8パラグラフによれば，_____**」

(A)「地域社会と政府は水の問題にそれぞれ独自に取り組むべきだ」▶第8段落第3文と不一致。

(B)「財政的支援は食の安全には必要でない」▶第7段落の内容と不一致。

(C)**「水の供給は，良好な資源の管理と効率的な技術により維持され得る」**▶第8段落第1・2文と一致。

(D)「地域の問題を解決しようとするとき，人々は全世界的な観点を持つ必要はない」▶第8段落第4文と不一致。

(6)「**本文に最もふさわしいタイトルは_____である**」

(A)「人口爆発」▶本文の前半，第2・第3・第4段落に言及があるが，後半にはない。

(B)**「水と食の安全」**▶本文全体において言及されている。

(C)「公衆衛生の分析」▶第7段落にしか記述がない。

(D)「アフリカの水不足」▶アフリカに限定する記述はない。

▼

それでは次に，段落ごとに詳しくみていこう。

第1段落 文の構造と語句のチェック

¹The United Nations has named March 22nd World Water Day (to **focus**
　　　　　　S　　　　　　V　　　　　O　　　　　　　C　　　　　①

attention **on** the importance 〔 of fresh, clean water 〕) and (to promote the
　　　　　　　　　　　　　　　　　　　　　　　　　　　　竹筏 ⓪

sustainable management 〔 of fresh water resources 〕).

語句

the United Nations	名	国際連合
name *A B*	熟	A を B と名づける，命名する
focus *A* on *B*	熟	A を B に集中させる
attention	名	注意，注目
importance	名	重要性
fresh	形	淡水の，真水の
clean	形	清潔な
promote	動	促進する，推進する
sustainable	形	持続可能な，環境に優しい
management	名	管理
resource	名	資源

第2段落 文の構造と語句のチェック

¹Almost one billion people — 〔 one seventh of the world's population 〕 — suffer
  S   V

(from constant hunger, a crisis 〔 that could become more intense (as the global
        └──── 同格 ────┘   関代   V   C   従接

population grows 〕〕). ²Our ability 〔 to increase food production 〕 will require
      S   V   S   V

sufficient water and ways 〔 to predict 〈 how much water will be available for
        O   等接 O   V'   O' 疑   S   V   C

people to grow food 〉〕. ³More than 70 percent of the water 〔 used in the world 〕
  S'   V'   O'   S

goes (towards agriculture). ⁴(In many developing countries), the amount 〔 used
  V   S

for agriculture 〕 is more than 90 percent.
                   V   C

語句

almost	副	ほぼ, ほとんど
billion	名	十億
population	名	人口
suffer from ～	熟	～に苦しむ
constant	形	絶え間ない
hunger	名	飢え
crisis	名	危機
intense	形	激しい, 強烈な
global	形	全世界の
grow	動	増大する
ability	名	能力
increase	動	増やす

production	名	生産
require	動	必要とする
sufficient	形	十分な
predict	動	予測する
available	形	入手可能な, 利用可能な
grow	動	栽培する
more than ～	熟	～以上, ～より多くの
percent	名	パーセント
go towards ～	熟	～に使われる
agriculture	名	農業
developing country	名	発展途上国
amount	名	量

第3段落　文の構造と語句のチェック

付帯状況

[1]Seven billion people live (on this planet), (with another 2 billion predicted (by
　　　S　　　　　　　V　　　　　　　　　　　　　　　　　　S′　　　　　V′

2050)). [2]Each one of us drinks two to four liters of water daily, but we consume
　　　　　　　　S　　　　　V　　　　　　O　　　　　　　　　　等接　S　　V

　　　　　　　　┌─関代 which 省略
much more (as part of the food [we eat]). [3]It takes around 1,500 liters of water
　O　　　　　　　　　　　　　　　S　V　　　仮S　V　　　　　　　O

⟨ to produce a kilo of wheat ⟩ and ten times that amount (for a kilo of beef).
真S　　　　　　　　　　　　　　等接　　　　　　O

> 訳 [1]地球上には70億人の人々が暮らしており, 2050年までにさらに20億人が増えると予測されている。[2]私たちの各自が毎日2～4リットルの水を飲むが, 私たちが食べる食べ物の一部として消費する量がずっと多い。[3]1キログラムの小麦を生産するのに, 1,500リットルくらいの水を要し, 1キログラムの牛肉にはその10倍の量を要する。

Check! 第1文の with は **【付帯状況】** を表す用法。⟨with＋A＋B⟩（A＝名詞, B＝分詞 [形容詞／副詞／前置詞＋名詞]）で **「A が B の状態で」** の意味。ここでは, A＝another 2 billion, B＝predicted となっている。

planet	名	惑星
another	形	さらに〜の
each	形	それぞれの
liter	名	リットル
daily	副	毎日, 日ごとに
consume	動	消費する

part	名	部分
take	動	要する
around	副	だいたい, およそ
produce	動	生産する
kilo	名	キログラム
wheat	名	小麦
beef	名	牛肉

第4段落　文の構造と語句のチェック

¹(As urban populations and economies increase), so do water demands 〔 for
　　従接　　　S　　　　等接　　　　　　　　　V　　　　V　　　　S

cities and industry 〕, (leaving less for agriculture).　²Competition 〔 between
　　　等接　　　　　　　　　　　　　　　　　　　　　　　　　S

　　　　　　　　　　　　　　　　　　　　　　　　　　┌─ 従接 that 省略
cities and the countryside 〕 is increasing.　³That means 〈 there will be less water
　　　　　　　　　　　　　　　　V　　　　　S　　V　O　　　　V　　　　S

(for small farmers and fishermen 〔 who cannot make a living (without it)〕)〉).
　　　　　　　等接　　　　　　　　関代　　V　　　　O

> 訳　¹都会の人口や経済が増大するにつれて, 都市や工業のための水の需要も増大し, 農業の
> ために残される量は少なくなる。²都市と田舎の間での競争が高まっている。³それは, 水が
> なくては生計を立てられない小規模農家や漁師のための水が少なくなるであろうことを意
> 味する。

Check! 第1文 so do water demands for cities and industry の部分は, ⟨so＋V＋S⟩
「S も V する」のパターン。

Check! 第1文 ..., leaving less for agriculture の部分は, 【結果】を表す分詞構文。前
から訳し,「…, そして (その結果) 〜する」の意味。

urban	形	都会の, 都市の
economy	名	経済
demand	名	需要
industry	名	産業, 工業
leave	動	残す

competition	名	競争
countryside	名	田舎
mean	動	意味する
farmer	名	農家, 農場経営者
fisherman	名	漁師
make a living	熟	生計を立てる

第5段落　文の構造と語句のチェック

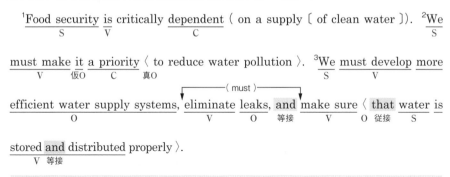

¹Food security is critically dependent (on a supply 〔 of clean water 〕). ²We
　　　S　　　V　　　　　　C

must make it a priority 〈 to reduce water pollution 〉. ³We must develop more
　V　仮O　C　　　　　真O　　　　　　　　　S　　　V

efficient water supply systems, eliminate leaks, and make sure 〈 that water is
　　　　　　O　　　　　　　　V　　　O　等接　V　　　O　従接　S

stored and distributed properly 〉.
　V　等接

> **訳** ¹食の安全は清潔な水の供給に決定的に左右される。²私たちは水質汚染を減らすことを優先事項としなければならない。³私たちは，より効率的な水の供給システムを開発し，水漏れをなくし，必ず水が適切に貯蔵，分配されるようにしなければならない。

Check! 第2文 We must make it a priority to reduce water pollution. は**仮目的語の構文**。〈make＋O＋C〉で「OをCにする」の意味。このOの部分に仮目的語のit を置き，後ろに真の目的語となる to do を置く。**〈make it＋C＋to do〉で「～することをCにする」**となる。同様のパターンをとる動詞に，find / think / believe / feel などがある。

語句

security	名	安全
critically	副	決定的に
be dependent on ～	熟	～次第である，～によって決まる
supply	名	供給（量）
priority	名	優先事項
reduce	動	減らす
pollution	名	汚染

develop	動	開発する
efficient	形	効率のよい
eliminate	動	排除する
leak	名	水漏れ
make sure that ...	熟	必ず…ようにする
store	動	蓄える
distribute	動	分配する
properly	副	適切に

第6段落 文の構造と語句のチェック

[1]We also need to protect the purity 〔 of water resources and wetlands 〔 that
S   V   O   ①   等接   ②   関代

support fisheries 〕〕. [2]They provide a significant source of protein (to 2.5 billion
V   O   S   V   O

people 〔 in developing countries〕).

> **訳** [1]私たちはまた, 養殖場を支えている水資源と沼沢地の清潔さを守る必要がある。[2]養殖場は発展途上国の25億人の人々にたんぱく質の重要な供給源を提供している。

語句

need to *do*	熟 ～する必要がある	fishery	名 漁場, 養殖場
protect	動 保護する	**provide**	動 提供する, 支給する
purity	名 清浄, 清潔	**significant**	形 重要な
wetland	名 湿地, 沼沢地	**source**	名 源, 供給源
support	動 支える	**protein**	名 たんぱく質

第7段落 文の構造と語句のチェック

[1]Water and sanitation should be priorities (in national development plans and
S   V   C   等接

strategies). [2]Money should also be provided (to meet these goals).
S   V

[3]Communities and governments should work (towards meeting the basic needs
S   等接   V

〔 of their people 〕)(to achieve food security).

> **訳** [1]水と公衆衛生は国家の開発計画・戦略において優先事項であるべきだ。[2]これらの目標を達成するために金銭も支給されるべきである。[3]地域社会および政府は食の安全を達成するために, 国民の基本的な必要を満たすことを目指して努力すべきである。

語句

sanitation	名	(公衆)衛生
national	形	国家の
development	名	開発
strategy	名	戦略
meet	動	達成する, 満たす
goal	名	目標

community	名	地域社会
government	名	政府
work towards ～	熟	～に向けて努力する
basic	形	基本的な
need(s)	名	必要
achieve	動	達成する

第8段落 文の構造と語句のチェック

[1]We need to increase water supplies (through better resource management).
S　　V　　　　　O

[2]We also need to reduce the demand for water (by employing more efficient
S　　　V　　　　　　O　　　　　　　　　V'　　　O'

irrigation technology). [3]Individuals, communities and governments must all work
　　　　　　　　　　　　　　　①　　　②　　　等接　③　　　S　　　　　V
　　　　　　　　　　　　　　　　　　　　　　　　　　　　　　　　　　　　　together. [4]Water scarcity is a global challenge, but the solutions are often local.
　　　　　　　　S　　　　V　　C　　　　等接　　S　　　V　　　C

> **訳** [1]私たちはよりよい資源管理を通じて水の供給量を増やす必要がある。[2]私たちはまた, より効率のよい灌漑(かんがい)技術を利用することにより水の需要を減らす必要もある。[3]個人, 地域社会および政府が皆, 協力しなければならない。[4]水不足は全世界的な課題であるが, その解決策は局地的なものであることが多い。

語句

employ	動	利用する
irrigation	名	灌漑
technology	名	技術
work together	熟	協力する

scarcity	名	不足
challenge	名	課題, 難題
solution	名	解決(策)
local	形	局地的な

文法事項の整理⑥　接続詞 as の識別

第2段落第1文の接続詞 as について見てみよう。

Almost one billion people — one seventh of the world's population — suffer from constant hunger, a crisis that could become more intense **as** the global population grows.

as には, 従属接続詞, 関係代名詞, 前置詞などの用法がある。従属接続詞の as は以下のような意味を表す。

① 【時】「～するときに, ～しながら」

例 As I was walking down the street, I met an old friend of mine.
「通りを歩いているときに, 旧友に出会った」

② 【理由】「～なので」

例 As it was raining heavily, the game was postponed.
「雨が激しかったので, 試合は延期された」

③ 【様態】「～ように, ～とおりに」

例 You must do as you are told.
「君は言われたとおりにやらなければならない」

④ 【比例】「～するにつれて」

例 As we grow older, we become weaker.
「私たちは年をとるにつれて弱くなる」

⑤ 【譲歩】〈形容詞or副詞＋as＋S＋V〉「～であるが」

例 Young as he is, he is an able man.
「彼は若いのだが, 有能な人だ」
（＝Though he is young, he is an able man.）

⑥ 【限定】〈名詞＋as＋S＋V〉「～ような」

例 English as we know it today has been influenced by French.
「今日私たちが知っているような英語は, フランス語の影響を受けてきた」

▶第2段落第1文の接続詞 as は【比例】を表す。**比較級**や**変化を表す動詞**とともに使われると,【比例】の意味になることが多い。

確認問題

1. 次の和訳と対応する英語の語句を, 頭文字を参考にして書き, 空欄を完成させよう。

(各1点×20)

	語句	品詞	和訳
①	p	動	促進する, 推進する
②	r	名	資源
③	p	名	人口
④	c	名	危機
⑤	p	動	予測する
⑥	a	形	入手可能な, 利用可能な
⑦	a	名	農業
⑧	c	動	消費する
⑨	w	名	小麦
⑩	u	形	都会の, 都市の
⑪	i	名	産業, 工業
⑫	p	名	汚染
⑬	e	形	効率のよい
⑭	p	動	保護する
⑮	s	形	重要な
⑯	d	名	開発
⑰	c	名	地域社会
⑱	a	動	達成する
⑲	t	名	技術
⑳	s	名	解決（策）

2. 次の[　]内の語句を並べ替えて, 意味の通る英文を完成させよう。(各5点×2)

① The United Nations has named March 22nd World Water Day to [on / the / of / attention / importance / focus] fresh, clean water.

② Food security is critically [a / on / of / supply / water / dependent / clean].

3. 次の英文を和訳してみよう。(10 点)

As urban populations and economies increase, so do water demands for cities and industry, leaving less for agriculture.

ディクテーションしてみよう！

今回学習した英文に出てきた単語を，音声を聞いて □□□ に書き取ろう。

🔊 27 ・ 34

27　The United Nations has named March 22nd World Water Day to focus attention on the importance of fresh, clean water and to ❶ p□□□□□□□ the sustainable management of fresh water resources.

28　Almost one billion people —— one seventh of the world's population —— suffer from constant hunger, a ❷ c□□□□□ that could become more intense as the global population grows. Our ability to increase food production will require sufficient water and ways to predict how much water will be ❸ a□□□□□□□ for people to grow food. More than 70 percent of the water used in the world goes towards agriculture. In many developing countries, the amount used for agriculture is more than 90 percent.

29　Seven billion people live on this planet, with another 2 billion predicted by 2050. Each one of us drinks two to four liters of water daily, but we ❹ c□□□□□ much more as part of the food we eat. It takes around 1,500 liters of water to produce a kilo of ❺ w□□□ and ten times that amount for a kilo of beef.

30　As urban populations and economies increase, so do water demands for cities and ❻ i□□□□□□ , leaving less for agriculture. Competition between cities and the countryside is increasing. That means there will be less water for small farmers and fishermen who cannot make a living without it.

31   Food security is critically dependent on a supply of clean water. We must make it a priority to reduce water ❼ p⬚⬚⬚⬚⬚⬚⬚⬚. We must develop more efficient water supply systems, eliminate leaks, and make sure that water is stored and distributed properly.

32   We also need to ❽ p⬚⬚⬚⬚⬚⬚ the purity of water resources and wetlands that support fisheries. They provide a significant source of protein to 2.5 billion people in developing countries.

33   Water and sanitation should be priorities in national ❾ d⬚⬚⬚⬚⬚⬚⬚⬚⬚ plans and strategies. Money should also be provided to meet these goals. Communities and governments should work towards meeting the basic needs of their people to ❿ a⬚⬚⬚⬚⬚ food security.

34   We need to increase water supplies through better resource management. We also need to reduce the demand for water by employing more efficient irrigation technology. Individuals, communities and governments must all work together. Water scarcity is a global challenge, but the solutions are often local.

確認問題の答 **1.** ① promote ② resource ③ population ④ crisis ⑤ predict
    ⑥ available ⑦ agriculture ⑧ consume ⑨ wheat ⑩ urban ⑪ industry
    ⑫ pollution ⑬ efficient ⑭ protect ⑮ significant ⑯ development ⑰ community
    ⑱ achieve ⑲ technology ⑳ solution

 2. ① focus attention on the importance of （第1段落　第1文）
    ② dependent on a supply of clean water （第5段落　第1文）

 3. 都会の人口や経済が増大するにつれて，都市や工業のための水の需要も増大し，農業のために残される量は少なくなる。（第4段落　第1文）

ディクテーションしてみよう！の答 ❶ promote ❷ crisis ❸ available ❹ consume
    ❺ wheat ❻ industry ❼ pollution ❽ protect ❾ development ❿ achieve

解答

問1	（ア）④	（イ）②	（ウ）②	（エ）①	（オ）②
問2	③	問3 ④	問4 (A) ①	(B) ③	
問5	(a) ②	(b) ①	(c) ①	(d) ①	

解説

問1

（ア）①「捕まえる」　②「失う」　③「逃す」　④「**進む**」

　目的格の関係代名詞 which が前にあるので，先行詞 a network of pathways はもともと空所に入る動詞の直後にあったと考える。また，後続の to get to them「そこ（お気に入りの場所）に着くために」もヒントになる。travel は他動詞で「（道のり）を進む，行く」の意味がある。

（イ）①「試み」　②「**障害**」　③「お気に入り」　④「象徴，記号」

　such A as B「（たとえば）B のような A 」では，B に A の具体例が入る。猫の行動圏について書かれているので，streets and buildings は行動を妨げるものと考えられる。cats are much more restricted の理由として挙げられている点も参考にして，②が適切。

（ウ）①「国／田舎」　②「**方向，方角**」　③「距離」　④「時間」

　go back in the （　ウ　） from which they originally came「もと来た（　ウ　）に戻る」とあるので，②が自然。なお，direction は in とセットで用い，in 〜 direction で「〜の方角に」の意味。which は関係代名詞（目的格）で，came from the direction の from が関係代名詞の前にきた形。

（エ）①「**避ける**」　　②「予期［期待］する」
　　③「理解する」　　④「見る，観察する」

　第3段落は複数の猫が同じ道を使うという問題の解決法について述べている。他の猫を見つけると，距離をおいて座ったり相手が行くのを待ったり，引

78

き返したりといった行動が挙げられている。よって，confrontation「顔を合わせること」を「避ける」と考える。

(オ)（以下，to 不定詞を後に続けた場合の意味）

①「～することを好む」　　②「**～しない**」

③「～し忘れる」　　　　　④「立ち止まって～する」

the pictured cat「絵に描かれた猫」は当然，合図を送っても反応しないはずなので，②が正解。fail to *do* は「～しない」という否定を表す。「失敗する」という意味ではないので注意（「～するのに失敗する」は fail in *doing*）。

問2

　　（ i ）　cat が主語，holds back ... disappeared が述部で upon spotting ... a path という分詞構文が挿入された文である。

「ほかの」という形容詞は，不特定なら another（複数の場合other），特定される場合は the other を用いる。「ほかのもの」という代名詞の場合，不特定なら another（複数の場合 others），特定される場合は the other（複数の場合 the others）を用いる（▶ 86 ページ「文法事項の整理⑦」参照）。

（ i ）は直前文の具体例の冒頭部分であり，「ほかの」の意味がないので **One**。

（ ii ）はこの時点では特定されていないほかの一匹の猫なので，**another**。この another は代名詞で，〈 spot＋O＋*doing* 〉「 O が…しているのを見つける」の O が代名詞になった文。

（ iii ）は（ ii ）の猫を指すので特定され，**the other**（ここでは形容詞の用法）。この the other は主語の one に対して「（二匹のうちの）もう一匹は」という意味になる。

問3

　　空所を含む英文には for example が挿入されており，直前の They try to (avoid) confrontation, even if one of the cats has already established itself as dominant to the other.「猫は，たとえ一方がすでに他方に対して優勢な立場を確立していたとしても，顔を合わせることを避けようとする」の具体例であることに注意する。そこで，優勢［上位］の猫が劣勢［下位］の猫の通過を待

つという内容にすべきだとわかる。空所を含む英文の後の文の主語 it が the superior cat を指していることもヒントになる。また，ほかの猫が道を通過するのを待つという内容なので，(v) には **clear** が適切。clear は「明確な」等の意味のほか，「妨げのない，（道が）自由に通れる」の意味がある。clean は「きれいな，清潔な」の意味。

問4

(A) sight of 〜 で「〜を見ること」の意味。また，its species とあるので，自らと同じ種の意味であると解釈できる。つまり，another of its species は「自分と同じ種の動物（猫）のほかの一匹」という意味。

(B) this は直前部分（searches behind the mirror）を指し，work は「うまくいく，効果がある」の意味。鏡に映った猫（自分の姿）を見て，鏡の後ろを探すことが役に立たない ⇒ 鏡の後ろを探しても見つからない，と考える。

問5

(a) 「田舎の猫は行動圏として非常に広い地域を使い，それをほかの猫と共有することはめったにない」
▶第2段落に several cats may use the same geographical area as a home range「複数の猫が行動圏として地理的に同じ地域を使う場合があり」とあるので，共有していることがわかる。よって，本文の内容と一致しない。

(b) 「二匹の猫が二つの道の合流点にお互いが接近しているのを見ると，同時に渡らないようにする」
▶第3段落第3文と一致。「距離をおいたところに座り，相手よりも長く待とうとする」を「同時に渡らないようにする」と言い換えている。

(c) 「猫は他の猫を別の動物と区別することができる」
▶第4段落第2文に cats know what cats look like「猫は猫の見た目を知っている」とあり，これと一致する。what … look like は「…がどんなふうに見えるか」という意味。

(d) 「猫が自分の輪郭を鏡で見ると，見えた『動物』の方へ歩いていく」
▶第4段落第4文と一致。walk up to 〜 は「〜の方へ歩いていく，〜に歩み寄る」の意味で，本文の approach を言い換えている。

▼

それでは次に, 段落ごとに詳しくみていこう。 35

第1段落 文の構造と語句のチェック

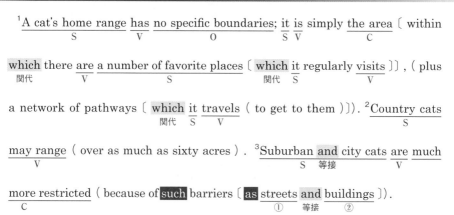

¹A cat's home range has no specific boundaries; it is simply the area 〔within
S   V   O   S V   C

which there are a number of favorite places 〔which it regularly visits 〕〕, (plus
関代   V   S   関代 S   V

a network of pathways 〔which it travels (to get to them)〕〕). ²Country cats
関代 S V   S

may range (over as much as sixty acres). ³Suburban and city cats are much
V   S   等接   V

more restricted (because of such barriers 〔as streets and buildings 〕).
C   ①   等接   ②

> 訳 ¹猫の行動圏には明確な境界線はない。それは単純に, 猫が定期的に訪れる数々のお気に入りの場所がある範囲内の区域に, それらの場所に行くために通る小道網を加えたものである。²田舎の猫は行動範囲が60エーカーをも超える場合がある。³郊外や都市部の猫は, 通りや建物といった障害物があるためにはるかに制限される。

語句

range	名	範囲／	**network**	名 ネットワーク, 網状組織
	動	(範囲が) 及ぶ	**pathway**	名 小道, 通路
specific	形	明確な	**travel**	動 進む, 行く
boundary	名	境界線	**acre**	名 エーカー (面積の単位,
simply	副	単に		1エーカー＝約4,046.86
a number of ～	熟	多くの～		平方メートル)
favorite	形	お気に入りの	**suburban**	形 郊外の
regularly	副	定期的に	**restrict**	動 制限する, 限定する
plus	前	～を加えて	**barrier**	名 障害, 障壁
			such A as B	熟 BのようなA

第2段落 文の構造と語句のチェック

¹(In either situation), though, several cats may use the same geographical
S   V   O

<u>area</u> (as a home range),(<u>each</u> <u>having</u> its own special <u>hunting grounds</u> <u>or</u>
　　　　　　　　　　　　　　S′　　V′　　　　　　　　　　O′　　　　　①　　等接

②
<u>resting places</u> (within it)).

訳 ¹だが，いずれの状況でも，複数の猫が行動圏として地理的に同じ地域を使う場合があり，その地域内にそれぞれの猫が自身の特別な狩場や休憩場所を持っている。

語句

either	形 どちらの~も		geographical	形 地理的な
situation	名 状況		hunt	動 狩りをする
though	副 しかし，~だけれども		▶hunting ground 狩場	
			rest	動 休憩する

第3段落 文の構造と語句のチェック

¹<u>Researchers</u> <u>have watched</u> 〈 <u>how</u> <u>cats</u> 〔 <u>whose</u> <u>ranges</u> <u>overlap</u> 〕 <u>solve</u>
　　S　　　　　　V　　　　　　O　疑　S　　関代　　S　　　V　　　　　V

<u>the problem</u> 〔 of using the same pathways 〕〉. ²<u>One cat</u>, (upon <u>spotting</u> <u>another</u>
　　　O　　　　　　　　　　　　　　　　　　　　S　　　　　　V′　　O′

<u>moving along a path</u>), <u>holds back</u> (<u>until</u> <u>the other cat</u> <u>has disappeared</u>). ³(<u>If</u>
　　　C′　　　　　　　　　　V　　　従接　　　S　　　　　V　　　　　　従接

<u>two cats</u> <u>see</u> <u>each other</u> <u>approaching a junction of two paths</u>), <u>both</u> <u>may sit down</u>
　S　　V　　　O　　　　　　　　　C　　　　　　　　　　　　　S　　①　V

(at a distance (from the crossroads)) <u>and</u> <u>try to wait</u> (longer than the other).
　　　　　　　　　　　　　　　　　　　　　②　　　　　　　　　　　　　　　　　
　　　　　　　　　　　　　　　　等接　　V

⁴<u>One cat</u> <u>may</u> eventually <u>make</u> <u>a fast run</u> (across the junction), or <u>both</u>
　　S　　　　V　　　　　　　　　O　　　　　　　　　　　　　　　　　　　　S

①
<u>may turn around</u> <u>and</u> <u>go back</u> (in the direction 〔 from <u>which</u> <u>they</u> originally
　　V　　　　　等接　②V　　　　　　　　　　　　　　　　関代　　S

<u>came</u> 〕). ⁵<u>They</u> <u>try to avoid</u> <u>confrontation</u>, (<u>even if</u> <u>one of the cats</u> <u>has already</u>
　V　　　　　S　　　V　　　　　O　　　　　　従接　　　S

<u>established</u> <u>itself</u> (as dominant to the other)). ⁶(<u>If</u>, (for example), <u>an inferior cat</u>
　　V　　　　O　　　　　　　　　　　　　　　　　　　従接　　　　　　　　　S

is already walking (down a pathway)(when a superior cat approaches)), the
　　　　　V　　　　　　　　　　　　　　　　従接　　　 S　　　　　 V

superior cat sits down and waits (until the road is clear). ⁷ Nor does it drive
　　 S　　　　 V　　　 等接　 V　　 従接　　 S　 V　 C　　 等接　(V) S　 V

an inferior cat away (from its own favorite sunning spot).
　　　 O

> **訳** ¹行動圏が重なる猫が同じ小道を使うという問題をどのように解決するのか, 研究者たちは観察を行ってきた。²ある猫が道でほかの猫が移動しているのを見つけるとすぐに, その猫が姿を消すまで引っ込む。³もし二匹の猫が二つの道の合流点にお互いが接近しているのを見た場合, 二匹とも交差点から距離をおいたところに座り, 相手よりも長く待とうとするかもしれない。⁴片方の猫が結局交差点を素早く走り抜けるかもしれないし, 二匹とも方向転換してもと来た方向へ戻るかもしれない。⁵猫は, たとえ一方がすでに他方に対して優勢な立場を確立していたとしても, 顔を合わせることを避けようとする。⁶たとえば, 上位の猫が接近してきたときに下位の猫がすでに道を歩いていた場合, 上位の猫は座って道が空くまで待つのだ。⁷上位の猫が自身のお気に入りの日なたぼっこの場所から下位の猫を追い払うということもない。

語 句

researcher	名	研究者
overlap	動	重なる
upon[on] *doing*	熟	～してすぐに
spot	動	見つける, 発見する
hold back	熟	引き下がる, 引っ込む
disappear	動	姿を消す
each other	熟	お互い
approach	動	接近する
junction	名	交差点, 合流点
at a distance (from ～)		
	熟	(～から)少し離れて
crossroad	名	十字路, 交差点
eventually	副	結局, 最終的に
make a run	熟	走る
turn around	熟	方向転換する, 向きを変える

direction	名	方向, 方角
originally	副	もともと, 最初に
avoid	動	避ける
confrontation	名	直面, 向き合うこと
even if ...	熟	たとえ…しても
establish	動	確立する
dominant	形	支配的な, 優勢な
inferior	形	劣った, 下位の
superior	形	優れた, 上位の
clear	形	妨げのない, (道が)自由に通れる
drive *A* away from *B*		
	熟	BからAを追い払う
sun	動	日なたぼっこ[日光浴]をする

¹(For many small animals), the mere sight 〔 of another of its species 〕 is not
　　　　　　　　　　　　　　　　　　S　　　　　　　　　　　　　　　　　　　　　V

enough (to cause aggressive behavior). ² 〈 That cats know 〈 what cats look like 〉〉
　C　　　　　　　　　　　　　　　　　　　　　S 従接　S　　V　　O　　　　S　　V

has been shown (by researchers 〔 who have watched feline reactions 〔 to
　　　V　　　　　　　　　　　　　　関代　　V　　　　　　　　O

pictures of variously shaped abstract forms and animal silhouettes 〕〕).
　　　　　　　　　　　　　①　　　　　　　　　等接　　　　②

³The usual behavior 〔 of a cat 〔 in this test situation 〕〕 is 〈 to approach the cat
　　　S　　　　　　　　　　　　　　　　　　　　　　　　　V C①

silhouette cautiously 〉 and then, sometimes, 〈 to make an angry sound (when
　　　　　　　　　　等接　　　　　　　　　　　　C②　　　　　　　　　　　　　　　従接

the pictured cat fails to respond (to its signals))〉. ⁴A cat 〔 who sees itself (in a
　　　S　　　　　　V　　　　　　　　　　　　　　　　　S　　関代　V　　O

mirror)〕 also approaches the "animal" 〔 it has just sighted 〕(in a friendly
　　　　　　　V　　　　　　O　　　　　　　S　　　　　V
　　　　　　　　　　　　　　　　　　─関代 which 省略

spirit). ⁵(Unable to locate a flesh-and-blood cat (in front of the mirror)),

the real cat often searches (behind the mirror), and (when this does not work),
　　S　　　　　V　　　　　　　　　　　　　　　　　等接　　従接　S　　V

it rapidly loses interest.
S　　　　V　　O

訳 ¹多くの小型動物にとって，同じ種のほかの個体をただ見るだけでは攻撃的な行動を起こすのに十分ではない。²猫は猫の見た目を知っているということは，さまざまな形の抽象的な物影と動物の輪郭の絵に対する猫の反応を観察した研究者によって示されてきた。³この試験の状況における猫の通常の行動はというと，猫の輪郭に用心深く近づき，その後，絵に描かれた猫がその合図に反応しないと怒ったような声を出すときもある。⁴自分の姿を鏡で見た猫も，視界に入ったばかりのその「動物」に友好的な気持ちをもって近づいていく。⁵鏡の前で生身の猫を見つけられないと，たいていの場合本物の猫は鏡の後ろを探し，これがうまくいかないと，すぐに興味を失う。

語句

mere	形	ほんの, 単なる
sight	名	見ること
species	名	(動物などの) 種
cause	動	引き起こす
aggressive	形	攻撃的な
behavior	名	行動
reaction	名	反応
variously	副	さまざまに
shaped	形	～の形をした
abstract	形	抽象的な
form	名	人影, 物影
silhouette	名	シルエット, 輪郭
cautiously	副	用心深く

make a sound	熟	音を立てる, 声を出す
picture	動	絵 [写真] で示す
fail to *do*	熟	～しない
respond to ～	熟	～に反応する
signal	名	合図
sight	動	～が目に入る
spirit	名	精神 (状態), 心
(be) unable to *do*	熟	～できない
locate	動	(場所) を突き止める
flesh-and-blood	形	生身の, 肉体を持つ
in front of ～	熟	～の前に
search	動	探す
rapidly	副	急速に
interest	名	興味

文法事項の整理 ⑦　other に関する表現

第3段落第2文の one / another / the other について見てみよう。

One cat, upon spotting **another** moving along a path, holds back until **the other** cat has disappeared.

otherに関する表現として, anotherやthe other, (the) others がある。以下のように整理しよう。

<基本的な考え方>

an-				
不特定・単数		other	（名詞）	-s
the				複数
特定				

※「特定」とは, ほかに組み合わせが考えられない, つまり, 残り全部という意味。

※ (an)other は後に名詞が付く場合は形容詞, 付かない場合は代名詞。

■頻出パターン

① 「(2者のうち) 1つは〜, もう1つは…」

one　　the other

例 I have two brothers. **One** is in Tokyo, and **the other** is in Osaka.
「私には兄弟が2人いる。1人は東京に, もう1人は大阪にいる」

② 「(3者以上のうち) 1つは〜, もう1つは…」

one　　　　　another

例 I have many foreign friends. **One** is from the U.S., and **another** is from Canada.

「私には多くの外国人の友だちがいる。1人はアメリカ, また別の1人はカナダ出身だ」

③「(3者のうち) 1つは～, もう1つは…, 残りの1つは…」

例 I have three sons. **One** is in Tokyo, **another** is in Nagoya, and **the other** is in Osaka.

「私には3人の息子がいる。1人は東京に, もう1人は名古屋に, 残りの1人は大阪にいる」

④「(多数のうち) ～するものもあれば, …するものもある」

例 **Some** people like baseball, and **others** like soccer.

〈others＝other people〉

「野球が好きな人もいれば, サッカーが好きな人もいる」

⑤「(多数のうち) ～するものもあれば, …するものもいて, さらに…するものもある」

例 **Some** people like baseball, **others** like soccer, and **still others** like tennis.

「野球が好きな人もいればサッカーが好きな人もいて, さらにテニスが好きな人もいる」

▶第３段落第２文の one (cat) と another は上記パターン②にあてはまり，この時点で２匹の猫の関係になるので，その後の the other (cat) は上記パターン①にあてはまる。１つのパターンに単純にあてはまるわけではなく，応用的に考える必要がある。問２の解説も参照。

確認問題

1. 次の和訳と対応する英語の語句を, 頭文字を参考にして書き, 空欄を完成させよう。

(各1点 × 20)

①	s		形	明確な
②	b		名	境界線
③	f		形	お気に入りの
④	r		副	定期的に
⑤	s		形	郊外の
⑥	b		名	障害, 障壁
⑦	g		形	地理的な
⑧	o		動	重なる
⑨	at a d	(from 〜)	熟	(〜から) 少し離れて
⑩	e		副	結局, 最終的に
⑪	d		名	方向, 方角
⑫	o		副	もともと, 最初に
⑬	e		動	確立する
⑭	i		形	劣った, 下位の
⑮	s		形	優れた, 上位の
⑯	c		形	妨げのない, (道が) 自由に通れる
⑰	a		形	攻撃的な
⑱	a		形	抽象的な
⑲	c		副	用心深く
⑳	s		名	精神 (状態), 心

2. 次の [ ] 内の語句を並べ替えて, 意味の通る英文を完成させよう。(各5点 × 2)

① A cat's home range has no specific boundaries; it is simply the area within [are / a / there / of / favorite / which / number] places which it regularly visits.

② For many small animals, [sight / mere / another / the / of / of] its species is not enough to cause aggressive behavior.

3. 次の英文を和訳してみよう。(10 点)

One cat, upon spotting another moving along a path, holds back until the other cat has disappeared.

ディクテーションしてみよう！

今回学習した英文に出てきた単語を，音声を聞いて □□□ に書き取ろう。

🔊 36・39

36 A cat's home range has no ❶ s⬚⬚⬚⬚⬚⬚ boundaries; it is simply the area within which there are a number of favorite places which it regularly visits, plus a network of pathways which it travels to get to them. Country cats may range over as much as sixty acres. Suburban and city cats are much more restricted because of such ❷ b⬚⬚⬚⬚⬚⬚ as streets and buildings.

37 In either situation, though, several cats may use the same geographical area as a home range, each having its own special hunting grounds or resting places within it.

38 Researchers have watched how cats whose ranges ❸ o⬚⬚⬚⬚⬚ solve the problem of using the same pathways. One cat, upon spotting another moving along a path, holds back until the other cat has disappeared. If two cats see each other approaching a junction of two paths, both may sit down at a ❹ d⬚⬚⬚⬚⬚⬚ from the crossroads and try to wait longer than the other. One cat may eventually make a fast run across the junction, or both may turn around and go back in the ❺ d⬚⬚⬚⬚⬚⬚ from which they originally came. They try to avoid confrontation, even if one of the cats has already ❻ e⬚⬚⬚⬚⬚⬚ itself as dominant to the other. If, for example, an inferior cat is already walking down a pathway when a superior cat approaches, the superior cat sits down and waits until the road is **❼** c⬚⬚⬚⬚. Nor does it drive an inferior cat away from its own favorite sunning spot.

39 For many small animals, the mere sight of another of its species is not enough to cause **❽** a⬚⬚⬚⬚⬚⬚⬚⬚⬚ behavior. That cats know what cats look like has been shown by researchers who have watched feline reactions to pictures of variously shaped **❾** a⬚⬚⬚⬚⬚⬚⬚ forms and animal silhouettes. The usual behavior of a cat in this test situation is to approach the cat silhouette cautiously and then, sometimes, to make an angry sound when the pictured cat fails to respond to its signals. A cat who sees itself in a mirror also approaches the "animal" it has just sighted in a friendly **❿** s⬚⬚⬚⬚. Unable to locate a flesh-and-blood cat in front of the mirror, the real cat often searches behind the mirror, and when this does not work, it rapidly loses interest.

確認問題の答 **1.** ① specific ② boundary ③ favorite ④ regularly ⑤ suburban
⑥ barrier ⑦ geographical ⑧ overlap ⑨ distance ⑩ eventually ⑪ direction
⑫ originally ⑬ establish ⑭ inferior ⑮ superior ⑯ clear ⑰ aggressive
⑱ abstract ⑲ cautiously ⑳ spirit

2. ① which there are a number of favorite （第1段落 第1文）
② the mere sight of another of （第4段落 第1文）

3. ある猫が道でほかの猫が移動しているのを見つけるとすぐに，その猫が姿を消すまで引っ込む。（第3段落 第2文）

ディクテーションしてみよう！の答 ❶ specific ❷ barriers ❸ overlap ❹ distance
❺ direction ❻ established ❼ clear ❽ aggressive ❾ abstract ❿ spirit

7 解答・解説

解答

問1	エ	問2	（A）①	（B）④		
問3	(1) ③	(2) ①	(3) ④	(4) ③	(5) ②	(6) ①
問4	①	問5	①			

解説

問1

（ア） helps の前に S が欠けているので，that は主格の関係代名詞。

（イ） lets の前に S が欠けているので，that は主格の関係代名詞。

（ウ） have caused の前に S が欠けているので，that は主格の関係代名詞。

（エ） Airbnb's growth（＝S）is slowing（＝V）となっており，この slow は「遅くなる」の意味の自動詞。よって，欠けている要素がないので，that は接続詞。ここでは signs の内容を説明する同格の用法。

問2

①「**たとえば**」 ②「したがって」 ③「他方で」 ④「**しかし**」

（A）は，直前文の some areas の具体例として New York を挙げているので，①が適切。

（B）は，第4段落が法的規制，第5段落がトラブルなどのリスクを説明しており，これらは所有者にとってのマイナス面である。ところが，空所の後は there are no signs that Airbnb's growth is slowing「Airbnb の成長が減速している兆候は見られない」と相反する内容が続く。よって，逆接を表す④が適切。

問3

(1)「Airbnb とは何か」

①「ホテルやアパートを経営する人々のための休暇用の予約サイトである」
②「人々が無料の部屋に関する情報を提供するためのウェブサイトである」
③「**人々が家やアパートを旅行者に貸し出せるようにするウェブサイトである**」
④「人々が金を儲ける目的で家やアパートを売却するためのウェブサイトである」
※ provide「提供する」／allow「可能にする」／make money「金を稼ぐ」
▶③が第1段落第7文〜第2段落に一致。

(2)「最近 Airbnb に何が起こったか」

①「**Airbnb の利用者数がかなり急速に増加した**」

②「Airbnb の設立者が会議においてとても人気が出た」

③「高価な家に滞在したいと思う人々の間で広まった」

④「190 か国の約 34,000 の都市が独自のウェブサイトを立ち上げた」

▶①が第 3 段落第 2 文に一致。

(3)「Airbnb はどのように金を儲けるか」

①「サービスがホストにもゲストにも無料である」

②「ウェブサイトにアクセスするのに一定額の金を請求する」

③「ウェブサイトの所有者が, 人々がログインするときに彼らに請求する」

④「**宿泊の手配が行われるとホストもゲストも手数料を支払う**」

※amount「量, 額」／log in「ログインする」／arrangement「準備, 手配」

▶④が第 3 段落第 5 文に一致。

(4)「**Airbnb のオーナーにとっての次のリスクのうち, 本文中に書かれていない
ものはどれか**」

①「オーナーから盗みを働く宿泊者がいるかもしれない」

②「オーナーの所有物が損傷するかもしれない」

③「**宿泊費の支払いを避けようとする宿泊客がいるかもしれない**」

④「オーナーの所有物がパーティーに使用されるかもしれない」

▶①及び②は第 5 段落第 2 文, ④は第 5 段落最終文に記述がある。③は本文中
に記述がない。

(5)「**誰が Airbnb のホストになれるか**」

①「家やアパートを持っていない人なら誰でも」

②「**家屋を旅行者に提供できる家屋所有者**」

③「自分の家に問題を抱えている人々」

④「市に税金を払っている人々」

▶②が第 1 段落最終文や第 2 段落第 1 文に一致。

（6）「Airbnb にとって将来はどうなるか」

　　①「**そのビジネスはおそらく拡大し続けるだろう**」

　　②「そのビジネスは数年のうちに確実に停滞するだろう」

　　③「Airbnb は生き残るためにはもっと中国人や出張旅行者を必要とするだろう」

　　④「人々は Airbnb に問題を抱えており，まもなくサービスを終了する可能性
　　　がある」

　　　※continue to *do*「～し続ける」／be certain to *do*「確実に～する」／

　　　　slow down「停滞［減速］する」／survive「生き残る，存続する」

　　▶①が最終段落全体に一致。

問4

①「**新しいタイプの宿泊システム**」

②「世界中で人気が出てきている旅行の仕方」

③「より安い滞在場所を見つける方法」

④「海外旅行でどこに滞在すべきか」

　本文は第１～２段落で Airbnb という新たな宿泊予約のサービスを紹介し，
第３段落でその歴史，第４～５段落で問題点，第６段落で現在および将来につ
いて説明している。そこで，①が正解となる。

問5

　Airbnb の利用者数については，第３段落第１～２文から，2008年に始まり，
開始以来人気が高まっていることがわかるので②と④は不正解。また，第６段
落第１文で成長が減速する兆候もないとあり，現在まで成長が続いていること
がわかるので，減速している③は不正解。以上により①が正解とわかる。

▼

それでは次に，段落ごとに詳しくみていこう。

第1段落　文の構造と語句のチェック

¹(When people travel), they sometimes prefer ⟨ not to stay in hotels ⟩. ²Then,
　　従接　　S　　　V　　　S　　　　　　　V　　　O

they stay (in other people's homes). ³These accommodations are called "Bed and
S　　V　　　　　　　　　　　　　　　　　S　　　　　　　　　V

Breakfast", or "B & B". ⁴These places are a nice way [to meet people], but it
　　　　　　　C　等接　　　S　　　　V　　C　　　　　　　　　　　　等接 仮S

is not always easy ⟨ to find the right one ⟩. ⁵Recently, a service has started [that
V　　　　　C　真S　V′　　O′　　　　　　　　　　　　　　S　　　　V　　　関代

helps people [find places [to stay (when they travel)]]]. ⁶The service is called
V　　O　　C　　　　　　　　　　従接　S　　V　　　　　　　S　　　　V

Airbnb. ⁷Airbnb has a free website [that lets people [find accommodation
C　　　　S　　V　　O　　　　関代　V　　O　　C

[which is similar (to a "B & B")](before they go (on their holidays))]]. ⁸It
関代　V　C　　　　　　　　　　従接　S　V　　　　　　　　　　　　　　　S

works (like any holiday booking site): travelers go online, select the dates [they
V　　　　　　　　　　　　　　　　　　　　S　　V　　　　V　　O　　　　S

wish to travel] and pick a place [to stay]. ⁹The places [on offer] tend to be the
V　　　　　等接　V　O　　　　　　　　S　　　　　　　V

apartments and houses [of ordinary people [who are looking to make
C　　　等接　　　　　　　　　　　　　　　関代　　　V

some extra money]].
O

> 訳 ¹人々は, 旅行をするとき, ホテルに滞在しないことを好む場合もある。²その場合, 他人の家に滞在する。³このような宿泊施設は「ベッドアンドブレックファースト」または「B&B」と呼ばれる。⁴このような場所は人と出会う良い方法であるが, 適切な場所を見つけるのは必ずしも容易ではない。⁵最近, 人々が旅行するときに滞在する場所を見つけるのに役立つサービスが始まった。⁶そのサービスは Airbnb(エアビーアンドビー)と呼ばれる。⁷Airbnb は, 人々が休暇に出かける前に「B&B」に似たような宿泊施設を見つけさせてくれる無料のウェブサイトを持つ。⁸それは休暇用の予約サイトのような働きをする。つまり, 人々はインターネットに接続し, 旅行をしたい日付を選択し, 滞在場所を選ぶ。⁹利用可能な場所は臨時収入を得ることを期待している一般人のアパートや家屋の傾向がある。

語 句

prefer to *do*	熟	~するほうを好む
accommodation	名	宿泊施設
right	形	適切な
recently	副	最近, 近頃
service	名	事業, サービス
free	形	無料の
website	名	ウェブサイト
let + O + *do*	熟	Oに~させる, Oに~させてやる
be similar to ~	熟	~に似ている, ~に類似している
booking	名	予約

site	名	ウェブサイト (=website)
go online	熟	インターネットに接続する
select	動	(画面上で) 選択する
date	名	日にち, 日付
pick	動	選ぶ
on offer	熟	売り出されて, 利用可能な
tend to *do*	熟	~する傾向がある
apartment	名	アパート [マンション] (の貸室)
ordinary	形	普通の, 一般的な
look to *do*	熟	~することを期待する
extra	形	余分の, 追加の

第2段落　文の構造と語句のチェック

¹Hosts can register (on the site) (for free), set a price 〔 per night 〕〔 for their
S　　　① V　　　　　　　　　　　　　　　② V　　O

accommodation 〕 and upload pictures 〔 of their homes 〕. ²They can even set
等接　③ V　　　O　　　　　　　　　　　　　S　　　　　　V

house rules. ³A stay 〔 in an Airbnb property 〕 is thought to be cheaper (than
O　　　　　　　S　　　　　　　　　　　　　　V　　　　　　　C

one 〔 in a hotel 〕).

> **訳** ¹ホスト [宿の主人] は無料でウェブサイトに登録し, 宿泊施設の1泊ごとの価格を設定
> し, 家の写真をアップロードすることができる。²家のルールを定めることさえできる。
> ³Airbnb での1泊はホテルでの1泊よりも安価だと考えられている。

語 句

host	名	(宿の) 主人, ホスト
register	動	登録する
for free	熟	無料で
set	動	定める, 設定する

per	前	~につき, ~ごとに [の]
upload	動	(データを) アップロードする
property	名	不動産 [家屋, 土地], 資産, 所有物

96

第3段落 文の構造と語句のチェック

¹Airbnb began (in 2008)(after two of its founders decided to offer
　S　　V　　　　　　　　　　従接　　　　　　S　　　　　　　　V

their San Francisco apartment (to travelers 〔 coming to the city (for a
　　　　　　　O

conference)〕)). ²(Since then) it has become very popular. ³People can now
　　　　　　　　　　　　　　　　　　S　　V　　　　C　　　　　　S

stay (in Airbnbs)(in 34,000 cities 〔 in 190 countries 〕). ⁴More than 40 million
 V　　　　　　　　　　　　　　　　　　　　　　　　　　　　　　S

people have booked a trip (using the site). ⁵Airbnb charges both its guests and
　　　　V　　　O　　　　　　　　　　　　　S　　V　　　　　　O₁

its hosts a fee 〔 for arranging stays 〕. ⁶Hosts are charged 3% 〔 of the cost 〔 of the
　　　　O₂　　　　　　　　　　　　　　S　　V　　　O

room 〕〕(to pay for expenses). ⁷Guests are charged 6−12% (depending on the
　　　　　　　　　　　　　　　　　S　　V　　　　O

price 〔 of the room 〕).

訳 ¹Airbnbは，設立者の2人が，会議のために市にやって来る旅行者に自分たちのサンフラ
ンシスコのアパートを提供しようと決めたあと，2008年に始まった。²それ以降 Airbnb は
大人気となった。³現在，人々は 190か国の 34,000の都市で Airbnb に宿泊できる。⁴これま
でに 4,000万人以上の人々がそのウェブサイトを利用して旅行の予約をした。⁵Airbnb はゲ
スト[宿泊客]とホストの両方に宿泊手配の手数料を請求する。⁶ホストは諸経費の支払いの
ため部屋代の3%を請求される。⁷ゲストは部屋代に応じて6〜12%を請求される。

語句

founder	名 設立者, 創設者	**charge**	動 請求する
offer	動 提供する	**guest**	名 宿泊客
conference	名 （大規模な）会議	**fee**	名 手数料, 料金
popular	形 人気のある,	**arrange**	動 手配する, 準備する
	広く普及した	**expense**	名 費用, 経費
book	動 予約する	**depending on 〜**	熟 〜次第で, 〜に応じて

第4段落　文の構造と語句のチェック

¹(In some areas 〔 in which Airbnb is operating 〕), there are rules 〔 about
　　　　　　　　　　　関代　　　S　　　V　　　　　　　　V　　　S

renting out a home 〕. ²New York, (for example), does not allow short-term rentals
　　　　　　　　　　　　　S　　　　　　　　　　　V　　　　　　　O

(fewer than 30 days) (unless the owner is also living there).
　　　　　　　　　　　従接　　　S　　　　　　V

> **訳** ¹Airbnb が営業を行っている地域の中には，家を貸し出すことに関する規則があるとこ
> ろもある。²たとえばニューヨークでは，オーナー[所有者]もそこに住んでいない限り，短期
> の賃貸(30日未満)は許されない。

語句

operate	動 営業する	**allow**	動 許す，許可する
rent out ～	熟 ～を貸し出す，	short-term	形 短期(間)の
	～を賃貸する	**unless**	接 ～しない限り
		owner	名 オーナー，所有者

第5段落　文の構造と語句のチェック

　　　　　　　　　　　　　　　　　　　　　　①　　等接　　　②
¹Other concerns include standards of local housing, laws and regulations, and
　　S　　　　　V　　　　　O①　　　　　　　　　O②　　　　　　等接

　　　　　　　　　　　　　　　　　　　　　　　　　　　　等接
security risks. ²There have been some cases 〔 of guests stealing or destroying
　O③　　　　　　　　　V　　　　　S　　　　　　S′　　　　V′

property 〕. ³Some owners have complained (about people renting houses (to
　O′　　　　　　S　　　　　V　　　　　　　　　　S′　　V′　　O′

hold parties 〔 that have caused damage (to homes)〕)).
　　　　　　関代　V　　　　O

> **訳** ¹ほかの懸念としては，地域の住環境の水準，法律や規制，治安のリスクがある。²これま
> でにゲストが所有物を盗んだり壊したりした事例もあった。³家屋に損傷を与えるほどのパ
> ーティーをするために家を借りる人々について苦情を言うオーナーもいた。

語句

concern	名	不安, 懸念
include	動	含む
standard	名	基準, 水準
local	形	地域の, 地方の
housing	名	住宅, 住環境
law	名	法律
regulation	名	規制, 規定

security	名	治安, 防犯
case	名	事例, 実例
destroy	動	破壊する, 壊す
complain	動	不平[苦情]を言う
rent	動	賃借[賃貸]する
hold	動	開催する
damage	名	損傷, 損害

第6段落 文の構造と語句のチェック

¹However, there are no signs 〈 that Airbnb's growth is slowing 〉. ²It has recently
started to use TV advertisements (in order to attract even more people (to the
site)). ³(In the future), Airbnb hopes to expand (into the Chinese and
the business travel markets).

> **訳** ¹しかし, Airbnb の成長が減速している兆候は見られない。²Airbnb は最近, さらに多くの人々をウェブサイトに引き寄せるためにテレビ広告を利用し始めた。³この先, Airbnb は中国市場や出張の市場へ拡大することを望んでいる。

語句

sign	名	形跡, 兆候
growth	名	成長, 発展
slow	動	遅くなる, 弱まる
advertisement	名	広告

in order to *do*	熟	～するために
attract	動	引き寄せる, 集める
expand	動	拡大する, 進出する
market	名	市場

文法事項の整理 ⑧ 〈名詞＋that節〉の識別

第1段落第5文の that について見てみよう。

Recently, a service has started **that** helps people find places to stay when they travel.

that には以下のように多くの用法がある。

①代名詞（「あれ，それ」と訳す）

②形容詞（「あの，その」と訳し，直後の名詞にかかる）

③副詞（「そんなに」と訳し，直後の形容詞または副詞にかかる）

④従属接続詞

⑤関係代名詞

⑥関係副詞

この中で，④〜⑥が節を導く用法。特に紛らわしい，「**名詞のあとに that 節がついている場合**」の識別方法を，以下に整理する。

1. that 以下が不完全な文（SやO，前置詞のあとの名詞などが欠けた文）

that は関係代名詞（節中のSが欠けていればthatは主格，Oや前置詞のあとの名詞が欠けていれば目的格）

> 例 This is the house that S was designed by my father. 【主格】
> 「これは私の父によって設計された家だ」
> ▶that 以下にSが欠けているので，that は主格の関係代名詞

> 例 This is the house that my father designed O . 【目的格】
> 「これは私の父が設計した家だ」
> ▶that以下にOが欠けているので，that は目的格の関係代名詞

> 例 This is the house that my father used to live in 名 . 【目的格】
> 「これは私の父がかつて住んでいた家だ」
> ▶that 以下に前置詞 in のあとの名詞が欠けているので，that は目的格の関係代名詞

▶ 冒頭の第1段落第5文では, 名詞 a service と that が離れているが, この that は helps の前に S が欠けているので主格の関係代名詞で, a service が先行詞である。

2. that 以下が完全な文
1) 前の名詞が【時】【場所】【理由 (reason)】【方法 (way)】の場合
⇒ **that は関係副詞**

例 I don't like the way that my brother talks to me.
「兄の私に対する話し方が気に入らない」

▶ that 以下は完全な文, 前に「方法 (way)」があるので, that は関係副詞

2) そのほかの場合
⇒ **that は同格の接続詞** (前の名詞の具体的な内容を説明する用法。「…という 名詞」と訳す)

例 I couldn't accept the idea that we were wrong.
「私は, 私たちが間違っているという考えを受け入れられなかった」

> 同格の接続詞 that を従える名詞
> fact「事実」/ conclusion「結論」/ belief「考え」/ idea「考え」/ thought「考え」/ claim「主張」/ opinion「意見」/ news「知らせ」/ hope「希望」/ possibility「可能性」/ chance「可能性」/ doubt「疑い」/ fear「恐れ」/ theory「理論」など

▶ **第1段落第7文**

Airbnb has a free website that lets people find accommodation which is similar to a "B & B" before they go on their holidays.

▶ 名詞 a free website の後に that が続き, that 以下は lets の前に S が欠けているので, that は主格の関係代名詞。

▶ **第5段落第3文**

Some owners have complained about people renting houses to hold parties that have caused damage to homes.

▶ 名詞 parties の後に that が続き，that 以下は have caused の前に S が欠けているので，that は主格の関係代名詞。

▶ **第6段落第1文**

However, there are no signs that Airbnb's growth is slowing.

▶ 名詞 signs の後に that が続き，that 以下は Airbnb's growth（=S）is slowing（=V）となっており，この slow は「遅くなる」の意味の自動詞。よって，欠けている要素がないので，that は接続詞。ここでは signs の内容を説明する同格の用法。

確認問題

1. 次の和訳と対応する英語の語句を,頭文字を参考にして書き,空欄を完成させよう。

/40点

（各1点×20）

①	p [　　　] to *do*	熟	～するほうを好む
②	a [　　　]	名	宿泊施設
③	be s [　　　] to ～	熟	～に似ている,～に類似している
④	on o [　　　]	熟	売り出されて,利用可能な
⑤	o [　　　]	形	普通の,一般的な
⑥	r [　　　]	動	登録する
⑦	for f [　　　]	熟	無料で
⑧	f [　　　]	名	設立者,創設者
⑨	c [　　　]	名	(大規模な)会議
⑩	c [　　　]	動	請求する
⑪	f [　　　]	名	手数料,料金
⑫	e [　　　]	名	費用,経費
⑬	d [　　　] on ～	熟	～次第で,～に応じて
⑭	c [　　　]	名	不安,懸念
⑮	r [　　　]	名	規制,規定
⑯	d [　　　]	動	破壊する,壊す
⑰	d [　　　]	名	損傷,損害
⑱	a [　　　]	名	広告
⑲	a [　　　]	動	引き寄せる,集める
⑳	e [　　　]	動	拡大する,進出する

2. 次の[　]内の語句を並べ替えて,意味の通る英文を完成させよう。（各5点×2）

① Airbnb charges both its guests [for / a / its / hosts / fee / and] arranging stays.

② There have been some [stealing / cases / guests / of / or] destroying property.

3. 次の英文を和訳してみよう。(10点)

Recently, a service has started that helps people find places to stay when they travel.

ディクテーションしてみよう！

今回学習した英文に出てきた単語を, 音声を聞いて 🔲 に書き取ろう。

41   When people travel, they sometimes prefer not to stay in hotels. Then, they stay in other people's homes. These ❶ a 🔲 are called "Bed and Breakfast", or "B & B". These places are a nice way to meet people, but it is not always easy to find the right one. Recently, a service has started that helps people find places to stay when they travel. The service is called Airbnb. Airbnb has a free website that lets people find accommodation which is similar to a "B & B" before they go on their holidays. It works like any holiday booking site: travelers go online, select the dates they wish to travel and pick a place to stay. The places on ❷ o 🔲 tend to be the apartments and houses of ordinary people who are looking to make some extra money.

42   Hosts can register on the site for ❸ f 🔲 , set a price per night for their accommodation and upload pictures of their homes. They can even set house rules. A stay in an Airbnb property is thought to be cheaper than one in a hotel.

43   Airbnb began in 2008 after two of its ❹ f 🔲 decided to offer their San Francisco apartment to travelers coming to the city for a conference. Since then it has become very popular. People can now stay in Airbnbs in 34,000 cities in 190 countries. More than 40 million people have booked a trip using the site. Airbnb charges both its guests and its hosts a ❺ f⬚⬚ for arranging stays. Hosts are charged 3% of the cost of the room to pay for expenses. Guests are charged 6-12% ❻ d⬚⬚⬚⬚⬚⬚⬚⬚ on the price of the room.

44 In some areas in which Airbnb is operating, there are rules about renting out a home. New York, for example, does not allow short-term rentals (fewer than 30 days) unless the owner is also living there.

45 Other ❼ c⬚⬚⬚⬚⬚ include standards of local housing, laws and regulations, and security risks. There have been some cases of guests stealing or destroying property. Some owners have complained about people renting houses to hold parties that have caused ❽ d⬚⬚⬚ to homes.

46 However, there are no signs that Airbnb's growth is slowing. It has recently started to use TV ❾ a⬚⬚⬚⬚⬚⬚⬚⬚⬚ in order to attract even more people to the site. In the future, Airbnb hopes to ❿ e⬚⬚⬚ into the Chinese and the business travel markets.

確認問題の答 **1.** ① prefer　② accommodation　③ similar　④ offer　⑤ ordinary　⑥ register　⑦ free　⑧ founder　⑨ conference　⑩ charge　⑪ fee　⑫ expense　⑬ depending　⑭ concern　⑮ regulation　⑯ destroy　⑰ damage　⑱ advertisement　⑲ attract　⑳ expand

2. ① and its hosts a fee for　（第3段落　第5文）
　② cases of guests stealing or　（第5段落　第2文）

3. 最近, 人々が旅行するときに滞在する場所を見つけるのに役立つサービスが始まった。 （第1段落　第5文）

ディクテーションしてみよう！の答 ❶ accommodations　❷ offer　❸ free　❹ founders　❺ fee　❻ depending　❼ concerns　❽ damage　❾ advertisements　❿ expand

解答

問1	(ア) ③	(イ) ④	(ウ) ④
問2	①	問3	③
問4	②, ⑥	問5	④	問6	①

解説

問1

(ア)

> While human beings race for fun or to win prizes, these animals primarily run $_{(ア)}$for their lives.

　文頭の接続詞 While は【対比】を表し,「…する一方で」の意味（▶116 ページ「文法事項の整理⑨」参照）。人間が競走をする目的が「楽しみ」「賞を獲得すること」であるのと対比して，動物たちが走るのは，そのような娯楽目的ではなく,「命のため」なのだ，と解釈する。正解は，③「**生きるために**」。

(イ)

> Although its greatest speed is only 60 miles per hour, the pronghorn has superb $_{(イ)}$endurance.

　superb endurance を具体化するのが直後の文（It can run at this speed for an hour.「この速度で1時間走ることができる」）で，速度はチーターほどでもないが，チーターよりも長時間走り続けることができる点を説明している。正解は，④「**持久力**」。

(ウ)

> The aerobic system of the pronghorn is five to ten times more $_{(ウ)}$efficient than the human aerobic system.

　pronghorn（プロングホーン）については，第2段落で，最も運動能力が優れ

た動物かもしれないと説明されている。そして, 第4段落第1文 (Every creature's speed and endurance depends on how well oxygen is transported by the aerobic system.) では,「すべての生物の速度と持久力は, いかに有効に酸素が酸素消費システムによって運ばれるかに左右される」とあるので, プロングホーンの酸素消費システムは人間より優れていると考えられる。選択肢のうち, プラスイメージのものは④「**効率のよい**」のみなので, これが正解となる。

問2

(A)To match the hummingbird's energy, a human being would have to work hard for a week without a minute's rest.

match は「～に匹敵する, ～と対等になる」の意味。直前の第3段落第2・3文で, 膨大な距離を移動するハチドリが長時間羽ばたきをし続けることが書かれており, この文では, 仮にハチドリの運動と同等のことを人間がするとしたらどうなるかを説明している。なお, 助動詞 would が用いられており, 内容も非現実的なので, この文は仮定法（1分も休まずに1週間働き続けるのは現実的でない)。正解は, ①「**ハチドリの活動量を人間に置き換えると, 人間は1週間の間1分も休まずに働き続けなくてはいけない**」。

問3

(B)This is the secret of the pronghorn's athletic superiority.

原則として, this は直前の文全体（または一部）の内容を指す。直前の文 (The aerobic system of the pronghorn is five to ten times more efficient than the human aerobic system.) には, プロングホーンの酸素消費システムの効率が優れていることが書かれている（問1 **(ウ)** の解説参照）。これは, the pronghorn's athletic superiority「プロングホーンの運動能力が優れていること」(→第2段落) の the secret「秘密, 秘訣」と言えるだろう。そこで, This は, 原則通り, 直前の文全体の内容を指すと考えられる。正解は, ②「**プロングホーンの酸素消費システムは人間よりも優れていること**」。

合致しないものを選ぶ点に注意。

① 「エチオピア出身のオリンピック選手 Haile Gebreselassie は毎日はだし で学校まで走ることでその能力を鍛えた」

　▶第1段落第4文（Haile developed his speed and endurance by running barefoot every day from his farm to his school six miles away.「ハイレ は, 農場から6マイル離れた学校まで毎日はだしで走ることによって, 速度と持久力を身につけた」）と一致。

② **「チーターとプロングホーンでは最高速度もその速度を持続できる時間も プロングホーンの方が勝っている」**

　▶第2段落第1・2文にチーター, 第3文以降にプロングホーンについて 書かれている。それによれば, 以下のようになる。

> チーター　　　　　：時速70マイルで走れるが数秒間しか持続しない
> プロングホーン：時速60マイルほどで1時間走れる

　よって, 本文の内容と合致しない（正解）。

③ 「長距離を追ってくるオオカミの群れから逃れようとして, プロングホー ンはその運動能力を伸ばしてきたと考えられる」

　▶第2段落最終文の引用の中に（They developed endurance to escape wolf packs, which hunted over long distances.「長距離にわたって狩り をするオオカミの群れから逃げるために持久力を発達させた」）とあり, これと一致する。

④ 「コビトジャコウネズミがもし人間と同じサイズなら, オリンピック選手 よりもはるかに速く走ることができるだろう」

　▶第3段落第8文（If the tiny shrew were the size of a human being, it could sprint a mile in about forty seconds.「もしこの小さなネズミが人 間の大きさだったら, 約40秒で1マイルを全力疾走できるだろう」）およ び最終文（Even the great Olympic runner Jesse Owens couldn't do that!「偉大なオリンピックランナーのジェシー・オーエンスでさえ, そ

んなことはできなかったのに！」と一致する。厳密には、「はるかに」速い
かどうかは本文から判断できないが、常識的に考えて正しいだろう。

⑤ 「動物の運動能力は、酸素がいかに有効に酸素消費システムに取り込まれ
るかに関係している」

▶第4段落第1文（ Every creature's speed and endurance depends on
how well oxygen is transported by the aerobic system.「すべての生物
の速度と持久力は、いかに有効に酸素が酸素消費システムによって運ば
れるかに左右される」）と一致する。

⑥ **「プロングホーンは万能な運動選手なので、体脂肪が少ないことは不利に
ならない」**

▶「体脂肪が少ない」は第5段落第2文。さらに、同段落最終文には、それ
が原因で飢え死にする可能性があると書かれている。よって、本文の内
容と合致しない（正解）。

問5

第4段落第2文以降の内容をまとめると、次のようになる。

❶ 呼吸
→❷ 酸素が肺に入る（第4段落第2文）
→❸ 酸素は肺から血液へ（同第3文前半）
→❹ 血流により酸素は心臓へ（同第3文後半）
→❺ 心臓により酸素を含む血液が筋肉へ（同第4文）
→❻ 酸素がエネルギーに変換（同第5文）

これを本問にあてはめると、以下のようになる。

❶ The animal takes a breath of air.
　「動物は空気を吸い込む」
→❷ (c) Oxygen goes into the lungs.
　「酸素が肺に入る」
→❸ The lungs carry oxygen into the bloodstream.

「肺は酸素を血流へと運ぶ」

→❹ **(b)** Blood carrying oxygen enters the heart.

「酸素を運んでいる血液が心臓に入る」

→❺ **(a)** The heart pumps oxygen-filled blood into the muscles.

「心臓は酸素で満たされた血液を筋肉へ注ぎ込む」

→❻ The oxygen turns into energy.

「酸素がエネルギーに変わる」

問6

① 「高い速度と持久力を持つ種」

　　▶本文全体の主題と言える。「種」の具体例として, チーター（第2段落）, プロングホーン（第2, 4, 5段落）, ハチドリ（第3段落）, コビトジャコウネズミ（第3段落）が, 人間と対比されながら紹介されている。

② 「歴史上最速の陸生動物」

　　▶最速の動物としては第2段落にチーターが挙げられているが, 「歴史上」であるかどうかは本文に書かれていない。

③ 「酸素はどのように体内を移動するか」

　　▶第4段落にしか書かれていないので, 主題とは言えない。

④ 「プロングホーンは何千年もの間どのように進化してきたか」

　　▶第2段落にしか書かれていないので, 主題とは言えない。

以上により, 正解は①。

▼

それでは次に, 段落ごとに詳しくみていこう。 47

第1段落　文の構造と語句のチェック

¹(If human beings train their bodies), they can become fine athletes. ²The
　　従接　　　S　　　　　　V　　　　O　　　　　　S　　　V　　　　　　C

best of us can achieve great feats 〔 of speed and endurance 〕. ³(For example),
　S　　　　　　V　　　　O　　　　　　①　　等接　　②

(in 1996), <u>an Ethiopian farm boy, Haile Gebreselassie,</u> <u>set</u> <u>an Olympic record</u>
　　　　　　　　 S 　　　└─同格─┘　　　　　　　 V 　　　　　 O

(in the 10-kilometer race). ⁴<u>Haile</u> <u>developed</u> <u>his speed</u> ^① and^{等接} endurance^② (by
　　　　　　　　　　　　　　　　 S 　　 V 　　　　　　　 O

running barefoot every day (from his farm to his school [six miles away])).

⁵<u>Yet</u> even <u>this elite runner</u> <u>would be left behind</u> (in a race [with certain
等接　　　　　 S 　　　　　　　 V

animals]). ⁶(While <u>human beings</u> <u>race</u> (for fun) or (to win prizes)), <u>these</u>
　　　　　　 従接　　 S 　　 V 　 ① 　 等接 　 ②

<u>animals</u> primarily <u>run</u> (for their lives).
　 S 　　　　　 V

訳 ¹もし人間が体を鍛えれば，優れたアスリートになることができる。²私たちの中で最も優れた人々は，速度と持久力のすばらしい偉業を達成することができる。³たとえば，1996年に，エチオピアの農場の少年，ハイレ・ゲブレセラシェは，10キロメートル競走でオリンピック記録を樹立した。⁴ハイレは，農場から6マイル離れた学校まで毎日はだしで走ることによって，速度と持久力を身につけた。⁵しかし，このエリートランナーでさえ，ある種の動物との競争では置いていかれてしまうだろう。⁶人間が楽しむため，または賞を獲得するために競走をする一方で，これらの動物は主として命のために走る。

語句

human being	名	人間
train	動	鍛える，訓練する
athlete	名	運動選手，アスリート
achieve	動	達成する
feat	名	偉業，離れ技
endurance	名	忍耐力，持久力
Ethiopian	形	エチオピア（人）の
set	動	（記録を）打ち立てる，樹立する
record	名	記録
race	名	レース，競争［競走］
	動	レースをする，競争［競走］する

develop	動	発展させる，伸ばす
barefoot	副	素足で，はだしで
yet	接	しかし
elite	形	エリートの，精鋭の
leave ～ behind	熟	～を取り残す，引き離す
certain	形	特定の，ある種の
for fun	熟	楽しみのために，遊びで
win	動	勝ち取る，獲得する
prize	名	賞
primarily	副	主として，第一に

111

[1]The cheetah, the world's swiftest land animal, can reach speeds [of 70 miles
 S └─ 同格 ─┘　　　　　　　　　　　　　V　　　　O

per hour]. [2]But it can sprint (at this top speed)(for only a few seconds).
　　　　　　　等接　S　　　V

[3]The American pronghorn antelope, however, may be the world's greatest all-
　　　　S　　　　　　　　　　　　　　　V　　　　　　C

round athlete. [4](Although its greatest speed is only 60 miles per hour), the
　　　　　　　　　従接　　　S　　　　　　V　　　　　C

pronghorn has superb endurance. [5]It can run (at this speed)(for an hour). [6]A
　S　　　V　　　O　　　　　　　S　　V

physiologist has explained the pronghorn's athletic superiority. [7]"Pronghorns
　S　　　　V　　　　　　O　　　　　　　　　　　S

have evolved (over millennia). [8](In ancient times), they probably developed
　V　　　　　　　　　　　　　　　　　　　　　　　　　S　　　　　　V

speed (to evade cheetahs). [9]They developed endurance (to escape wolf packs,
　O　　　　　　　　　　　　　S　　V　　　O

[which hunted (over long distances)])."
　関代　　V

訳 [1]チーターは世界最速の陸生動物であり, 時速 70 マイルの速度に達することができる。
[2]しかし, この最高速度での全力疾走はわずか数秒間しか持続できない。[3]しかし, プロング
ホーンは, おそらく世界最高の万能アスリートかもしれない。[4]最高速度は時速 60 マイル
ほどだが, プロングホーンは持久力に優れている。[5]この速度で 1 時間走ることができる。
[6]ある生理学者がプロングホーンの運動能力の優秀さを説明した。[7]「プロングホーンは何千
年もの間進化してきました。[8]大昔は, おそらくチーターから逃れるために速度を発達させ
ました。[9]そして, 長距離にわたって狩りをするオオカミの群れから逃げるために持久力を
発達させたのです」。

語 句

cheetah	名	チーター
swift	形	速い, すばやい
per	前	〜あたり, 〜につき
sprint	動	全力疾走する

all-round	形	万能の
superb	形	見事な, すばらしい
physiologist	名	生理学者
explain	動	説明する
athletic	形	運動能力の, 運動選手の

superiority	名 優越, 優位	**ancient**	形 古代の, 大昔の
evolve	動 進化する	**evade**	動 避ける, 逃れる
millennium	名 千年(間)(＊複数形 millennia)	**distance**	名 距離

第3段落　文の構造と語句のチェック

¹Much smaller animals are also superb athletes. ²The tiny California
   S   V   C   S

hummingbird, (for instance), migrates (enormous distances). ³(To do this),
            V
           └─ 前置詞 for 省略

it beats its wings (thousands of times per minute) (for 24 hours) (at a time).
S V O

⁴(To match the hummingbird's energy), a human being would have to work
                S   V

hard (for a week) (without a minute's rest). ⁵Another example is the
                S   V

Etruscan shrew. ⁶This mouse-like creature is only two inches long and thin as a
 C   S   V   C①   等接 C②

dime. ⁷Yet it can run (more swiftly than the fastest human). ⁸(If the tiny
   等接 S V   従接   S

shrew were the size of a human being), it could sprint a mile (in about forty
 V   C   S V   O

seconds). ⁹Even the great Olympic runner Jesse Owens couldn't do that!
        S   └─同格─┘   V   O

> **訳** ¹はるかに小さな動物にもすばらしいアスリートがいる。²たとえば, 小さなカリフォルニアハチドリは, 膨大な距離を移動する。³これをするために, 一度に24時間, 毎分数千回羽ばたく。⁴ハチドリのエネルギーと対等になるには, 人間は1分も休まず1週間懸命に働かなければならない。⁵もう1つの例はコビトジャコウネズミだ。⁶このネズミのような生き物はわずか体長2インチで, 10セントコインのように薄い。⁷しかし, このコビトジャコウネズミは最も足の速い人間よりも速く走ることができる。⁸もしこの小さなネズミが人間の大きさだったら, 約40秒で1マイルを全力疾走できるだろう。⁹偉大なオリンピックランナーのジェシー　オーエンスでさえ, こんなことはできなかったのに！

tiny	形	とても小さい	at a time	熟	一度に	
for instance	熟	たとえば	match	動	匹敵する, 対等になる	
migrate	動	移動する, 移住する	rest	名	休憩, 休息	
enormous	形	莫大な, 膨大な	creature	名	動物, 生き物	
beat	動	(羽を)上下に動かす	thin	形	薄い, 細い	
wing	名	翼, 羽	swiftly	副	速く, すばやく	

第4段落 文の構造と語句のチェック

¹Every creature's speed and endurance depends (on ⟨ how well oxygen is
transported (by the aerobic system)⟩⟩. ²Each breath of air [we take] contains
oxygen [that passes (into the lungs)]. ³The oxygen travels (from the lungs)
(into the blood); then the bloodstream moves the oxygen (into the heart).

⁴The heart pumps this oxygen-filled blood (into the muscles). ⁵There, the life-
giving oxygen is transformed (into energy). ⁶The aerobic system [of the
pronghorn] is five to ten times more efficient (than the human aerobic system).

⁷This is the secret [of the pronghorn's athletic superiority].

> **訳** ¹すべての生物の速度と持久力は, いかに有効に酸素が酸素消費システムによって運ばれるかに左右される。²私たちが呼吸をするたびに, その空気には肺に送り込まれる酸素が含まれている。³酸素は肺から血液に移動し, その後血流が酸素を心臓に移動させる。⁴心臓はこの酸素で満たされた血液を筋肉に注ぎ込む。⁵そこで, 命を与える酸素はエネルギーに変換される。⁶プロングホーンの酸素消費システムは, 人間の酸素消費システムよりも5〜10倍効率がよい。⁷これがプロングホーンの運動能力が優れている秘密だ。

語句

depend on ～	熟	～次第だ, ～によって決まる
oxygen	名	酸素
transport	動	運ぶ, 輸送する
aerobic	形	酸素消費の, 有酸素の
breath	名	呼吸, 吸気
pass into ～	熟	～に入り込む, ～に運ばれる
lung	名	肺
travel	動	移動する

blood	名	血, 血液
bloodstream	名	血流
pump	動	注ぎ込む, 注入する
muscle	名	筋肉
transform A into B	熟	AをBに変換する
efficient	形	効率がよい
secret	名	秘密, 秘訣

第5段落 文の構造と語句のチェック

[1]Unfortunately, the peerless pronghorn pays a high price (for its aerobic efficiency). [2]The pronghorn has almost no body fat. [3]Therefore, (while it can outrun its enemies), it may starve (to death) (in a harsh winter).

訳 [1]残念ながら, ほかに類を見ないプロングホーンは酸素消費効率に高い代償を払っている。[2]プロングホーンはほとんど体脂肪がない。[3]そのため, 敵より速く走ることはできるが, 過酷な冬には飢え死にする可能性がある。

語句

unfortunately	副	残念ながら
peerless	形	ほかに類を見ない, 比類のない
price	名	代償, 犠牲
efficiency	名	効率
fat	名	脂肪

therefore	副	それゆえに, したがって
outrun	動	より速く走る, 引き離す
enemy	名	敵
starve to death	熟	飢え死にする
harsh	形	厳しい, 過酷な

文法事項の整理 ⑨　接続詞 while の意味

第1段落最終文の while について見てみよう。

While human beings race for fun or to win prizes, these animals primarily run for their lives.

　接続詞 while は【時】【譲歩】【対比】の意味を表す。

1. 【時】：…している間に

　例　You should visit Kyoto **while** you are staying in Japan.
　　　「日本に滞在している間に京都を訪れるべきだ」

2. 【譲歩】：…だけれど

　例　**While** I admit that she is right, I will not support her.
　　　「彼女が正しいことは認めるけれど，支持するつもりはない」

3. 【対比】：…する一方で

　例　**While** some of the students are shy, others are very sociable.
　　　「内気な学生がいる一方で，社交的な学生もいる」

　▶【譲歩】【対比】のいずれの意味にも取れる場合も多い。

▶第1段落最終文の While は【対比】の意味。人間と動物を対比している。
▶第5段落最終文の while は【譲歩】の意味。

Therefore, **while** it can outrun its enemies, it may starve to death in a harsh winter.

確認問題

1. 次の和訳と対応する英語の語句を, 頭文字を参考にして書き, 空欄を完成させよう。

（各1点×20）

①	h		b		名	人間
②	a				名	運動選手, アスリート
③	a				動	達成する
④	e				名	忍耐力, 持久力
⑤	d				動	発展させる, 伸ばす
⑥	l	~	b		熟	～を取り残す, 引き離す
⑦	s				形	速い, すばやい
⑧	e				動	説明する
⑨	s				名	優越, 優位
⑩	e				動	進化する
⑪	a				形	古代の, 大昔の
⑫	d				名	距離
⑬	t				形	とても小さい
⑭	c				名	動物, 生き物
⑮	t				動	運ぶ, 輸送する
⑯	l				名	肺
⑰	b				名	血, 血液
⑱	e				形	効率がよい
⑲	f				名	脂肪
⑳	s		t	d	熟	飢え死にする

2. 次の[ ]内の語句を並べ替えて, 意味の通る英文を完成させよう。(各5点×2)

① Each [of / breath / take / air / contains / we] oxygen that passes into the lungs.

② Unfortunately, the peerless pronghorn [high / its / pays / for / a / price] aerobic efficiency.

3. 次の英文を和訳してみよう。(10 点)

While human beings race for fun or to win prizes, these animals primarily run for their lives.

ディクテーションしてみよう！

今回学習した英文に出てきた単語を, 音声を聞いて [ ] に書き取ろう。

48
52

48   If human beings train their bodies, they can become fine athletes. The best of us can achieve great feats of speed and endurance. For example, in 1996, an Ethiopian farm boy, Haile Gebreselassie, set an Olympic record in the 10-kilometer race. Haile developed his speed and endurance by running barefoot every day from his farm to his school six miles away. Yet even this elite runner would be ❶ l[　　　] b[　　　　] in a race with certain animals. While human beings race ❷ f[　] f[　　] or to win prizes, these animals primarily run for their lives.

49   The cheetah, the world's swiftest land animal, can reach speeds of 70 miles per hour. But it can sprint at this top speed for only a few seconds. The American pronghorn antelope, however, may be the world's greatest all-round athlete. Although its greatest speed is only 60 miles per hour, the pronghorn has superb endurance. It can run at this speed for an hour. A physiologist has ❸ e[　　　　　] the pronghorn's athletic superiority. "Pronghorns have ❹ e[　　　　　] over millennia. In ancient times, they probably developed speed to evade cheetahs. They developed endurance to escape wolf packs, which hunted over long distances."

50   Much smaller animals are also superb athletes. The tiny California hummingbird, for instance, migrates ❺ e[　　　　　] distances. To do this, it beats its wings thousands of times per minute for 24 hours at a time. To match the hummingbird's energy, a human being would have to work hard for a week without a minute's rest. Another example is the Etruscan shrew. This mouse-like **❻** c⬚⬚⬚⬚⬚⬚⬚ is only two inches long and thin as a dime. Yet it can run more swiftly than the fastest human. If the tiny shrew were the size of a human being, it could sprint a mile in about forty seconds. Even the great Olympic runner Jesse Owens couldn't do that!

51 Every creature's speed and endurance depends on how well oxygen is transported by the aerobic system. Each breath of air we take **❼** c⬚⬚⬚⬚⬚⬚ oxygen that passes into the lungs. The oxygen travels from the lungs into the blood; then the bloodstream moves the oxygen into the heart. The heart pumps this oxygen-filled blood into the muscles. There, the life-giving oxygen is **❽** t⬚⬚⬚⬚⬚⬚⬚⬚ into energy. The aerobic system of the pronghorn is five to ten times more efficient than the human aerobic system. This is the secret of the pronghorn's athletic superiority.

52 **❾** U⬚⬚⬚⬚⬚⬚⬚⬚⬚⬚, the peerless pronghorn pays a high price for its aerobic efficiency. The pronghorn has almost no body fat. Therefore, while it can outrun its enemies, it may starve to death in a **❿** h⬚⬚⬚ winter.

確認問題の答 **1.** ① human being ② athlete ③ achieve ④ endurance ⑤ develop
⑥ leave, behind ⑦ swift ⑧ explain ⑨ superiority ⑩ evolve ⑪ ancient
⑫ distance ⑬ tiny ⑭ creature ⑮ transport ⑯ lung ⑰ blood ⑱ efficient
⑲ fat ⑳ starve to death
2. ① breath of air we take contains （第4段落　第2文）
② pays a high price for its （第5段落　第1文）
3. 人間が楽しむため，または賞を獲得するために競走をする一方で，これらの動物は主として命のために走る。（第1段落　最終文）

ディクテーションしてみよう！の答 ❶ left behind ❷ for fun ❸ explained ❹ evolved
❺ enormous ❻ creature ❼ contains ❽ transformed ❾ Unfortunately ❿ harsh

解 答

問1	②	問2	②	問3	④	問4	④	問5	①
問6	③	問7	③	問8	③	問9	①	問10	④

解 説

問1

第1段落第3文に memory loss can begin when someone is in their twenties「物忘れは20代で始まる場合もある」と書かれているので②が正解。

問2

combine は「組み合わせる，結合させる」の意味。「4つの要素を組み合わせる」に最も近いのは「4つの要素を含む」なので②が正解となる。なお，combine を知らなかったとしても，combine の名詞形 combination が同段落最終文にあり，「コンビネーション」は日本語になっているので推測可能であろう。

問3

プログラムの内容は第2段落第4文（His program combines four elements: a special diet, daily physical activity, stress relieving exercises and, of course, memory exercises.）に書かれている。ここに含まれる4つの要素とは，(1) 特別な食事，(2) 日々の身体的活動，(3) ストレスを軽減する訓練，(4) 記憶力の訓練である。選択肢①は (2)，②は (1)，③は (4) に該当するが，選択肢④に該当するものはない。

問4

① 「彼女の記憶力は同じ年齢の平均的な人よりもずっと悪い」
　　▶第3段落第3〜4文によれば，彼女の記憶力は，最初は同年齢の平均で，プログラム終了後に20歳と同程度になったので，誤り。
② 「スモール医師は，彼の記憶力の訓練で彼女の記憶力を改善することができなかった」
　　▶第3段落第4文に，プログラム終了後に20歳の記憶力と同等になったとある。そのあとに書かれている彼女の変化からも，改善できたとわか

120

るので, 誤り。

③ 「彼女には, それぞれ10代の子どもを育てている3人の子どもがいる」

　　▶第3段落第2文に10代の3人の子どもがいると書かれているが, その子どものそれぞれが子育てをしているという記述はない。

④ **「彼女は子どもたちの勉強を手伝うことによって脳を鍛えている」**

　　▶第3段落最終文と一致。

問5

① **「方法, 方式」**

② 「記録」

③ 「指導, 手引き」

④ 「競技会, コンテスト」

　strategy は「戦略, 戦術」の意味から, 一般的に（戦いに関係しない文脈で）「方策, 方針」の意味を表す。この選択肢の中では①が最も近い。

問6

　下線部 **(ウ)** の does は, 後に change という動詞の原形があるので, 【動詞の強調】を表す助動詞の用法である (▶128ページ「文法事項の整理⑩」参照)。

① 「彼はふだん, 夕食後に宿題をする」

　　▶「する」という意味。第3文型 (S＋V＋O) で用いられている一般動詞。

② 「タバコが有害無益であることは広く知られている」

　　▶「～に…を与える, 及ぼす」という意味。第4文型 (S＋V＋O＋O) で用いられている一般動詞。do ～ harm で「～に害を与える」, do ～ good で「～に利益を与える」。したがって, do ～ more harm than good で「～にとって有害無益だ」の意味になる。

③ **「彼は本当に妻を愛しているのだが, 妻は愛していない」**

　　▶動詞の原形の前に does があるので, 【動詞の強調】を表す助動詞の用法。これが正解。なお, 後続の doesn't の does も助動詞（強調を表す用法ではない）で, あとに love her husband を補って考えるとよい。

④ 「私は兄よりも上手に書ける」

　　▶前に出た動詞の代わりをする代動詞の用法。ここでは writes の代用。

問7

① 「17人がこの研究で調べられた」

  ▶第4段落第2文と一致。

② 「スモール医師は2週間のプログラムをするのに8人を選んだ」

  ▶同段落第4文と一致。

③ **「テストの前，被験者のうち何人かは記憶に問題を抱えていた」**

  ▶同段落第3文参照。「全員」が記憶に不満を抱えていたので some が不適。

④ 「9人が比較のために選ばれ，特別なことを何もしなかった」

  ▶同段落最終文と一致。

問8

　①と②は本文中に記述がない。③は第5段落第2文と一致。④は同段落最終文と逆の内容（less forgetful は「忘れにくくなった」の意味になる）。

問9

① **「遅くする，遅らせる」**

② 「明るくする，軽くする」

③ 「保護する」

④ 「解決する」

　delay は「延ばす，遅らせる」の意味。slow は「（速度を）遅くする，遅らせる」という意味があり，delay の意味に最も近い。

問10

① 「記憶と運動」

② 「年齢と物忘れ」

③ 「脳細胞とは何か」

④ **「脳の短期集中訓練」**

　この文章は The Boot Camp for the Brain（脳の短期集中訓練）について，第2段落で内容を説明し，第3～5段落で具体的な調査とその結果，最終段落でそれに関する考察を述べている。

それでは次に，段落ごとに詳しくみていこう。 53

第1段落　文の構造と語句のチェック

¹Many people worry (about memory loss). ²It is normal 〈 to lose memory (as
　　　 S　　　　 V　　　　　　　　　　　　　　　 仮S V　　C　　真S　　　　　　　 従接

you get older)〉. ³(In fact), memory loss can begin (when someone is (in their
　 S　 V　　C　　　　　　　　　 S　　　　　　 V　　 従接　　 S　　 V

twenties)). ⁴But how much of your memory do you have to lose, and (how
　　　　　　　　　 等接　 疑　　　　　　 O　　　(V) S　　 V　　　　 等接　 疑

quickly) does it have to happen? ⁵Research 〔 on the brain and memory 〕 is
　　　　　　(V) S　　 V　　　　　　 S　　　　①　　　　　 等接　②　　　　 V

a huge area (these days). ⁶Doctors are looking for ways 〔 to help people improve
　 C　　　　　　　　　　　　 S　　　 V　　　　 O　　　　　　　　　　　　　①

their memory and possibly prevent loss 〕.
　　　　　　　②
　　　　　 等接

> 訳 ¹多くの人々が物忘れに悩む。²年をとるにつれて物忘れをするのは正常である。³実際，物忘れは20代で始まる場合もある。⁴しかし，記憶のうちどれほど多くを失わなければならないのか，また，どれほど速く物忘れが起こらなければならないのだろうか。⁵今日，脳や記憶に関する研究は大きな分野である。⁶医師たちは，人々が記憶力を改善したり，ひょっとしたら物忘れを防いだりするのを助ける方法を探している。

語句

memory	名 記憶，記憶力	brain	名 脳
loss	名 喪失	huge	形 巨大な
▶memory loss	記憶喪失，物忘れ	area	名 (学問の) 分野，領域
normal	形 ふつうの，正常な	these days	熟 近頃では，今日では
in fact	熟 実際に	look for ~	熟 ~を探す
in *one's* twenties	熟 20代で	improve	動 改善する，向上させる
quickly	副 速く，すぐに	possibly	副 ひょっとしたら
research	名 研究，調査	prevent	動 防ぐ，予防する

¹Let us look at one program [to help memory], [called The Boot Camp for the
　　V　　　　　　O

Brain]. ²What is The Boot Camp for the Brain? ³It is a two-week program
　　　　　　疑
　　　　　　C　V　　　　　S　　　　　　　　S　V　　　　　　C

[developed by a psychiatrist [named Gary Small]]. ⁴His program combines
　　　　　　　　　　　　　　　　　　　　　　　　　　　　　　S　　　　　V

four elements: a special diet, daily physical activity, stress relieving exercises and ,
　　O　　　　　①　　　　　　　②　　　　　　　　　③　　　　　　　　　　　等接

(of course), memory exercises. ⁵The memory exercises take about 15 minutes (a
　　　　　　　④　　　　　　　　　　　S　　　　　　　　V　　　　O

day). ⁶Dr. Small claims ⟨ that this combination can improve your brain's function ⟩.
　　　　　S　　　　V　O　従接　　　S　　　　　　　V　　　　　　O

> 訳 ¹脳の短期集中訓練と呼ばれる，記憶力を助けるプログラムを１つ見てみよう。²脳の短期
> 集中訓練とは何だろうか。³それはゲイリー・スモールという精神科医によって開発された
> ２週間のプログラムである。⁴彼のプログラムは４つの要素を組み合わせる。それは，特別な
> 食事，日々の身体的活動，ストレスを軽減する訓練，そしてもちろん記憶力の訓練だ。⁵記憶
> 力の訓練は１日に約15分を要する。⁶スモール医師はこの組み合わせによって脳の機能が改
> 善できると主張する。

語 句

program	名 プログラム, 計画	**physical**	形 身体的な
boot camp	名 短期集中訓練	**activity**	名 活動
develop	動 開発する	**relieve**	動 軽減する, 和らげる
combine	動 組み合わせる, 結合させる	**exercise**	名 運動, 訓練／動 運動する
element	名 要素	**claim**	動 主張する
diet	名 日々の食事	**combination**	名 組み合わせ, 結合
		function	名 働き, 機能

¹Michele Rubin is one of Dr. Small's success stories. ²Rubin is a 46-year-old mother
　　S　　　　V　　　　　　C　　　　　　　　　　S　　V　　　　　C

[of three teenagers]. ³(At the start of the program), her memory tested (as
　　　　　　　　　　　　　　　　　　　　　　　　　　　　　S　　　　V

average (for her age)). ⁴(When she took memory tests (after the program)),
従接 S V O

her memory was equal (to a 20-year-old person). ⁵Rubin says ⟨ that (a few years
S V C S V O 従接

① ②
ago) she started to feel ⟨ that she was forgetting things ⟩ and ⟨ that her memory
S V O 従接 S V O 等接 O 従接 S

was not as good as it used to be ⟩⟩. ⁶She says ⟨ that the program was life-changing ⟩.
V C S V O 従接 S V C

① ①
⁷(Since completing the program), (in addition to ⟨ exercising more ⟩ and
等接

② ①
⟨ improving her diet ⟩), she has started ⟨ using memory strategies ⟩, (reading non-
S V O

②
fiction and doing crossword puzzles). ⁸She also helps her children (with their
等接 S V O

math homework)(as a way [to work her brain]).

訳 ¹ミシェル・ルービンはスモール医師の成功談の１例である。²ルービンは３人の10代の子どもを持つ46歳の母親だ。³プログラムの最初, 彼女の記憶力のテストの結果は年齢としては平均だった。⁴プログラム終了後に記憶力のテストを受けたとき, 彼女の記憶力は20歳の人と同等であった。⁵ルービンは, 数年前, 物忘れをするようになり, また記憶力が以前ほどよくないと感じ始めたと言う。⁶そのプログラムは人生を変えるものだったと彼女は言う。⁷プログラムを完了して以来, 彼女は運動量を増やしたり食事を改善することに加え, ノンフィクションを読んだりクロスワードパズルをしたりして記憶戦略を使い始めた。⁸彼女はまた, 自分の脳を働かせる方法として, 子どもの数学の宿題を手伝っている。

語句

success story	名 成功談, サクセスストーリー		be equal to ~	熟 ~に等しい
teenager	名 ティーンエージャー(10代の若者)		used to *do*	熟 かつては~だった
at the start of ~	熟 ~の最初に		life-changing	形 人生を変えるような
test	動 テスト[試験, 検査]の結果が~となる		complete	動 終える, 修了する
			in addition to ~	熟 ~に加え, ~だけでなく
	名 テスト[試験, 検査]		strategy	名 戦略
average	形 平均的な		non-fiction	名 ノンフィクション
for *one's* age	熟 年齢の割に, 年齢を考慮すると		work	動 (身体の一部などを)動かす, 働かせる

¹Dr. Small says 〈 that he has evidence 〈 that the two-week boot camp program
S　　V　　O　従接　S　V　　　O　　　従接（同格）　　　　　　S

does in fact change the brain 〉〉. ²He did a study 〔 with 17 volunteers 〕.
　　　　V　　　　O　　　　　　　　　　　　　S　V　　O

³All of the volunteers had mild memory complaints. ⁴Dr. Small randomly chose
　　　S　　　　　　　V　　　　O　　　　　　　　　　　S　　　　　　　V

eight people 〔 to participate in The Boot Camp for the Brain 〕, and
　　O　　　　　　　　　　　　　　　　　　　　　　　　　　　　　　等接

the remaining nine people did nothing different.
　　　　　　S　　　　　　　V　　　O

> **訳** ¹スモール医師は，2週間の短期集中訓練で実際に脳に変化が起こるという証拠があると言う。²彼は17人のボランティア被験者に対して研究を行った。³被験者の全員が軽度の記憶の不満を抱えていた。⁴スモール医師は脳の短期集中訓練に参加する8人を無作為に選び，残りの9人は何も違うことをしなかった。

語句

evidence	名	証拠
volunteer	名	ボランティア
mild	形	（症状が）軽い
complaint	名	不平，不満

randomly	副	無作為に
choose	動	選ぶ
	*活用：choose-chose-chosen	
participate (in ～)	熟	（～に）参加する
remaining	形	残りの

¹They did brain scans 〔 on all 17 people 〕 (before and after the program).
S　V　　O　　　　　　　　　　　　　　　　　　　　①　　　　②
　　　　　　　　　　　　　　　　　　　　　　　　　　等接

²Dr. Small says 〈 that the eight people 〔 who participated 〕 developed
　　S　　　　V　　O　従接　　　　S　　　　　関代　　　V　　　　　V

significantly more efficient brain cell activity 〔 in a front part of the brain 〔 that
　　　　　　　　　　　　O　　　　　　　　　　　　　　　　　　　　　　　　　　　関代

controls everyday memory tasks 〕〕〉. ³The people 〔 who participated 〕 also said
　V　　　　　O　　　　　　　　　　　　　　S　　　　　関代　　　V　　　　　　V

〈 that they felt less forgetful (after the program)〉.
O 従接　　S　 V　　　　C

> **訳** ¹彼らはプログラムの前後に17人全員に脳のスキャンを行った。²スモール医師は，参加した8人が，毎日の記憶作業を制御する脳の前部において著しくより効率的な脳細胞活動を発達させたと言う。³参加者もまた，プログラム終了後は以前ほど物忘れがひどくないと感じると言った。

語句

scan	名	スキャン(脳や内臓の精密検査)
develop	動	発達[発展]させる
significantly	副	著しく，かなり
efficient	形	効率の良い，効率的な
cell	名	細胞

front	形	前の，前方の
control	動	制御する，操る
everyday	形	毎日の
task	名	作業，任務
forgetful	形	忘れっぽい，物忘れがひどい

第6段落　文の構造と語句のチェック

¹Dr. Small emphasizes 〈① that this study was very small 〉 and 〈② that
S　　　　　V　　　　 O 従接　　S　 V　　　C　　　　等接 O 従接

a larger study is needed 〉. ²But he still feels 〈 that the results are important 〉.
　　　S　　　　V　　　等接 S　 V O 従接　 S　　 V　　　C

　　　　　　　　　　┌── 従接 that 省略
³Other scientists say 〈 they are cautiously optimistic (about Small's approach)〉.
S　　　　　 V O S　 V　　　　C

　　①　┌── 従接 that 省略　　　　 ②　┌── 従接 that 省略
⁴They feel 〈 more research is needed 〉, but say 〈 it is possible 〈 that The Boot
S　 V O　　 S　　　　 V　　等接 V O仮S V　 C　真S 従接

Camp for the Brain could delay serious memory problems 〉〉.
S　　　　　　　　V　　　　 O

> **訳** ¹スモール医師はこの研究が非常に小規模のものであり，より大規模な研究が必要だと強調する。²しかし，彼はそれでも，この調査結果は重要だと感じている。³ほかの科学者たちはスモール医師の手法に慎重ながらも楽観的だと言う。⁴彼らはさらなる調査が必要だと感じているが，脳の短期集中訓練が深刻な記憶障害を遅らせる可能性はあると言う。

語句

emphasize	動	強調する
result	名	結果
scientist	名	科学者
cautiously	副	用心深く，慎重に

optimistic	形	楽観的な
approach	名	取り組み(方)，研究方法
possible	形	可能性がある
delay	動	遅らせる
serious	形	深刻な，重大な

文法事項の整理⑩　強調のdo

第4段落第1文の does について見てみよう。

Dr. Small says that he has evidence that the two-week boot camp program **does** in fact change the brain.

　〈**do [does / did] ＋動詞の原形**〉は【動詞の強調】を表し,「**確かに [実際に／本当に] ～する**」などと訳す。また, 命令文の場合は「**ぜひ [必ず] ～しなさい**」のように訳す。

例　He <u>does</u> understand what you said.
　　「彼はあなたが言ったことをちゃんと理解していますよ」

例　"You didn't say that." 「君はそんなことは言わなかったよ」
　　"I <u>did</u> say that!" 「いや, 確かに言った！」

例　<u>Do</u> come to see us. 「ぜひ会いにいらっしゃい」

▶第4段落第1文の does は, 直後の in fact を取り除くと, その後に動詞の原形 change があるので,【動詞の強調】を表すことがわかる。

確認問題

1. 次の和訳と対応する英語の語句を,頭文字を参考にして書き,空欄を完成させよう。

（各1点×20）

①	n	形	ふつうの, 正常な
②	i	動	改善する, 向上させる
③	c	動	組み合わせる, 結合させる
④	e	名	要素
⑤	d	名	日々の食事
⑥	p	形	身体的な
⑦	r	動	軽減する, 和らげる
⑧	f	名	働き, 機能
⑨ be e to ～		熟	～に等しい
⑩	c	動	終える, 修了する
⑪ in a to ～		熟	～に加え, ～だけでなく
⑫	s	名	戦略
⑬	e	名	証拠
⑭	v	名	ボランティア
⑮	r	副	無作為に
⑯ p （in ～）		熟	（～に）参加する
⑰	f	形	忘れっぽい, 物忘れがひどい
⑱	e	動	強調する
⑲	o	形	楽観的な
⑳	d	動	遅らせる

2. 次の[ ]内の語句を並べ替えて,意味の通る英文を完成させよう。（各5点×2）

① Doctors are looking for ways [their / people / memory / help / to / improve] and possibly prevent loss.

② She also helps her [their / with / as / children / homework / math] a way to work her brain.

3. 次の英文を和訳してみよう。(10 点)

Dr. Small says that he has evidence that the two-week boot camp program does in fact change the brain.

*boot camp「短期集中訓練」

ディクテーションしてみよう！

🔊 54・59

今回学習した英文に出てきた単語を，音声を聞いて ☐☐ に書き取ろう。

54　Many people worry about memory loss. It is ❶ n☐☐☐☐☐☐ to lose memory as you get older. In fact, memory loss can begin when someone is in their twenties. But how much of your memory do you have to lose, and how quickly does it have to happen? Research on the brain and memory is a huge area these days. Doctors are looking for ways to help people ❷ i☐☐☐☐☐☐☐ their memory and possibly prevent loss.

55　Let us look at one program to help memory, called The Boot Camp for the Brain. What is The Boot Camp for the Brain? It is a two-week program developed by a psychiatrist named Gary Small. His program combines four ❸ e☐☐☐☐☐☐☐☐ : a special diet, daily physical activity, stress ❹ r☐☐☐☐☐☐☐☐☐☐☐ exercises and, of course, memory exercises. The memory exercises take about 15 minutes a day. Dr. Small claims that this combination can improve your brain's function.

56　Michele Rubin is one of Dr. Small's success stories. Rubin is a 46-year-old mother of three teenagers. At the start of the program, her memory tested as average for her age. When she took memory tests after the program, her memory was ❺ e☐☐☐☐☐ to a 20-year-old person. Rubin says that a few years ago she started to feel that she was forgetting things and that her memory was not as good as it used to be. She says that the program was life-changing. Since **❻** `c` [   ] the program, in addition to exercising more and improving her diet, she has started using memory strategies, reading non-fiction and doing crossword puzzles. She also helps her children with their math homework as a way to work her brain.

57 Dr. Small says that he has evidence that the two-week boot camp program does in fact change the brain. He did a study with 17 **❼** `v` [   ]. All of the volunteers had mild memory complaints. Dr. Small **❽** `r` [   ] chose eight people to participate in The Boot Camp for the Brain, and the remaining nine people did nothing different.

58 They did brain scans on all 17 people before and after the program. Dr. Small says that the eight people who participated developed significantly more efficient brain cell activity in a front part of the brain that controls everyday memory tasks. The people who participated also said that they felt less **❾** `f` [   ] after the program.

59 Dr. Small emphasizes that this study was very small and that a larger study is needed. But he still feels that the results are important. Other scientists say they are cautiously optimistic about Small's approach. They feel more research is needed, but say it is possible that The Boot Camp for the Brain could **❿** `d` [   ] serious memory problems.

確認問題の答 **1.** ① normal ② improve ③ combine ④ element ⑤ diet ⑥ physical
⑦ relieve ⑧ function ⑨ equal ⑩ complete ⑪ addition ⑫ strategy ⑬ evidence
⑭ volunteer ⑮ randomly ⑯ participate ⑰ forgetful ⑱ emphasize ⑲ optimistic
⑳ delay

2. ① to help people improve their memory （第1段落　最終文）
② children with their math homework as （第3段落　最終文）

3. スモール医師は，2週間の短期集中訓練で実際に脳に変化が起こるという証拠があると言う。
（第4段落　第1文）

ディクテーションしてみよう！の答 ❶ normal ❷ improve ❸ elements ❹ relieving
❺ equal ❻ completing ❼ volunteers ❽ randomly ❾ forgetful ❿ delay

解答

問1	(ア) ②	(イ) ①	(ウ) ③	(エ) ④
問2	(a) ④	(b) ③	(c) ④	問3　②
問4	(a) ①	(b) ③	問5　③	

解説

問1

(ア) ① at　② **as**　③ loudly　④ what

Min-ho laughs（　ア　）he checks some funny photos …
S　　V　　　　　　　S　　V　　　　　O

　文の構造を確認すると，空所の前後に SV があることから，前置詞である① at や副詞である③ loudly は除外。また，④の what は疑問詞／関係代名詞だが，いずれの場合も名詞節を作り，後ろには不完全な文（S や O など名詞要素が欠ける文）が続く。ここでは，laugh が自動詞なので，そのあとに目的語として名詞節を続けることはできないし，空所のあとは SVO の完全な文となっている。以上により，正解は② **as**。ここでは【時】を表す接続詞の用法で，「…するときに，…しながら」の意味。

(イ) ① **between**　② among　③ for　④ at

Members of Gen-Z are people born（　イ　）the mid-1990s and the early 2000s.

　空所のあとの and に注目。 between *A* and *B* で「AとBの間に」となるので，正解は①。「～の間に」の意味を表す前置詞の区別は，between ＝ 2 者間／among ＝ 3 者間以上。

(ウ) ① work　② bad　③ **enough**　④ effect

But her parents' eyes are not（　ウ　）to make her stop using social media.

空所直後に to 不定詞が続いている点に注目。 be enough to *do* で「～するのに十分 (な量 [数])」の意味。

次の文（ Valerie knows how to limit what her parents can see about her on the social networking sites she uses.「ヴァレリーは, 自分が使用しているソーシャルネットワーキングサイト［SNS］で両親が自分について見ることができる内容を制限する方法を知っている」）によれば, ヴァレリーは両親からの監視をすり抜けて SNS を利用していることがわかる。そこで, 両親の監視（この eyes「目」は比喩的に監視のことを指している）では不十分, との内容にすれば文脈にも合う。以上により, 正解は③ **enough**。

(エ) ① Before ② Although ③ When ④ **Because**

(**エ**) they	grew up	using social media, maybe	Generation Z	will be	better …
S	V		S	V	C

文構造を見ると, 接続詞が入ることはすぐにわかる。選択肢はいずれも接続詞の用法を持つので, これだけでは選択肢を絞れない。そこで, 文の内容を見ると, 前半 (ソーシャルメディアを利用しながら育った) と後半 (個人情報を守るのが上手) には原因⇒結果の関係が成立していると考えられる。以上により, 正解は④ **Because** とわかる。

問2

(a)「イェシム・ユルマズについて, 以下のうちどれがあてはまるか」

① 「彼女はよく朝食を抜く」

② 「彼女はZ世代に属していない」

③ 「彼女は時々教科書を電車に置き忘れる」

④ **「彼女は宿題をし忘れた場合でも動揺しない」**

▶第1段落第3～5文で, 教科書を読んでくるという宿題を忘れても動じることなく, オンラインの教科書をダウンロードしている様子が書かれている。正解は④。

(b)「パク・ミンホについて, 以下のうちどれが記述されていないか」

① 「彼はテキストメッセージの入力が得意だ」

② 「彼はいつも携帯電話を持ち歩いている」

③ **「彼はよくおもしろい写真を撮って友だちに見せる」**

④ 「彼はバスの中で，携帯電話でゲームをする」

▶①は第2段落第2文，②は同段落第3文，④は同段落第7文にある。③は書かれていない。同段落第5文（ Min-ho laughs as he checks some funny photos his friend Jae-sung has just posted online.「ミンホは友だちのジェソンがウェブ上に投稿したばかりのおもしろい写真をチェックしながら笑う」）によれば，ミンホは友だちが撮った写真を見ている側である。

(c) **「ヴァレリー・チェンについて，以下のうちどれがあてはまるか」**

① 「彼女の両親は彼女がオンラインでしていることを心配していない」

② 「彼女の両親は彼女がソーシャルメディアを使っていることを知らない」

③ 「彼女はソーシャルメディアを使って両親に連絡を取っている」

④ **「彼女は自分の極秘情報を両親に隠すことに成功している」**

▶④が第6段落最終文と一致。この選択肢のsensitiveは「極秘の」の意味。本文の knows how to limit what her parents can see about her「両親が彼女について見ることができる内容を制限する方法を知っている」は，どうしても見られたくない情報を隠していると解釈できる。①は同段落第5文と不一致。両親は心配だから監視しようとしているのだろう。②は本文に書かれていないが，同段落後半の内容から判断して，ソーシャルメディアを使っていることを知っているからこそ監視しようとしているように思われる。③は本文に書かれていない。

問3

① 「Z世代が自分の個人情報を親から秘密にすることはますます難しくなるだろう」

▶第7段落第1文に「唯一の課題ではない」とあるが，ますます難しくな

るという記述はない。

② **「人々は，オンラインに投稿する内容によって仕事を得るチャンスを逃さ
ないように注意するべきだ」**

▶第7段落第2～3文と一致。

③ 「ソーシャルメディアはZ世代にマーケティング会社から個人情報を保護
する方法を教えるだろう」

▶第7段落第4文に「ソーシャルメディアを使いながら成長したため個人
情報を保護するのが上手になるかもしれない」とあるが，ソーシャルメ
ディアに教えられているわけではない。

④ 「Z世代でも個人情報を守ることは不可能になるだろう」

▶Z世代が個人情報をよりよく保護できるかどうかについて，第7段落最
終文に Only time will tell.「時間が経ってみないとわからない」とある。
つまり，Z世代はこれまでの世代よりも上手に守れると予測はするが（第
4文），最終的に本文では肯定も否定もしていない。

問4

(a) 「この記事は主に（　　　）についてである」

① **「Z世代とそのテクノロジーの利用」**

② 「仕事を見つけるためにテクノロジーを利用する方法」

③ 「ソーシャルメディアはZ世代の親たちにどのように影響するか」

④ 「Z世代に属する人々とその親たちとの違い」

▶第1～3段落で実際のZ世代の人を例に挙げ，彼らのテクノロジー利用
法を紹介。さらに第4～第7段落では，彼らのソーシャルメディアとの
関わりと，それをターゲットにするマーケティング会社についてなどが
書かれている。よって，①**「Z世代とそのテクノロジーの利用」**が正解。

　　ほかの選択肢も見ておこう。②「仕事を見つけるためにテクノロジー
を利用する方法」については書かれていない。第7段落で，個人情報が
就職に不利になり得るリスクの説明があるのみ。③「ソーシャルメディ
アはZ世代の親たちにどのように影響するか」は，本文で直接的には書
かれていない。第6段落で若者のソーシャルメディア利用を監視したが

る親と，それを避けようとする若者との関係が書かれているのみ。④「Z
世代に属する人々とその親たちの違い」は，第4段落第1・2文に音楽
やゲームとの付き合い方の違いが書かれているが，この箇所のみなの
で，主な内容とは言えない。

(b)「Z世代に属する人々の多くは（　　　　）」

① 「マーケティング会社によってソーシャルメディアの使用にもっと時
　間を費やすよう促されている」

② 「ソーシャルネットワーキングのサイト上での友人のアドバイスに基
　づいて何の商品を購入すべきかを決める」

③ **「マーケティング会社によってどれほど多くの自分の個人情報が収集**
　されているかを気にしないようだ」

④ 「親よりもマーケティング会社によってプライバシーが侵害されるこ
　とを恐れるようだ」

▶③が第6段落第3文（ Not many seem to be very worried about
companies knowing how to sell things to them.「彼らの多くは，企業
が彼らに商品を売りつける方法を知っていることをあまり心配してい
ないようだ」）と一致。①②は本文中に記述なし。④については，第6段
落第4文（ Many Gen-Z members are more concerned about keeping
their private information from their parents.「多くのZ世代に属する
人々は，自分の個人情報を親から守ることをむしろ気にしている」）と
不一致。

問5

① 「Z世代に属する人々のほとんどは，ビデオテープレコーダーやデスクトッ
　プパソコンを使ったことがない」

　▶ビデオテープレコーダーについては第3段落第3文に「見たことがな
　　い」とあるので正しいが，デスクトップパソコンについては記述がない。

② 「Z世代の親たちはコンピュータを利用できる環境ではなかった」

　▶そのような記述はない。

③「**Z世代に属する人々の一部は21世紀生まれだ**」

▶第3段落最終文に the early 2000s とあるので正しい。

④「**Z世代の親たちは子どものころ, 家に電話がなかった**」

▶第4段落第1文に「家の電話で通話した」とあるので, これと矛盾する。

▼

それでは次に, 段落ごとに詳しくみていこう。

第1段落　文の構造と語句のチェック

¹(In Istanbul), Yesim Yilmaz is getting ready (for class). ²Her mother
　　　　　　　　　S　　　　　　V　　　C　　　　　　　　　　S

┌─she is 省略
brings her some breakfast, which Yesim eats (while looking at her e-mail on
V　　O₁　　O₂　　　　関代　　S　　V　　従接

her phone). ³She has forgotten 〈 to read a chapter (for her biology class)〉. ⁴No
　　　　　　　　S　　　V　　　　O

problem. ⁵She opens up her laptop and downloads a chapter (from her online
　　　　　　S　　V　　　O　　等接　　V　　　O

textbook)(to read on the train).

> **訳** ¹イスタンブールで, イェシム・ユルマズが授業の準備をしている。²彼女の母親が朝食を
> 持ってきて, イェシムは携帯電話でメールを見ながらそれを食べる。³彼女は生物学の授業
> のための章を読むのを忘れてしまった。⁴問題はない。⁵彼女はノートパソコンを開き, オン
> ラインの教科書から1つの章をダウンロードして電車で読む。

語句

get ready for ～	熟	～の準備をする
chapter	名	(書物などの)章
biology	名	生物学

laptop	名	ノートパソコン
download	動	ダウンロードする
textbook	名	教科書

第2段落　文の構造と語句のチェック

¹(On Sunday afternoon)(next to his apartment complex in Seoul), Min-ho
　　　　　　　　　　　　　　　　　　　　　　　　　　　　　　　　　　S

Park is waiting (for the bus). ²(At lightning speed), he types a text message
<u>Park</u> <u>is waiting</u>
V   S V   O

(to <u>let</u> <u>his friend</u> <u>know</u> 〈 he's on his way 〉). ³<u>Min-ho</u> <u>is</u> never (without his
      V′   O′   C′   S   V

┌─従接 that 省略

phone). ⁴(In fact), <u>he's</u> already <u>bought</u> <u>a ticket</u> (on his phone)(for a movie
                        S   V   O

┌─関代 which 省略

〔 <u>he and his friends</u> <u>will see</u> (this afternoon)〕). ⁵<u>Min-ho</u> <u>laughs</u> (<u>as</u> <u>he</u> <u>checks</u>
       S   V   S   V   as S   V
                                                                                        従接

┌─関代 which 省略

<u>some funny photos</u> 〔 <u>his friend Jae-sung</u> <u>has just posted</u> online 〕). ⁶<u>His bus</u> soon
        O   S   V   S

<u>arrives</u>. ⁷<u>Min-ho</u> <u>gets on</u>, <u>sits down</u>, <u>opens</u> <u>a game app</u> (on his phone), <u>and</u>
   V   S   V①   V②   V③   O   等接

<u>puts</u> <u>his earphones</u> (in his ears). ⁸<u>Most of the other people</u> 〔 on the bus 〕〔 <u>who</u>
 V④   O   S   関代

<u>are</u> <u>Min-ho's age</u> 〕 <u>are doing</u> exactly <u>the same thing</u>.
 V   C   V   O

> **訳** ¹日曜日の午後, ソウルにある自分が住むアパートの建物の横で, パク・ミンホはバスを待っている。²彼は友だちに, 自分が向かっている旨の連絡をするために, 超高速でテキストメッセージを入力する。³ミンホは携帯電話を常に持っている。⁴実際, 彼は友だちと今日の午後に見る映画のチケットを, すでに携帯電話で購入している。⁵ミンホは友だちのジェソンがウェブ上に投稿したばかりのおもしろい写真をチェックしながら笑う。⁶やがて彼のバスが到着する。⁷ミンホは乗り込んで座り, 携帯電話でゲームアプリを開き, イヤホンを耳に差し込む。⁸バスに乗っている, ミンホと同年代のほかの多くの人々もまったく同じことをしている。

語句

next to 〜 熟 〜の隣で, 〜に接して
complex 名 (複数の施設が入った)ビル, 団地
at lightning speed 熟 超高速で, 瞬時に
type 動 (文字を)打ち込む, 入力する

text message 名 テキストメッセージ(携帯電話で送受信するメッセージ, メール)
post 動 (ウェブ上に)投稿する, アップする
app 名 アプリ, アプリケーション
exactly 副 まさに, まったく

第3段落 文の構造と語句のチェック

¹<u>Yesim</u> <u>and</u> <u>Min-ho</u> <u>are</u> <u>members</u> 〔 of Generation Z 〕. ²<u>They</u> <u>are</u> sometimes
       S   等接   V   C   S

called "digital natives" (because they have grown up (with the Internet,
  V   C   従接   S   V   ①

mobile phones, **and** social media)(**since** they were children)). ³(In fact),
  ②   等接   ③   従接   S   V   C

many have never seen a VCR **or** a telephone 〔 with a dial 〕. ⁴Members 〔 of
S   V   O① 等接   O②   S

Gen-Z 〕 are people 〔 born **between** the mid-1990s **and** the early 2000s 〕.
          V   C

> **訳** ¹イェシムとミンホはZ世代に属する人々だ。²彼らは時に「デジタルネイティブ」と呼ばれることもある。なぜなら彼らは子どものころからインターネット，携帯電話，ソーシャルメディアとともに成長してきたからだ。³実際，彼らの多くはビデオテープレコーダーやダイヤルのついた電話機を見たことがない。⁴Z世代に属する人々は，1990年代中盤から2000年代初頭に生まれた人々だ。

語 句

generation 名 世代 | native 名 出身者

第4段落　文の構造と語句のチェック

¹Their parents spent most of their teenage years (listening to cassette players),
     S   V   O   ①

(playing early video games), **and** (calling friends on their families' telephones).
     ②   等接   ③

²Generation Z, however, is connected (to its music, videos, games, **and** friends)
 S   V   C   ①   ②   ③ 等接   ④

online all day, every day. ³Recent surveys show 〈 **that** young people 〔 in Asia 〕
                         S   V O 従接   S

spend an average of 9.5 hours (per day) online 〉. ⁴And marketing companies
 V   O   等接   S

know this.
 V   O

> **訳** ¹彼らの両親は，カセットプレーヤーで音楽を聴いたり，初期のテレビゲームをしたり，家の電話で友だちと通話したりして，10代のほとんどを過ごした。²しかし，Z世代は音楽，

動画, ゲーム, 友だちとオンラインで一日中, 毎日つながっている。³最近の調査によると, アジアの若者は平均して1日に9.5時間をオンラインで過ごしている。⁴そして, マーケティング会社はこれを知っている。

第5段落　文の構造と語句のチェック

¹(従接 Every time they open their page 〔 on a social networking site 〕), Gen-Z
S V O

members don't see only friends' updates ① and 等接 ② photos. ²They also see ads 〔 for
S V O S V O

┌─関代 which 省略
products 〔 they might want to buy 〕〕. ³Marketing companies work (with social
S V S V

media sites) (to find out ① 疑 〈 where their customers live 〉, ② 疑 〈 what movies, books,
S V O

等接 ③ 疑
and music they like 〉, and 〈 who their friends are 〉). ⁴The companies use this
S V 等接 C S V S V

┌─関代 which 省略
information (to show their customers the advertisements 〔 they want them to
O V' O'₁ O'₂ S V O

see 〕).
C

訳 ¹Z世代に属する人々が, ソーシャルネットワーキングサイト[SNS]のページを開くたびに目にするのは, 友だちの更新情報や写真だけではない。²自分たちが購入したいと思うかもしれない製品の広告も目に入ってくるのだ。³マーケティング会社は, 顧客がどこに住んでいて, どんな映画や本, 音楽が好きで, 友だちは誰であるかを調べるために, ソーシャルメディアサイトと協力している。⁴企業は顧客に見てほしい広告を表示するためにこの情報を活用する。

| find out ～ | 熟 | ～を調べる，探り出す | information | 名 | 情報 |
| customer | 名 | 顧客 | | | |

第6段落　文の構造と語句のチェック

¹What does this generation think (about marketing companies knowing so
　O　(V)　　S　　　　　V　　　　　　　S'　　　　　　V'

much (about them))? ²Are they worried (about losing their privacy)? ³Not
O'　　　　　　　　　　　　V　S　　C

many seem to be very worried (about companies knowing 〈 how to sell things
S　　V　　　　C　　　　　　　　S'　　　V'　　O'

to them 〉). ⁴Many Gen-Z members are more concerned (about keeping their
　　　　　　　　S　　　　　　V　　C

private information (from their parents)). ⁵(For example), Valerie Chen 〔 in
　　　　　　　　　　　　　　　　　　　　　　　　　　　　　　S

　　　　　　　　　　　　　　　　　　　　　　　　関代 that 省略┐
Kaohsiung 〕 is upset (because her parents want to watch everything〔she does
　　　　　V　C　従接　　S　　　　　V　　　　O　　S　does

online 〕). ⁶But her parents' eyes are not enough (to make her stop using social
　　　　　等接　　S　　　　　V　C　　　V'　O'　　　C'

media). ⁷Valerie knows 〈 how to limit 〈 what her parents can see (about her)
　　　　　　S　　V　O　　　　　　関代　S　　　V

　　　　　　　　　┌関代 which 省略
(on the social networking sites〔 she uses 〕)〉〉.
　　　　　　　　　　　　　　　S　V

訳 ¹この世代は，マーケティング会社が自分たちについてそれほど多くを知っていることをどう考えているのだろうか。²彼らはプライバシーを失うことを心配しているだろうか。³彼らの多くは，企業が彼らに商品を売りつける方法を知っていることをあまり心配していないようだ。⁴多くのZ世代に属する人々は，自分の個人情報を親から守ることをむしろ気にしている。⁵たとえば，高雄市のヴァレリー・チェンは，自分がオンラインでやっていることのすべてを両親が見たがるので，不安を感じている。⁶しかし，彼女の両親の目は，彼女がソーシャルメディアを使用するのをやめさせるには十分ではない。⁷ヴァレリーは，自分が使用しているソーシャルネットワーキングサイト [SNS] で両親が自分について見ることができる内容を制限する方法を知っている。

語 句

be worried about ～ 熟 ～を心配して	**be concerned about ～** 熟 ～を気にして, ～を心配して
privacy 名 プライバシー, 私生活	**upset** 形 不安になって, 動揺して
	limit 動 制限する, 限定する

第7段落 文の構造と語句のチェック

¹However, 〈 keeping information private (from parents)〉 may not be the only
　　　　　　S　　　V′　　　　　O′　　　　　C′　　　　　　　　　　　　　　　V

challenge. ²Many people are now finding out 〈 that 〈 posting funny pictures (on
C　　　　　　S　　　　　　V　　　　　O 従接　S

the Web)〉 can be a problem (when they finish school and start looking for a
　　　　　　V　　C　　　　従接　S　　V　　O　等接　V　　　　O

job)〉. ³(In fact), some studies show 〈 that more than 70% of companies reject
　　　　　　　　　　S　　　V　O 従接　　　　　　　S　　　　　V

people 〔 who are looking for jobs 〕(because of 〈 what they can see (about
O　　関代　　V　　　O　　　　　　　　　　　関代　S　　V

young people) online)〉〉. ⁴(Because they grew up (using social media)),
　　　　　　　　　　　　　　　従接　　S　　V

maybe Generation Z will be better (at protecting their personal information
　　　　S　　　　V　　C

online) than the generation before them. ⁵Only time will tell.
　　　　　　　　　　　　　　　　　　　　　S　　V

> **訳** ¹しかしながら, 親から情報を秘密にすることが唯一の課題なのではないかもしれない。
> ²多くの人々は, 学校を卒業して仕事を探し始める際に, ウェブ上でおもしろい写真を投稿
> したことが問題になり得ることを今わかり始めている。³実際, いくつかの調査が示すよう
> に, 70%以上の企業が, 若者に関してオンラインでわかることを理由に, 求職者を不採用に
> している。⁴ソーシャルメディアを使いながら成長したため, もしかしたらZ世代は前の世
> 代よりもオンラインで自分の個人情報を保護するのが上手になるかもしれない。⁵これは時
> 間が経ってみないとわからない。

語 句

challenge 名 課題	**be good at ～** 熟 ～が得意だ, ～が上手い
reject 動 断る, 不採用にする	**protect** 動 保護する
maybe 副 もしかすると	**personal** 形 個人の

文法事項の整理 ⑪　関係代名詞／疑問詞 what

第6段落最終文の what について見てみよう。

Valerie knows how to limit **what** her parents can see about her on the social networking sites she uses.

what には大きく分けて関係代名詞と疑問詞がある。疑問詞は疑問代名詞と疑問形容詞に分かれる。

①　関係代名詞 what

名詞節を作り，「…すること［もの］」の意味を表す。 the thing(s) which に置き換え可能。

例　**What** I want is a new car.
　　　　S　　　V　C

「私がほしいものは新車だ」

（= **The thing which** I want is a new car. ）

②　疑問代名詞 what

「何が［を］…するか」の意味を表す。

（1）　節を作らない場合⇒文中でS・O・Cになる。

例　**What** do you have in your hand?
　　　O　　S　V

「手に何を持っているのですか」

（2）　節を作る場合⇒名詞節を作る。

例　He asked me **what** I had done the day before.
　　S　V　O₁　　O₂

「彼は私が前日に何をしたのかと尋ねた」

※関係代名詞とも疑問代名詞とも取れる場合がある。

例　Tell me **what** our teacher said yesterday.

関係代名詞：「昨日先生が言ったことを教えてください」

疑問代名詞：「昨日先生が何を言ったのか教えてください」

③ **疑問形容詞 what**

　直後の名詞とセットで,「何の［どんな］名詞が［を］…するか」の意味を表す。

　(1)　節を作らない場合⇒文中で S・O・C になる。

　　　例　<u>What</u> <u>subject</u> do <u>you</u> <u>like</u>?
　　　　　　O　　　　　　 S　 V
　　　　　「何の教科が好きですか」

　(2)　節を作る場合⇒名詞節を作る。

　　　例　<u>I</u> <u>don't know</u> **what** <u>kind of music you like</u>.
　　　　　S　　V　　　　　　　　　 O
　　　　　「私はあなたがどんな種類の音楽を好きか知らない」

▶第５段落第３文

Marketing companies work with social media sites to find out where their customers live, <u>what</u> movies, books, and music they like, and who their friends are.

▶疑問形容詞で, 直後の名詞 (movies, books, and music) とセットになり, 名詞節を作っている (find out に対する O)。

▶第６段落第１文

<u>What</u> does this generation think about marketing companies knowing so much about them?

▶疑問代名詞で, 節を作らないタイプ。 think に対する O になっている。

▶第６段落最終文

Valerie knows how to limit <u>what</u> her parents can see about her on the social networking sites she uses.

▶関係代名詞。 what から文末までが名詞節で，limit に対する O になっている。

▶第7段落第3文

> In fact, some studies show that more than 70% of companies reject people who are looking for jobs because of <u>what</u> they can see about young people online.

▶関係代名詞。 what から文末までが名詞節で，前置詞句 because of に対する O になっている。

確認問題

1. 次の和訳と対応する英語の語句を、頭文字を参考にして書き、空欄を完成させよう。

/40点

(各1点×20)

①	b		名	生物学
②	t		名	教科書
③	e		副	まさに、まったく
④	g		名	世代
⑤	t		形	10代の
⑥	r		形	最近の
⑦	s		名	（聞き取り）調査
⑧	a		名	広告
⑨	a		名	広告　※⑧の短縮形
⑩	p		名	製品
⑪	c		名	顧客
⑫	p		名	プライバシー、私生活
⑬	be c	about ～	熟	～を気にして、～を心配して
⑭	u		形	不安になって、動揺して
⑮	l		動	制限する、限定する
⑯	c		名	課題
⑰	r		動	断る、不採用にする
⑱	m		副	もしかすると
⑲	p		動	保護する
⑳	p		形	個人の

2. 次の [ ] 内の語句を並べ替えて，意味の通る英文を完成させよう。なお，文頭に来るべき語も小文字で示している。（各5点×2）

① [open / time / their / every / they / page] on a social networking site, Gen-Z members don't see only friends' updates and photos.

② Valerie knows [her / to / how / what / limit / parents] can see about her on the social networking sites she uses.

3. 次の英文を和訳してみよう。（10点）

Min-ho laughs as he checks some funny photos his friend Jae-sung has just posted online.

*Min-ho「ミンホ」(人名)　*Jae-sung「ジェソン」(人名)

ディクテーションしてみよう！

🔊
61
～
67

今回学習した英文に出てきた単語を，音声を聞いて □□□ に書き取ろう。

61　In Istanbul, Yesim Yilmaz is getting ready for class. Her mother brings her some breakfast, which Yesim eats while looking at her e-mail on her phone. She has forgotten to read a chapter for her ❶ b□□□□ class. No problem. She opens up her laptop and downloads a chapter from her online textbook to read on the train.

62　On Sunday afternoon ❷ n□□□ to his apartment complex in Seoul, Min-ho Park is waiting for the bus. At lightning speed, he types a text message to let his friend know he's on his way. Min-ho is never without his phone. In fact, he's already bought a ticket on his phone for a movie he and his friends will see this afternoon. Min-ho laughs as he checks some funny photos his friend Jae-sung has just posted online. His bus soon arrives. Min-ho gets on, sits down, opens a game app on his phone, and puts his earphones in his ears. Most of the other people on the bus who are Min-ho's age are doing ❸ e□□□□□ the same thing.

63　Yesim and Min-ho are members of Generation Z. They are sometimes

147

called "digital natives" because they have grown up with the Internet, mobile phones, and social media since they were children. In fact, many have never seen a VCR or a telephone with a dial. Members of Gen-Z are people born ❹ b   the mid-1990s and the early 2000s.

64   Their parents spent most of their teenage years listening to cassette players, playing early video games, and calling friends on their families' telephones. Generation Z, however, is connected to its music, videos, games, and friends online all day, every day. Recent ❺ s   show that young people in Asia spend an average of 9.5 hours per day online. And marketing companies know this.

65   Every time they open their page on a social networking site, Gen-Z members don't see only friends' updates and photos. They also see ads for ❻ p   they might want to buy. Marketing companies work with social media sites to find out where their customers live, what movies, books, and music they like, and who their friends are. The companies use this information to show their ❼ c   the advertisements they want them to see.

66   What does this generation think about marketing companies knowing so much about them? Are they worried about losing their ❽ p   ? Not many seem to be very worried about companies knowing how to sell things to them. Many Gen-Z members are more concerned about keeping their private information from their parents. For example, Valerie Chen in Kaohsiung is ❾ u   because her parents want to watch everything she does online. But her parents' eyes are not enough to make her stop using social media. Valerie knows how to limit what her parents can see about her on the social networking sites she uses.

67   However, keeping information private from parents may not be the only ❿ c   . Many people are now finding out that posting funny pictures on the Web can be a problem when they finish school and start looking for a job. In fact, some studies show that more than 70% of

companies **⑪**[r] people who are looking for jobs because of what they can see about young people online. Because they grew up using social media, maybe Generation Z will be better at protecting their personal information online than the generation before them. Only time will tell.

1. ① biology ② textbook ③ exactly ④ generation ⑤ teenage ⑥ recent ⑦ survey ⑧ advertisement ⑨ ad ⑩ product ⑪ customer ⑫ privacy ⑬ concerned ⑭ upset ⑮ limit ⑯ challenge ⑰ reject ⑱ maybe ⑲ protect ⑳ personal [private]

2. ① Every time they open their page （第5段落　第1文）
② how to limit what her parents （第6段落　最終文）

3. ミンホは友だちのジェソンがウェブ上に投稿したばかりのおもしろい写真をチェックしながら笑う。
（第2段落　第5文）

ディクテーションしてみよう！の答 ❶ biology ❷ next ❸ exactly ❹ between ❺ surveys
❻ products ❼ customers ❽ privacy ❾ upset ❿ challenge ⓫ reject

11 解答・解説

解 答

| 問1 | ① | 問2 | ① | 問3 | 3 | ② | 4 | ⑤ |

| 問4 | ① | 問5 | ② |

解 説

問1

「オックスフォードは，| 1 |と考えている」

① 「**連続したドリル学習は退屈である**」

② 「用語の解説を読むことは役立つ」

③ 「学生は科学に興味がない」

④ 「ワークブックを使って勉強することが成功につながる」

▶前半第 1 段落最終文… this sort of repetitive learning is dull and demotivating.「…このような繰り返しの学習は退屈で，やる気をなくさせます」と①が一致する。 this sort of repetitive learning はワークブックを用いる反復学習を指すので，continuous drilling と言い換えられる。また，dull と boring はともに「退屈な，つまらない」の意味。

問2

「リーが論じた研究では，学生は最後の学習セッションの| 2 |後にテストを受けた」

①「**4週間**」　②「すぐ」　③「1日」　④「1週間」

▶後半第3段落最終文に 28 days after the last learning session「最後の学習セッションから28日後」とあるので，28日を「4週間」と言い換えた①が正解。

問3

「リーが| 3 |間隔で学習することを伴う間隔学習を紹介しているのは，オックスフォードが論じた| 4 |学習の欠点を克服するためだ。（選択肢①〜⑥のうち，最も適切なものをそれぞれの| |に選びなさい。）」

①「文脈の」　　②「**長期の**」　　③「固定的な」　　④「不規則な」

⑤「**集中的な**」　　⑥「実用的な」

▶後半第2段落で，リーはオックスフォードの例では学習期間が短く，注意が薄れる点を指摘し，間隔を長くすることを提唱している。つまり，　3　には②が入る（extended は「長期にわたる，延長された」の意味）。また，リーはオックスフォードの論じた学習が massed learning「集中学習」であると後半第1段落第4文で述べているので，　4　には⑤が入る。

問4

「**両方の筆者ともに，　5　が新しい情報を記憶するのに役立つという点で一致している**」

①「**体験による学習**」

②「適切な休息をとること」

③「長期的な注目」

④「ワークブックを使う学習」

▶前半第2段落第2文でオックスフォードは体験による学習（＝文脈学習）を提唱しており，後半第1段落第1・2文で，リーはこれが有益であることに同意している。よって，①が正解となる。

問5

「**どの追加情報がリーの間隔学習に対する主張をさらに裏付けるのに最適か**」

6

①「理科の授業を魅力的にする主な要因」

②「**間隔学習で最も効果的な間隔の長さ**」

③「学生のワークブックに視覚資料が含まれているかどうか」

④「オックスフォードの学生が情報をうまく記憶できなかった理由」

▶リーは間隔学習における学習の間隔について，後半第2段落最終文では3日，第3段落第3文では1週間を例として挙げており，最も効果的な間隔の日数が不明である。そこで，これを明確にすればさらに説得力が増すと考えられる。よって，正解は②。

それでは次に，段落ごとに詳しくみていこう。

68

前置き／前半のタイトル　文の構造と語句のチェック

¹Your teacher has asked you to read two articles 〔 about effective ways to study 〕.
　　S　　　　　V　　　　O　　　　　　　　　　　　　　　C

²You will discuss 〈 what you learned 〉(in your next class).
　S　　V　　　　O　関代　S　　V

³**How to Study Effectively: Contextual Learning!**

⁴Tim Oxford

⁵*Science Teacher, Stone City Junior High School*

訳 ¹先生が効果的な勉強法に関する記事を２つ読むように言いました。²次の授業では，学んだことを話し合います。

³効果的な勉強の仕方：文脈学習！
⁴ティム・オックスフォード
⁵ストーンシティ中学校　理科教員

語句
article　名 記事
effective　形 効果的な
contextual　形 文脈の，背景的な

前半　第１段落　文の構造と語句のチェック

¹(As a science teacher), I am always concerned (about 〈 how to help students
　　　　　　　　　　　　　S V　　　　　C

〔 who struggle (to learn)〕〉). ²Recently, I found 〈 that their main way 〔 of
　関代　V　　　　　　　　　　　　　S　V　O　従接　　　S

learning 〕was 〈 to study new information repeatedly (until they could recall it
　　　　　V C　　　　　　　　　　　　　　　　　　　従接　S　　V

all 〉〉〉. ³(For example), (when they studied (for a test)), they would use a
O　　　　　　　　　従接　S　　V　　　　　　　　　S　　V　　①

workbook [like the example below] and repeatedly say the terms [that go
O　　　　　　　　　　　　　　　　等接　　　　　　　V　　O　　関代　V
②

(in the blanks)] : ⁴"Obsidian is igneous, dark, and glassy. ⁵Obsidian is igneous,

dark, and glassy...." ⁶These students would feel (as if they had learned the
　　　　　　　　　　　S　　　　　V　　従接　S　　V
　　　　　　　　　　　①　　　　　　　　　②

information), but would quickly forget it and get low scores (on the test).
O　　　　　等接　　　　　V　　　O　等接　V　　O

⁷Also, this sort of repetitive learning is dull and demotivating.
　　　　S　　　　　　　　　　　V　C
　　　　　　　　　　　　　①　等接　②

> **訳** ¹理科の教師として，私はいつも，勉強に苦労している学生を助ける方法を気にかけています。²最近，彼らの主な学習方法は，新しい情報をすべて思い出せるようになるまで繰り返し勉強することだとわかりました。³たとえば，テスト勉強をするときは，下の見本のようなワークブックを使い，空欄に入る用語を繰り返し言っていました。⁴「黒曜石は火成岩，黒色，ガラス質。⁵黒曜石は火成岩，黒色，ガラス質…」。⁶このような学生は，情報を覚えたように感じても，すぐに忘れてしまい，テストでは低い点数を取ってしまうのです。⁷また，このような繰り返しの学習は退屈で，やる気をなくさせます。

語 句

be concerned about ~	熟 ~を気にして，~を心配して	blank	名 空欄
		obsidian	名 黒曜石
struggle	動 奮闘する，苦労する	igneous	形 火成の
recently	副 最近	glassy	形 ガラス質［状］の，ガラスのような
repeatedly	副 繰り返して	as if ...	接 …かのように
recall	動 思い出す／名 思い出すこと，想起	repetitive	形 反復の
		dull	形 退屈な，つまらない
term	名 言葉，用語	demotivating	形 やる気を失わせる

前半　第2段落　文の構造と語句のチェック

¹(To help them learn), I tried (applying "contextual learning)," ²(In this
　　V′　O′　C′　S　V　O

kind of learning), new knowledge is constructed (through students' own
　　　　　　　　　　S　　　　　　V

experiences). ³(For my science class), <u>students</u> <u>learned</u> <u>the properties</u> 〔 of

　　　　　　　　　　　　　　　　　　　　　　　S　　　V　　　　O

different kinds of rocks 〕. ⁴(Rather than <u>having</u> <u>them</u> <u>memorize the terms</u>

　　　　　　　　　　　　　　　　　　　　　　V'　　O'　　　　C'

(from a workbook)), <u>I</u> <u>brought</u> <u>a big box</u> 〔 of various rocks 〕(to the class).

　　　　　　　　　　　　S　　V　　　O

⁵<u>Students</u> <u>examined</u> <u>the rocks</u> <u>and</u> <u>identified</u> <u>their names</u> (based on the

　　S　　　V　　　　O　　等接　　V　　　　O

　　　　　　　　　┌─ 関代 which 省略

characteristics 〔 <u>they</u> <u>observed</u> 〕).

　　　　　　　　　　S　　V

訳 ¹彼らの学習を助けるために, 私は「文脈学習」を応用してみました。²この種の学習では, 学生自身の体験を通して新しい知識が構築されていきます。³私の理科の授業では, 学生たちはさまざまな種類の岩石の特性を学びました。⁴私は, ワークブックで用語を暗記させるのではなく, さまざまな岩石の入った大きな箱を教室に持ってきました。⁵学生たちは岩石を調べ, 観察した特徴からその名前を特定しました。

語句

apply	動	適用する, 応用する
knowledge	名	知識
construct	動	組み立てる, 構築する
experience	名	経験, 体験
property	名	(通例-ties)特性, 特質
rather than 〜	熟	〜よりむしろ

memorize	動	暗記する
examine	動	調べる, 検査する
identify	動	特定する
based on 〜	熟	〜に基づいて
characteristic	名	特徴, 特色
observe	動	観察する

前半　第3段落　文の構造と語句のチェック

　　　　　　　　　　　　　　　　　　　┌─ 従接 that 省略

¹(Thanks to this experience), <u>I</u> <u>think</u> 〈 these students <u>will</u> always <u>be able to</u>

　　　　　　　　　　　　　　　S　V　O　　　S　　　　　　　　　V

　　　　　　　　　　　　　　　　　　┌─ 関代 which 省略

<u>describe</u> <u>the properties</u> 〔 of the rocks 〔 <u>they</u> <u>studied</u> 〕〕〉. ²<u>One issue</u>, however, <u>is</u>

　　　　　　O　　　　　　　　　　　　S　　V　　　　S　　　　　　　V

〈 <u>that</u> <u>we</u> <u>don't</u> always <u>have</u> <u>the time</u> 〔 to do contextual learning 〕, <u>so</u> <u>students</u>

C　従接　S　　　　　　V　　　O　　　　　　　　　　　　　　　　　　等接　S

<u>will</u> still <u>study</u> (by doing drills)〉. ³<u>I</u> <u>don't think</u> 〈 <u>this</u> <u>is</u> <u>the best way</u> 〉. ⁴<u>I'm</u>

　　　　V　　　　　　　　　　　　　　　S　　V　　O　S　V　　C　　　　　　　S

still searching for ways 〔 to improve their learning 〕.
　　　　　V　　　　　　O

> **訳** ¹この体験のおかげで，この学生たちは自分たちが学習した岩石の特性をいつでも説明できるようになるだろうと思います。²ただ，1つ問題なのは，文脈学習をする時間がいつもあるわけではないので，学生たちは今後もなお，ドリルをすることによって勉強をするということです。³私はこれが一番よい方法だとは思いません。⁴彼らの学習をよりよいものにするための方法を，私はまだ模索しています。

語 句

thanks to 〜	熟	〜のおかげで
describe	動	説明する
issue	名	問題

drill	名	（問題練習の）ドリル
search for 〜	熟	〜を探し求める
improve	動	改善する，向上させる

後半のタイトル　文の構造と語句のチェック

¹**How to Make Repetitive Learning Effective**

²Cheng Lee

³*Professor, Stone City University*

> **訳**
> ¹反復学習を効果的にする方法
> ²チェン・リー
> ³ストーンシティ大学教授

後半　第1段落　文の構造と語句のチェック

¹Mr. Oxford's thoughts 〔 on contextual learning 〕 were insightful. ²I agree
　　　S　　　　　　　　　　　　　　　　　　　　　V　　C　　　S　V

〈 that it can be beneficial 〉. ³Repetition, though, can also work well. ⁴However,
O 従接 S　V　　C　　　　　　　　S　　　　　　　can　　　V

　　　　　　　　　　　　　　　　　　　　┌─ 関代 which 省略
the repetitive learning strategy 〔 he discussed 〕, 〔 which is called "massed
　　　　　　　S　　　　　　　　　　　S　discussed　　　関代　V

learning," 〕 is not effective. ⁵There is another kind of repetitive learning 〔 called
C　　　　　　V　　C　　　　　　　V　　　　　　　　　S

155

"spaced learning," 〔 in **which** students memorize new information **and** then
　　　　　　　　　　　　関代　　　 S　　　 V①　　　　　　O　　　　　等接

review it (over longer intervals)〕〕.
V②　 O

訳 ¹文脈学習に関するオックスフォード氏の考えは, 洞察に富んでいました。²それが有益な
ものとなり得ることには同意します。³ただ, 反復学習も役に立ち得るのです。⁴しかし, 彼
が論じた「集中学習」と呼ばれる反復学習戦略は, 効果的ではありません。⁵反復学習にはほ
かに,「間隔学習」と呼ばれる種類があり, この方法では学生は新しい情報を記憶したあと,
より長い間隔を置いて復習します。

語 句

thought	名	考え
insightful	形	深い理解を示す, 洞察に富む
beneficial	形	有益な
repetition	名	反復
though	副	でも, けれども
strategy	名	戦略, 方策
massed	形	集中的な, 結集した
spaced	形	間隔を置いた
review	動	復習する
interval	名	間隔, 休止期間

後半　第2段落　文の構造と語句のチェック

¹The interval 〔 between studying 〕 is the key difference. ²(In Mr. Oxford's
　 S　　　　　　　　　　　　　　 V　　　 C

example), his students probably used their workbooks (to study (over a short
　　　　　　 S　　　　　　　 V　　 O

period of time)). ³(In this case), they might have paid less attention (to the
　　　　　　　　　　　　　　　　　 S　　　 V　　　　 O

content) (**as** they continued to review it). ⁴The reason 〔 for this 〕 is 〈 **that**
　　　　　　従接　 S　　　 V　　　　 O　　　 S　　　　　　　　 V C　 従接

the content was no longer new **and** could easily be ignored 〉. ⁵(In contrast),
　 S　　 V　　　　　　　 C　 等接　　　　　　　 V

(**when** the intervals are longer), the students' memory 〔 of the content 〕 is
　 従接　 S　　　 V　 C　　　　　 S　　　　　　　　　　　 V

weaker. ⁶Therefore, they pay more attention (**because** they have to make a
　 C　　　　　　　 S　 V　　 O　　　　　 従接　 S　　 V

greater effort (to recall 〈 **what** they had learned before 〉)). ⁷(For example),
　 O　　　　　　　　　 関代　 S　　 V

156

前置詞 for 省略

(if students study (with their workbooks), wait (three days), and then
　従接　　S　　　V①　　　　　　　　　　　　　　　　　V②　　　　　　　　　　　等接

study again), they are likely to learn the material better.
　V③　　　　　 S　　　　V　　　　　　　　O

訳 ¹学習と学習の間隔が重要な違いです。²オックスフォード氏の例では, 学生たちはおそらく短期間で学習するためにワークブックを使用したのでしょう。³この場合, 復習を続けるうちに, 内容への注意が薄れてしまっていたのかもしれません。⁴その理由は, その内容がもはや新しいものではなく, 容易に無視することができたからなのです。⁵それとは異なり, 間隔がもっと長くなると, 内容についての学生の記憶は薄れます。⁶そのため, 以前に学習した内容を思い出すために, より大きな努力をしなければならないので, より多くの注意を払うことになります。⁷たとえば, ワークブックを使って勉強したあと, 3日待ってからもう一度勉強すると, 教材をよりよく覚えられる可能性が高いです。

語句

key	形	重要な	**in contrast**	熟	対照的に, それとは違って
difference	名	違い	**memory**	名	記憶
period	名	期間	**therefore**	副	したがって, そのため
pay attention to ~	熟	~に注意を払う	**make an effort**	熟	努力する
content	名	内容	**be likely to _do_**	熟	~しそうだ, ~する可能性が高い
no longer	熟	もはや~ない			
ignore	動	無視する	**material**	名	題材, 教材

後半　第3段落　文の構造と語句のチェック

¹Previous research has provided evidence [for the advantages [of spaced
　　　S　　　　　　　V　　　　　　O

learning]]. ²(In one experiment), students [in Groups A and B] tried to
　　　　　　　　　　　　　　　　　　　　　　S

memorize the names [of 50 animals]. ³Both groups studied (four times), but
　V　　　　O　　　　　　　　　　　　　　　　S　　　　　V　　　　　　　　　　　等接

Group A studied (at one-day intervals) (while Group B studied (at one-week
　S　　　V　　　　　　　　　　　　　　　　　従接　　S　　　　V

intervals)). ⁴(As the figure [to the right] shows), (28 days after the last
　　　　　　　　　従節　　　S　　　　　　　　　V

learning session), the average ratio [of recalled names [on a test]] was
　　　　　　　　　　　　　　S　　　　　　　　　　　　　　　　　　　　　　V

157

<u>higher</u> (for the spaced learning group).
  C

> **訳** ¹これまでの研究でも, 間隔学習が有利であるという証拠が出されています。²ある実験で, AグループとBグループの学生が, 50 の動物の名前を暗記しようとしました。³両グループとも 4 回学習しましたが, Aグループは 1 日間隔で, 他方, Bグループは 1 週間間隔で学習しました。⁴右の図が示すように, 最後の学習セッションから 28 日後, テストで名前が思い出された割合は, 平均で, 間隔学習のグループの方が高かったのです。

語句

previous	形	以前の
provide	動	提供する, もたらす
evidence	名	証拠
advantage	名	利点, 有利
experiment	名	実験

figure	名	図
session	名	セッション(集団活動の機会・期間)
average	形	平均の
ratio	名	割合, 比率

後半　第4段落　文の構造と語句のチェック

¹<u>I</u> <u>understand</u> 〈 that <u>students</u> often <u>need to learn</u> <u>a lot of information</u> (in a
 S   V   O 従接   S   V   O

short period of time), and <u>long intervals</u> 〔 between studying 〕 <u>might not be</u>
              等接   S   V

<u>practical</u> 〉. ²<u>You</u> <u>should understand</u>, though, 〈 that <u>massed learning</u> <u>might not</u>
 C   S   V   O 従接   S   V

<u>be good</u> (for long-term recall)〉.
  C

> **訳** ¹学生はしばしば短期間に多くの情報を習得する必要があり, 長い学習間隔が現実的でないかもしれないということはわかります。²でも, 集中学習は, 長期記憶には有利でないかもしれないということを理解した方がよいでしょう。

語句

practical	形	実際的な, 現実的な
long-term	形	長期の

文法事項の整理 ⑫ 接続副詞

前半第３段落第２文の however について見てみよう。

One issue, **however**, is that we don't always have the time to do contextual learning, ...

接続副詞とは，前の文との論理関係を示す副詞のこと。以下のようなものがある。

❶逆接 ： however「しかし」／ though「けれども」／
nevertheless「にもかかわらず」
❷具体例 ： for example「たとえば」／ for instance「たとえば」
❸言い換え： in other words「言い換えれば」／
that is (to say)「つまり」／ namely「つまり」
❹対比 ： in[by] contrast「対照的に」／ on the other hand「他方」
❺因果関係： therefore「したがって」／ consequently「その結果」／
as a result「その結果」

これらは接続詞に似ているが，文中での位置が比較的自由で，文頭だけでなく文中や文末にも置かれる。日本語に訳すときは最初に訳す。

例 My brother loves playing video games. **However**, he needs to focus on his studies.

例 My brother loves playing video games. He needs to focus, **however**, on his studies.

例 My brother loves playing video games. He needs to focus on his studies, **however**.
「弟はテレビゲームをするのが好きです。しかし，勉強に集中する必要があります」

▶前半　第３段落第２文

One issue, however, is that we don't always have the time to do contextual learning, ...

▶文の途中に however があるが，日本語に訳すときは最初に訳す。

▶後半　第１段落第３文

Repetition, though, can also work well.

▶文の途中に though があるが，日本語に訳すときは最初に訳す。この though は従属接続詞（節を作る）ではなく副詞の用法である点にも注意。

▶後半　第１段落第４文

However, the repetitive learning strategy he discussed, which is called "massed learning," is not effective.

▶文頭に However がある。日本語でも最初に訳す。この位置では，等位接続詞 but と同様に考えてよい。

▶後半　第２段落第６文

Therefore, they pay more attention because they have to make a greater effort ...

▶文頭に Therefore がある。日本語でも最初に訳す。この前後の文の In contrast や For example も同様。

▶後半　第４段落最終文

You should understand, though, that massed learning might not be good for long-term recall.

▶文の途中に副詞の though があるが，日本語に訳すときは最初に訳す。

確認問題

1. 次の和訳と対応する英語の語句を，頭文字を参考にして書き，空欄を完成させよう。

（各1点×20）

①	s		動	奮闘する，苦労する
②	r		副	繰り返して
③	d		形	退屈な，つまらない
④	k		名	知識
⑤	e		名	経験，体験
⑥	m		動	暗記する
⑦	i		動	特定する
⑧	o		動	観察する
⑨	t	t 〜	熟	〜のおかげで
⑩	i		動	改善する，向上させる
⑪	b		形	有益な
⑫	r		動	復習する
⑬	i		名	間隔，休止期間
⑭	p	a to 〜	熟	〜に注意を払う
⑮	c		名	内容
⑯	m	an e	熟	努力する
⑰	a		名	利点，有利
⑱	e		名	実験
⑲	a		形	平均の
⑳	p		形	実際的な，現実的な

2. 次の [ ] 内の語句を並べ替えて，意味の通る英文を完成させよう。なお，文頭に来るべき語も小文字で示している。（各5点×2）

① As a science teacher, I am always [about / how / students / to /

161

concerned / help / who] struggle to learn.

② [this / reason / that / for / the / is] the content was no longer new and could easily be ignored.

3. 次の英文を和訳してみよう。(10点)

You should understand, though, that massed learning might not be good for long-term recall.

*massed learning「集中学習」

ディクテーションしてみよう！

今回学習した英文に出てきた単語を, 音声を聞いて ⬚⬚⬚ に書き取ろう。

69 Your teacher has asked you to read two articles about effective ways to study. You will discuss what you learned in your next class.

How to Study Effectively: Contextual Learning!
Tim Oxford
Science Teacher, Stone City Junior High School

70 As a science teacher, I am always ❶c⬚⬚⬚⬚⬚⬚⬚ a⬚⬚⬚⬚⬚ how to help students who struggle to learn. Recently, I found that their main way of learning was to study new information repeatedly until they could recall it all. For example, when they studied for a test, they would use a workbook like the example below and repeatedly say the terms that go in the blanks: "Obsidian is igneous, dark, and glassy. Obsidian is igneous, dark, and glassy...." These students would feel as if they had learned the information, but would quickly forget it and get low scores on the test. Also, this sort of ❷r⬚⬚⬚⬚⬚⬚⬚⬚ learning is dull and demotivating.

71 To help them learn, I tried applying "contextual learning." In this kind of learning, new knowledge is ❸c⬚⬚⬚⬚⬚⬚⬚⬚⬚

through students' own experiences. For my science class, students learned the properties of different kinds of rocks. Rather than having them memorize the terms from a workbook, I brought a big box of various rocks to the class. Students examined the rocks and identified their names based on the characteristics they **❹** o▯▯▯▯▯▯▯.

72　Thanks to this experience, I think these students will always be able to **❺** d▯▯▯▯▯▯ the properties of the rocks they studied. One issue, however, is that we don't always have the time to do contextual learning, so students will still study by doing drills. I don't think this is the best way. I'm still searching for ways to improve their learning.

73　　　　**How to Make Repetitive Learning Effective**

Cheng Lee

Professor, Stone City University

74　Mr. Oxford's thoughts on contextual learning were insightful. I agree that it can be beneficial. Repetition, though, can also work well. However, the repetitive learning **❻** s▯▯▯▯▯▯ he discussed, which is called "massed learning," is not effective. There is another kind of repetitive learning called "spaced learning," in which students memorize new information and then review it over longer intervals.

75　The interval between studying is the key difference. In Mr. Oxford's example, his students probably used their workbooks to study over a short period of time. In this case, they might have paid less attention to the content as they continued to review it. The reason for this is that the content was **❼** n▯ l▯▯▯▯▯ new and could easily be ignored. In contrast, when the intervals are longer, the students' memory of the content is weaker. Therefore, they pay more attention because they have to **❽** m▯▯ a greater e▯▯▯▯▯ to recall what they had learned before. For example, if students study with their workbooks, wait three days, and then study again, they are likely to learn the material better.

76　Previous research has **❾** p▯▯▯▯▯▯▯ e▯▯▯▯▯▯▯

for the advantages of spaced learning. In one experiment, students in Groups A and B tried to memorize the names of 50 animals. Both groups studied four times, but Group A studied at one-day intervals while Group B studied at one-week intervals. As the figure to the right shows, 28 days after the last learning session, the average **⑩** r▢▢▢▢ of recalled names on a test was higher for the spaced learning group.

77   I understand that students often need to learn a lot of information in a short period of time, and long intervals between studying might not be practical. You should understand, though, that massed learning might not be good for long-term recall.

確認問題の答   1. ① struggle   ② repeatedly   ③ dull   ④ knowledge   ⑤ experience
⑥ memorize   ⑦ identify   ⑧ observe   ⑨ thanks to   ⑩ improve   ⑪ beneficial
⑫ review   ⑬ interval   ⑭ pay attention   ⑮ content   ⑯ make, effort   ⑰ advantage
⑱ experiment   ⑲ average   ⑳ practical

2. ① concerned about how to help students who （前半　第1段落　第1文）
② The reason for this is that （後半　第2段落　第4文）

3. でも，集中学習は，長期記憶には有利でないかもしれないということを理解した方がよいでしょう。
（後半　第4段落　最終文）

ディクテーションしてみよう！の答   ❶ concerned about   ❷ repetitive   ❸ constructed
❹ observed   ❺ describe   ❻ strategy   ❼ no longer   ❽ make, effort
❾ provided evidence   ❿ ratio

解 答

問1	①	問2	④ → ⑤ → ① → ③
問3	①, ③	問4	④	問5	①

解 説

問1

「　1　にあてはまる最も適切な選択肢を選びなさい」

① 「ルーシーに絵のコツを教える」

② 「ルーシーによく自分の絵を描かせる」

③ 「週末はルーシーと一緒に絵を描いて過ごす」

④ 「ルーシーに芸術家として活動してほしいと思っている」

▶①が第4段落第4文（He was no artist himself, but sometimes gave her advice, … ）と一致。 tip は「助言, ヒント, アドバイス」の意味で, 本文の advice とほぼ同じ意味。②については, 第3段落第2文（She did her first drawing of her father when she was in kindergarten. ）に幼いころに父の絵を描いたとあるが, その後父が頻繁に描かせたとは書かれていない。③④は本文に記述がない。

問2

「5つの説明（①〜⑤）のうち4つを選び, 起こった順序に並べ替えなさい」

① 「彼女は絵を描くことに欲求不満を感じるようになる」

② 「彼女は自分の描いた絵を誰にも見せないと決める」

③ 「彼女は目だけでなく, 感情も使って描く」

④ 「彼女は絵をプレゼントとして描くのが楽しい」

⑤ 「彼女は自分の絵の才能を証明するために努力している」

▶④が第3段落最終文（ …, Lucy spent many happy hours drawing pictures to give to Mommy and Daddy. ）, ⑤が第4段落最終文（Lucy tried hard, wanting to improve her technique and please her father. ）お

よび第5段落第2〜4文（She thought that if she won, her artistic ability would be recognized. ...），①が第8段落第1文（Lucy continued to draw, but her art left her feeling unsatisfied.），③が第10段落最終文（It had caught Cathy exactly, not only her odd expression but also her friend's kindness and her sense of humor — the things that are found under the surface.）にそれぞれ対応するので，この順序になる。②は本文に記述がない。

問3

「 6 と 7 にあてはまる最も適切な2つの選択肢を選びなさい。(順番は問わない)」

① 「(その姿を)スケッチせずにはいられなかった友人」

② 「小説から受け取ったメッセージ」

③ 「母親からもらったアドバイス」

④ 「彼女が友人を笑わせようとしたこと」

⑤ 「室内で絵を描いて週末を過ごすこと」

▶ ルーシーが絵を上達させた要因を選ぶ。コンテストで優勝できなかったのは，ルーシーが単に，見えた題材を正確に模写するだけだったからであり，そのあと，目に見えない部分もとらえる必要があるという母親のアドバイスを受ける（第7段落後半）。それでも自分の絵に欠けているものが理解できなかったが，キャシーという友人と出会い，あまりにも楽しくて思わずデッサンを描いた（第9段落後半）ことがきっかけで，内面まで描くことができるようになった（第10段落）。以上により，①と③が正解。

問4

「 8 にあてはまる最も適切な選択肢を選びなさい」

① 「父が期待するほど練習しなかった」

② 「コンテストに参加するのを父が嫌がっているのを知っていた」

③ 「父のアドバイスに従うべきだったと思った」

④ 「自分が父をがっかりさせたのではないかと心配した」

▶第2段落最終文の "Oh Daddy, I'm sorry I didn't win." 「ああパパ, 優勝できなくてごめんなさい」というルーシーの発言は, 第4段落最終文 (Lucy tried hard, wanting to improve her technique and please her father.) にあるように, 父を喜ばせたくて絵を描いていたため, 優勝できなかったことにより父をがっかりさせてしまったのではないかという気持ちの表れであると考えられる。以上により, ④が正解。

問5

「　9　にあてはまる最も適切な選択肢を選びなさい」

① 「人に対する理解を深める」

② 「自分の感情をより深く分析する」

③ 「自分の周りで起きていることを正確に表現する」

④ 「状況に応じて異なる技術を使う」

▶このストーリーを選んだ理由としては, ストーリーの中で主人公ルーシーが絵を描くことを通じて, 描く対象の表面に現れない, 内面に目を向けることを学ぶという部分であろう(第7段落後半, 第9～10段落参照)。これは声優を目指す「私」にとっても, 演じるキャラクターをリアルにする上で重要と考えられる。以上により, ①が正解。

▼

それでは次に, 段落ごとに詳しくみていこう。 78

前置き　文の構造と語句のチェック

¹Your English teacher has told everyone 〔 in your class 〕 to choose a short story
　　　　S　　　　　　　V　　　O

〔 in English 〕〔 to read 〕. ²You will introduce the following story (to your
　　　　　　　　　　　　　S　　　V　　　　　　　O

classmates), (using a worksheet).

語句

following	形 次の，以下の	worksheet 名 ワークシート（学習用のプリント）

第1段落 文の構造と語句のチェック

¹Becoming an Artist

²Lucy smiled (in anticipation). ³(In a moment) she would walk (onto the
　S　　V　　　　　　　　　　　　　　　　　　　　　　　S　　would walk
　　　　　　　　　　　　　　　　　　　　　　　　　　　　　　　V

stage) and receive her prize (from the mayor and the judges of the drawing
　　　　等接　V　　　O　　　　　　　　①　　等接　　②

contest). ⁴The microphone screeched and then came the mayor's announcement.
　　　　　　S　　　　　　　　V　　　等接　　　V　　　　S

⁵"And the winner 〔 of the drawing contest 〕 is... Robert McGinnis!
　等接　　S　　　　　　　　　　　　　　　　V　　　　C

⁶Congratulations!"

語句

artist	名 画家，芸術家		drawing	名 絵，絵画
anticipation	名 期待		microphone	名 マイク
in a moment	熟 すぐに，即座に		screech	動 甲高い音を立てる，キーと音を立てる
prize	名 賞		announcement	名 発表
mayor	名 市長		winner	名 勝者，優勝者
judge	名 審査員		Congratulations	間 おめでとう

第2段落　文の構造と語句のチェック

¹Lucy stood up, (still smiling). ²Then, (her face blazing red (with
　　S　　　V　　　　　　　　　　　　　　　　　S′　　　V′

┌─ she 省略
↓　S
embarrassment)), abruptly sat down again. ³What? ⁴There must be a mistake!
　　　　　　　　　　　　　V　　　　　　　　　　　　　　　　　V　　　S

⁵But the boy 〔 named Robert McGinnis 〕 was already (on the stage), (shaking
　　　S　　　　　　　　　　　　　　　　V

hands with the mayor) and (accepting the prize). ⁶She glanced (at her
　　　　　　　　　　　　　　　　　　　　　　　　　　　　　　S　　V

parents), (her eyes filled with tears of disappointment). ⁷They had expected
　　　　　　　　　　　　　　　　　　　　　　　　　　　　　　　S　　V

　　　　　　　　　　　　　　　　　　　　　　　┌─ 従接 that 省略
　　　　　　　　　　　　　　　　　　　　　　　↓
her to do well, especially her father. ⁸"Oh Daddy, I'm sorry (I didn't win)," she
O　C　　　　　　　　　　　　　　　　　　　　　　　S V　C　　S　　V　　　　S

whispered.
　V

> **訳** ¹ルーシーはまだ笑顔のまま立ち上がった。²そして，恥ずかしさのあまり顔を真っ赤に
> して，また突然座り込んでしまった。³何なの？　⁴何かの間違いがあったに違いない！
> ⁵しかし，ロバート・マクギニスという名の少年はすでに壇上に上がり，市長と握手をして
> 賞品を受け取っていた。⁶彼女は両親の顔をちらっと見た。その目を落胆の涙でいっぱいに
> して。⁷両親，特に父親は，彼女のよい結果を期待していたのだ。⁸「ああパパ，優勝できなく
> てごめんなさい」と彼女は小さい声で言った。

語句

blaze	動	燃える，ギラギラする	tear	名 (通例-s) 涙
embarrassment	名	恥ずかしさ，気まずさ	disappointment	名 失望，落胆
abruptly	副	突然，急に	expect	動 期待する
shake hands	熟	握手する	do well	熟 よい結果を出す，
accept	動	受け取る		好成績を挙げる
glance at ~	熟	~をちらっと見る	especially	副 特に
			whisper	動 ささやく，小声で話す

第3段落　文の構造と語句のチェック

¹Lucy had enjoyed drawing (since she was a little girl). ²She did
　　S　　　V　　　　　　O　　　　　従接　　　　　　　　　　　　　　S　　V

her first drawing 〔 of her father 〕(when she was (in kindergarten)).
O　　　　　　　　　　　　　　　　　　従接　S　V

³(Although it was only a child's drawing), it really looked (like him). ⁴He
従接　S　V　　　　C　　　　　　　　S　　　　V　　　　　　　　　　　S

was delighted, and, (from that day), Lucy spent many happy hours (drawing
V　　C　　　　　　　　　　　　　　　S　　V　　　　O

pictures 〔 to give to Mommy and Daddy 〕).

訳　¹ルーシーは幼いころから絵を描くのが趣味だった。²幼稚園のときに初めて父の絵を描
いた。³ただの子どもの絵なのに, 本当に父に似ていた。⁴父は喜び, その日から, ルーシーは
ママとパパにプレゼントする絵を描いて多くの楽しい時間を過ごした。

語句
kindergarten　名 幼稚園

look like ~　熟 ~に似ている
delighted　形 喜んで

第4段落　文の構造と語句のチェック

¹(As she got older), her parents continued to encourage her. ²Her mother, a
従接　S　V　C　　　　　　　S　　　　　　V　　　　　　　　O　　　　S└─同格─┘

busy translator, was happy (that her daughter was doing something creative).
V　　C　　従接　　S　　　　　V　　　　　O

³Her father bought her art books. ⁴He was no artist himself, but sometimes
S　　　V　　O₁　O₂　　　　　S　V　　C　　　　　等接

gave her advice, (suggesting ⟨ that she look very carefully (at ⟨ what she was
V　O₁　O₂　　　　　　　　　従接　S　V　　　　　　　　　　関代　S

drawing ⟩) and copy as accurately as possible ⟩). ⁵Lucy tried hard, (wanting
V　　　　等接　V　　　　　　　　　　　　　　　　S　　V

to improve her technique and please her father).
V′　　　O′　　等接　V′　　O′

訳　¹ルーシーが成長しても, 両親は彼女を励まし続けた。²忙しい翻訳家である母親は, 娘が
創造的なことをしていることを喜んだ。³父親は彼女に画集を買い与えた。⁴彼自身は絵を描
く人ではなかったが, 彼女にアドバイスすることもあり, 描いている物をとても注意深く見

て, できるだけ正確に模写するよう提案した。⁵ルーシーは, 自分の技術を向上させて父を喜ばせたいと思い, 懸命に努力した。

語句

continue	動	続ける
encourage	動	励ます
translator	名	翻訳家
creative	形	創造的な
art book	名	画集, 美術書
suggest	動	提案する

copy	動	写し取る, 模写する
as ... as possible	熟	できるだけ…
accurately	副	正確に
improve	動	改善する, 向上させる
technique	名	技術
please	動	喜ばせる

第5段落　文の構造と語句のチェック

¹It had been Lucy's idea 〈 to enter the town drawing contest 〉. ²She thought
仮S　V　　　　C　　　　　　　真S　　　　　　　　　　　　　　　　S　　V

〈 that (if she won), her artistic ability would be recognized 〉. ³She practiced
従接 O　従接 S　V　　　　S　　　　　　V　　　　　　　　　　　S　　V

(every evening)(after school). ⁴She also spent all her weekends (working
　　　　　　　　　　　　　　　　　　S　　　　V　　　all her weekends O　working

quietly on her drawings), (copying her subjects (as carefully as she could)).
　　　　　　　　　　　　　　　V′　　O′

訳 ¹町の絵画コンテストに参加するのは, ルーシーの思いつきだった。²もし優勝すれば, 自分の芸術的能力が認められると思ったのだ。³放課後, 毎日夕方に練習をした。⁴週末も黙々と絵を描き, できるだけ丁寧に題材を模写した。

語句

enter	動	参加する, 入る
artistic	形	芸術の
ability	名	能力
recognize	動	認める, 評価する

work on ~	熟	~に取り組む
quietly	副	静かに, 黙って
subject	名	題材
as ... as ~ can	熟	(~が)できるだけ…

第6段落　文の構造と語句のチェック

¹Her failure to do well came (as a great shock). ²She had worked (so hard)
　　　　S　　　　　　　V　　　　　　　　　　　　　　S　　　V

and her parents had been so supportive. ³Her father, however, was puzzled.
等接　　S　　　　V　　　　C　　　　　S　　　　　　　　V　　C

⁴Why did Lucy apologize (at the end of the contest)? ⁵There was no need 〔 to
疑　(V)　S　　V　　　　　　　　　　　　　　　　　　　V　　S

do so 〕. ⁶Later, Lucy asked him 〈 why she had failed to win the competition 〉.
　　　　　　　S　　V　　O₁　O₂　疑　S　　　V　　　　　　　O

⁷He answered sympathetically, "(To me), your drawing was perfect." ⁸Then he
S　　V　　　　　　　　　　　　　　　　S　　　　V　　C　　　　　S

smiled, and added, "But perhaps you should talk (to your mother). ⁹She
V①　　等接　V②　　等接　　　S　　V　　　　　　　　　　　S

understands art (better than I do)."
V　　　O　　　　　　　S　V

> 訳　¹よい結果を残せなかったことが大きなショックとなった。²彼女はとても頑張ったし、両親もとても応援してくれていたのだ。³しかし、父親は困惑していた。⁴なぜ、ルーシーはコンテストの最後に謝ったのだろうか。⁵そんなことする必要はなかったのに。⁶後日、ルーシーは父親に、なぜ自分はコンテストで優勝できなかったのかと尋ねた。⁷彼は同情しながら「私には、あなたの絵は完璧だったよ」と答えた。⁸そしてほほえんで、付け加えた。「だが、もしかすると母さんに相談した方がいいかもしれない。⁹母さんは私より芸術を理解しているよ」。

語句

failure 名 ～しない［できない］こと	**at the end of ～** 熟 ～の終わりに、～の最後に
come as ～ 熟 ～となる	**sympathetically** 副 同情して、共感して
supportive 形 協力的な、支えとなって	**add** 動 付け加える、付け加えて言う
puzzled 形 困惑して、戸惑って	
apologize 動 謝る、謝罪する	

第7段落　文の構造と語句のチェック

¹Her mother was thoughtful. ²She wanted to give Lucy advice (without
S　　　V　　C　　　S　　V　　　　　O₁　O₂

damaging her daughter's self-esteem). ³"Your drawing was good," she told her,
V'　　　　　　　　O'　　　　　　　　　　　S　　　　V　　C　　S　　V　　O

┌─従接 that 省略　　　　　　　　　　┌─従接 that 省略
"but I think 〈 it lacked something 〉. ⁴I think 〈 you only drew 〈 what you could
等接 S　V　O　S　V　　　O　　　　S　　V　O　S　　　V　　O　関代　S　　V

172

see 〉〉. ⁵(When I translate a novel), I need to capture not only the meaning,
　　　　従接　S　　V　　　　O　　　　 S　　　V

but also the spirit of the original. ⁶(To do that), I need to consider the meaning
　O　　　　　　　　　　　　　　　　　　　 S　　　V　　　　　　 O

〔 behind the words 〕. ⁷Perhaps drawing is the same; you need to look (under
　　　　　　　　　　　　　　　　　　S　　V　 C　　 S　　 V

the surface)."

> **訳** ¹彼女の母親は思慮深かった。²娘の自尊心を傷つけることなく、ルーシーに助言を与え
> たいと思ったのだ。³「あなたの絵はよかったのよ」。母親は娘に向かって言った。「でも, 何
> かが足りなかったのだと思うの。⁴あなたは目に見えたものしか描いてないように思うわ。
> ⁵私が小説を翻訳するときは, 原作の意味だけでなく, 精神的な部分もとらえなければなら
> ないの。⁶それをするためには, 言葉の裏にある意味を考える必要があるわ。⁷たぶん, 絵を
> 描くことも同じで, 表面の裏に隠れているものを見る必要があるのかもしれないわね」。

語句

thoughtful	形 思慮深い, 慎重な	capture	動 とらえる
damage	動 傷つける, 損なう	not only A but also B	熟 AだけでなくBも
self-esteem	名 自尊心	meaning	名 意味
lack	動 欠ける	spirit	名 精神, 真意
translate	動 翻訳する	original	名 原作, 原文
novel	名 小説	consider	動 考慮する
		surface	名 表面

第8段落　文の構造と語句のチェック

¹Lucy continued to draw, but her art left her feeling unsatisfied. ²She couldn't
　S　　　V　　　　　 等接　S　　 V　　 O　　　　 C　　　　 S

understand 〈 what her mother meant 〉. ³What was wrong (with drawing
　V　　　　 O　 関代　 S　　　 V　　 疑S　 V　　 C

〈 what she could see 〉)? ⁴What else could she do?
　関代 S　 V　　　　　 O　　(V) S　V

> **訳** ¹ルーシーは絵を描き続けたが, 彼女の気持ちは絵を描いても満たされないままだった。
> ²母の言おうとしていることが理解できなかったのだ。³目に見えるものを描くことの何が
> 間違っていたのか。⁴ほかに何ができたのだろうか。

第9段落　文の構造と語句のチェック

¹(Around this time), <u>Lucy</u> <u>became</u> <u>friends</u> (with a girl [called Cathy]). ²<u>They</u>
　　　　　　　　　　　　　S　　　V　　　C　　　　　　　　　　　　　　　　　　　　S

<u>became</u> <u>close friends</u> <u>and</u> <u>Lucy</u> <u>grew to appreciate</u> <u>her</u> (for her kindness <u>and</u>
　V　　　　C　　　　等接　　S　　　　V　　　　　　　O　　　　　①　　　　　　等接

humorous personality). ³<u>Cathy</u> often <u>made</u> <u>Lucy</u> <u>laugh</u>, (telling jokes), (saying
　　　②　　　　　　　　　　S　　　　　V　　O　　C　　　　　　　　　　　　①

ridiculous things), <u>and</u> (making funny faces). ⁴(One afternoon), <u>Cathy</u> <u>had</u>
　　②　　　　　　　等接　　　　③　　　　　　　　　　　　　　　　　　　　　S　　V

┌── 従接 that 省略

<u>such</u> a funny expression (on her face) <u>that</u> <u>Lucy</u> <u>felt</u> ⟨ <u>she</u> <u>had to draw</u> <u>it</u> ⟩.
　　　　　　O　　　　　　　　　　　　　　　　　　S　　V　　O　　　V　　　　O

⁵"<u>Hold</u> <u>that pose!</u>" <u>she</u> <u>told</u> <u>Cathy</u>, laughing. ⁶<u>She</u> <u>drew</u> quickly, (<u>enjoying</u> <u>her</u>
　　V　　　O　　　S　　V　　O　　　　　　　　　S　　V　　　　　　　　V′

<u>friend's expression</u> <u>so</u> much <u>that</u> <u>she</u> <u>didn't really think</u> (about ⟨ <u>what</u> <u>she</u> <u>was</u>
　　O′　　　　　　　　　　　　　　　S　　　　V　　　　　　　　　　　疑　　S

<u>doing</u> ⟩)).
　V

> **訳** ¹このころ, ルーシーはキャシーという女の子と友だちになった。²彼女たちは親友になり, ルーシーは彼女の優しさとユーモアのある性格がすばらしいと思うようになった。³キャシーは, 冗談を言ったり, ばかげたことを言ったり, 変な顔をしたりして, よくルーシーを笑わせた。⁴ある日の午後, キャシーの表情がとてもおかしかったので, ルーシーはそれを描かなければと思った。⁵「そのポーズのままでいて！」と彼女は笑いながらキャシーに言った。⁶ルーシーはキャシーの表情があまりにも楽しくて, 自分が何をしているかをあまり考えることもなく, 素早く描いた。

語句

close	形	親しい, 親密な	**personality**	名	性格, 人格
grow to *do*	熟	～するようになる	**ridiculous**	形	ばかげた, 滑稽な
appreciate	動	評価する, よさを認める	**funny**	形	おもしろい, おかしな
kindness	名	優しさ, 親切さ	**expression**	名	表情
humorous	形	ユーモラスな, おもしろい	**hold**	動	保つ, 続ける
			pose	名	ポーズ, 姿勢, 格好

第10段落　文の構造と語句のチェック

¹(When Lucy entered art college (three years later)), she still had that
　　　　従接　　S　　V　　　　O　　　　　　　　　　　　　　　　　　　S　　　　　V

sketch. ²It had caught Cathy exactly, not only her odd expression but also her
O　　　　　S　　V　　　O

friend's kindness and her sense of humor — the things 〔 that are found (under
①　　　　　　　等接　　②　　　　　　　　　　　　　関代　　　V

the surface)〕.

> **訳** ¹ 3年後, ルーシーが美術大学に入学したとき, 彼女はそのスケッチをまだ持っていた。
> ² そのスケッチは, キャシーのおかしな表情だけでなく, 友人の優しさやユーモアのセンス
> といった, 内面に見られることまでも, 正確にとらえていた。

語句

art college	名 美術大学	catch	動 とらえる
sketch	名 スケッチ, デッサン	odd	形 奇妙な, おかしな
		humor	名 ユーモア

ワークシート部分　文の構造と語句のチェック

Your worksheet:

1. Story title

"Becoming an Artist"

2. People in the story

Lucy: She loves to draw.

Lucy's father: He gives Lucy some drawing tips.

Lucy's mother: She is a translator and supports Lucy.

Cathy: She becomes Lucy's close friend.

3. What the story is about

Lucy's growth as an artist:

> She has fun making drawings as gifts.
>
> She works hard to prove her talent at drawing.
>
> She becomes frustrated with her drawing.
>
> She draws with her feelings as well as her eyes.

Her drawing improves thanks to a friend she couldn't help sketching and advice she received from her mother.

4. My favorite part of the story

When the result of the contest is announced, Lucy says, "Oh Daddy, I'm sorry I didn't win."

This shows that Lucy was worried she had disappointed her father.

5. Why I chose this story

Because I want to be a voice actor and this story taught me the importance of trying to achieve a better understanding of people to make the characters I play seem more real.

訳 あなたのワークシート

1. 物語のタイトル
「芸術家になること」

2. 登場人物
ルーシー：絵を描くのが大好き。
ルーシーの父：ルーシーに絵のコツを教える。
ルーシーの母：翻訳家であり，ルーシーを応援。
キャシー：ルーシーの親友になる。

3. 物語の主題
ルーシーの芸術家としての成長：
彼女は絵をプレゼントとして描くのが楽しい。
彼女は自分の絵の才能を証明するために努力している。
彼女は絵を描くことに欲求不満を感じるようになる。
彼女は目だけでなく，感情も使って描く。

スケッチせずにはいられなかった友人と母親からもらったアドバイスのおかげで彼女の絵は上達する。

4. 物語の中で一番好きなところ

コンテストの結果が発表されると, ルーシーは "Oh Daddy, I'm sorry I didn't win." と言う。これは, ルーシーが自分が父をがっかりさせたのではないかと心配したことを示している。

5. この物語を選んだ理由

私は声優になりたいと思っていて, この物語で, 自分の演じるキャラクターをよりリアルに見せるために人に対する理解を深めるよう心がけることの大切さを学んだからである。

語句

what ~ is about	熟 ~の中心/本質/主目的	voice actor	名 声優
result	名 結果	importance	名 重要性, 大切さ
announce	動 発表する	character	名 キャラクター, 登場人物

文法事項の整理 ⑬ so[such] ~ that S + V

第9段落第4文の such ~ that S + Vについて見てみよう。

One afternoon, Cathy had **such** a funny expression on her face **that** Lucy felt she had to draw it.

so ~ that S + V, such ~ that S + V はいずれも「とても~なのでSはVする」【結果】または「SがVするほど~」【程度】の意味を表す。 so ~ that S + V の「~」は形容詞または副詞, such ~ that S + V の「~」は(形容詞+)名詞がくる。

例　He is **so** rich **that** he can buy the house.

　　「彼はとても金持ちなのでその家を買える」【結果】

　　「彼はその家を買えるほど金持ちだ」【程度】

　※ so と that の間は形容詞 rich 。

　※【結果】【程度】は基本的にどちらで解釈してもよいが, 否定文の場合は

【程度】。

例　He isn't **so** rich **that** he can buy the house.
　　「彼はその家を買えるほど金持ちではない」【程度】

例　He is **such** a rich man **that** he can buy the house.
　　「彼はとても金持ちの男なのでその家を買える」【結果】
　　「彼はその家を買えるほど金持ちの男だ」【程度】

　※ such と that の間には名詞 man がある。

▶第9段落第4文

One afternoon, Cathy had <u>such</u> a funny expression on her face <u>that</u> Lucy felt she had to draw it.

▶such ～ that S＋V が【結果】または【程度】を表す。 such と that の間には名詞 expression がある。

▶第9段落最終文

She drew quickly, enjoying her friend's expression <u>so</u> much <u>that</u> she didn't really think about what she was doing.

▶so ～ that S＋V が【結果】または【程度】を表す。 so と that の間には副詞 much がある。

確認問題

1. 次の和訳と対応する英語の語句を, 頭文字を参考にして書き, 空欄を完成させよう。

/40点

（各1点×20）

①	a		名	期待
②	w		名	勝者, 優勝者
③	s	h	熟	握手する
④	g	a	〜 熟	〜をちらっと見る
⑤	w		動	ささやく, 小声で話す
⑥	k		名	幼稚園
⑦	e		動	励ます
⑧	t		名	翻訳家
⑨	a		副	正確に
⑩	i		動	改善する, 向上させる
⑪	a		動	謝る, 謝罪する
⑫	m		名	意味
⑬	s		名	表面
⑭	a		動	評価する, よさを認める
⑮	k		名	優しさ, 親切さ
⑯	p		名	性格, 人格
⑰	r		形	ばかげた, 滑稽な
⑱	e		名	表情
⑲	o		形	奇妙な, おかしな
⑳	h		名	ユーモア

2. 次の [ ] 内の語句を並べ替えて, 意味の通る英文を完成させよう。（各5点×2）

① She wanted to give Lucy [without / her / damaging / self-esteem / advice / daughter's] .

179

② One afternoon, Cathy had [funny / her / such / expression / face / on / a] that Lucy felt she had to draw it.

3. 次の英文を和訳してみよう。(10点)

Lucy spent many happy hours drawing pictures to give to Mommy and Daddy.

ディクテーションしてみよう！

今回学習した英文に出てきた単語を, 音声を聞いて □□□ に書き取ろう。

79　Your English teacher has told everyone in your class to choose a short story in English to read. You will introduce the following story to your classmates, using a worksheet.

80　　　　　　　　　**Becoming an Artist**

Lucy smiled in anticipation. ❶ I a m she would walk onto the stage and receive her prize from the mayor and the judges of the drawing contest. The microphone screeched and then came the mayor's announcement. "And the winner of the drawing contest is... Robert McGinnis! Congratulations!"

81　Lucy stood up, still smiling. Then, her face blazing red with embarrassment, abruptly sat down again. What? There must be a mistake! But the boy named Robert McGinnis was already on the stage, ❷ s h with the mayor and accepting the prize. She ❸ g a her parents, her eyes filled with tears of disappointment. They had expected her to do well, especially her father. "Oh Daddy, I'm sorry I didn't win," she whispered.

82　Lucy had enjoyed drawing since she was a little girl. She did her first drawing of her father when she was in ❹ k . Although it was only a child's drawing, it really looked like him. He was delighted, and, from that day, Lucy spent many happy hours drawing pictures to give to Mommy and Daddy.

83 As she got older, her parents continued to encourage her. Her mother, a busy translator, was happy that her daughter was doing something creative. Her father bought her art books. He was no artist himself, but sometimes gave her advice, suggesting that she look very carefully at what she was drawing and copy as **❺** a⬚⬚⬚⬚⬚⬚⬚⬚⬚ as p⬚⬚⬚⬚⬚⬚⬚. Lucy tried hard, wanting to improve her technique and please her father.

84 It had been Lucy's idea to enter the town drawing contest. She thought that if she won, her artistic ability would be recognized. She practiced every evening after school. She also spent all her weekends working quietly on her drawings, copying her **❻** s⬚⬚⬚⬚⬚⬚⬚ as carefully as she could.

85 Her **❼** f⬚⬚⬚⬚⬚⬚ to do well came as a great shock. She had worked so hard and her parents had been so supportive. Her father, however, was puzzled. Why did Lucy **❽** a⬚⬚⬚⬚⬚⬚⬚⬚ at the end of the contest? There was no need to do so. Later, Lucy asked him why she had failed to win the competition. He answered sympathetically, "To me, your drawing was perfect." Then he smiled, and added, "But perhaps you should talk to your mother. She understands art better than I do."

86 Her mother was **❾** t⬚⬚⬚⬚⬚⬚⬚⬚⬚. She wanted to give Lucy advice without damaging her daughter's self-esteem. "Your drawing was good," she told her, "but I think it lacked something. I think you only drew what you could see. When I translate a novel, I need to capture not only the meaning, but also the spirit of the **❿** o⬚⬚⬚⬚⬚⬚⬚. To do that, I need to consider the meaning behind the words. Perhaps drawing is the same; you need to look under the surface."

87 Lucy continued to draw, but her art left her feeling unsatisfied. She couldn't understand what her mother meant. What was wrong with drawing what she could see? What else could she do?

88   Around this time, Lucy became friends with a girl called Cathy. They became close friends and Lucy grew to **⑪** a [＿＿＿＿＿＿＿＿] her for her kindness and humorous personality. Cathy often made Lucy laugh, telling jokes, saying **⑫** r [＿＿＿＿＿＿＿] things, and making funny faces. One afternoon, Cathy had such a funny expression on her face that Lucy felt she had to draw it. "Hold that pose!" she told Cathy, laughing. She drew quickly, enjoying her friend's expression so much that she didn't really think about what she was doing.

89   When Lucy entered art college three years later, she still had that sketch. It had caught Cathy exactly, not only her **⑬** o [＿＿] expression but also her friend's kindness and her sense of humor — the things that are found under the surface.

90   Your worksheet:

1. Story title

"Becoming an Artist"

2. People in the story

Lucy: She loves to draw.

Lucy's father: He gives Lucy some drawing tips.

Lucy's mother: She is a translator and supports Lucy.

Cathy: She becomes Lucy's close friend.

3. What the story is about

Lucy's growth as an artist:

    She has fun making drawings as gifts.

    She works hard to prove her talent at drawing.

    She becomes frustrated with her drawing.

    She draws with her feelings as well as her eyes.

Her drawing improves thanks to a friend she couldn't help sketching and advice she received from her mother.

4. My favorite part of the story

When the result of the contest is announced, Lucy says, "Oh Daddy, I'm sorry I didn't win."

This shows that Lucy was worried she had disappointed her father.

5. Why I chose this story

Because I want to be a voice actor and this story taught me the importance of trying to achieve a better understanding of people to make the characters I play seem more real.

確認問題の答 1. ① anticipation　② winner　③ shake hands　④ glance at　⑤ whisper
　　⑥ kindergarten　⑦ encourage　⑧ translator　⑨ accurately　⑩ improve
　　⑪ apologize　⑫ meaning　⑬ surface　⑭ appreciate　⑮ kindness　⑯ personality
　　⑰ ridiculous　⑱ expression　⑲ odd　⑳ humor

2.　① advice without damaging her daughter's self-esteem　（第7段落　第2文）
　　② such a funny expression on her face　（第9段落　第4文）

3.　ルーシーはママとパパにプレゼントする絵を描いて多くの楽しい時間を過ごした。　（第3段落　最終文）

ディクテーションしてみよう！の答　❶ In, moment　❷ shaking hands　❸ glanced at
　　❹ kindergarten　❺ accurately, possible　❻ subjects　❼ failure　❽ apologize
　　❾ thoughtful　❿ original　⓫ appreciate　⓬ ridiculous　⓭ odd